To Bruce -
Thanks for your
Harkonessian review of
the manuscript.

Regards,
Martin

Joseph Conrad
and Psychological Medicine

A man suffering from indigestion, suggested by little characters and demons tormenting him. Colored etching by G. Cruikshank, 1835, after A. Crowquill. (The Wellcome Library, London)

"The decency of our life is for a great part a matter of good taste, of the correct appreciation of what is fine in simplicity. The intimate influence of conscientious cooking by rendering easy the processes of digestion promotes the serenity of mind, the graciousness of thought, and that indulgent view of our neighbours' failings which is the only genuine form of optimism."

—Joseph Conrad, from the preface to Jessie Conrad's *A Handbook of Cookery for a Small House*

Joseph Conrad and Psychological Medicine

Martin Bock

Texas Tech University Press

This book was set in ITC Garamond. The paper used in this book meets
the minimum requirements of ANSI/NISO Z39.48-1992 (R1997). ∞

Printed in the United States of America

Design by Brandi Price

Library of Congress Cataloging-in-Publication Data
    Bock, Martin, 1951–
      Joseph Conrad and psychological medicine / Martin Bock.
        p. cm.
      Includes bibliographical references and index.
      ISBN 0-89672-483-2 (alk. paper)
          1. Conrad, Joseph, 1857–1924—Knowledge—Psychology.
    2. Psychological fiction, English—History and criticism.
    3. Novelists, English—20th century—Psychology. 4. Conrad,
    Joseph, 1857–1924—Psychology. 5. Psychology in literature.
    I. Title.
    PR6005.O4 Z4598 2002
    823'.912—dc21

                                        2001006418

        02 03 04 05 06 07 08 09 10 / 9 8 7 6 5 4 3 2 1

Texas Tech University Press
Box 41037
Lubbock, Texas 79409-1037 USA

1-800-832-4042

ttup@ttu.edu

www.ttup.ttu.edu

Contents

Illustrations

Foreword

In *Joseph Conrad and His Circle,* Jessie Conrad offers an amusing account of Conrad's awkward courtship and sudden proposal of marriage. After taking her into the National Gallery, he suggested "without any preamble" that they should "get married at once and get over to France": "All the points in favour of haste he put forward, such as the weather, his health, his work."[1] In his subsequent meeting with her mother, Conrad repeated his desire for haste on the grounds that "he hadn't very long to live," affirming, in addition, that "there would be no family" (15). Jessie elaborates on Conrad's recent medical history to explain his anxieties about his health and his sense of urgency. She observes:

> I had heard from several of his friends how nearly he had died from dysentery while being carried to the coast when he left the Congo. Of the many months he had lain between life and death in the German Hospital in London. I knew also that he had been lately staying at Champel in Geneva under medical treatment, and that he suffered from gout—but as to what particular form of illness this might be I was entirely ignorant. (13)

In the first section of *Joseph Conrad and Psychological Medicine,* Martin Bock explores some of Conrad's particular forms of illness and situates them within their contemporary context. His research into neurasthenia and into the medical staff and culture of the German Hospital in London suggests why this might have been a congenial hospital for the neurasthenic Conrad, while his detailed account of the "medical treatment" at Champel-les-Bains in Geneva places Conrad back into the late-nineteenth-century European culture of balneotherapy and hydrotherapy that he shared with his friend and collaborator, Ford Madox Ford, and that provides the background for Ford's best-known novel, *The Good Soldier.* Rightly resisting the siren-calls of psychoanalysis, Bock also avoids the temptation to provide the "true" medical meaning of Conrad's symptoms. Rather he takes pains to map contemporary diagnosis onto contemporary treatment and, thereby, to reconstruct contemporary understandings of particular forms of illness. By this means, Bock attempts to approach ways in which Conrad might have understood his own physical and mental being. Thus Bock's attentive reading of Conrad's symptoms and of contemporary medical and psychological discourses helps us to understand (among other things) why Conrad insisted that there should be "no family."

From his early years in exile in Vologda and Chernikhov, with first his mother and then his father dying of tuberculosis, while his own health broke down and required treatment in Kiev and Nowofastow, illness, medicine, and doctors run like a scarlet thread through Conrad's life. Furthermore, many of Conrad's health problems relate directly to the area of psychological medicine. There were, for example, the fits he seems to have experienced as a child.[2] There was also the mysterious illness that affected him on the *Highland Forest* after he was apparently struck by a falling spar. In *The Mirror of the Sea*, he describes how this left him with "inexplicable periods of powerlessness, sudden accesses of mysterious pain" that required him to lie up for a couple of months in the Singapore hospital.[3] Bock focuses on Conrad's poor state of health on his return from the Congo—the swollen leg and the "thinness" of hair that he reported to his uncle Tadeusz Bobrowski; the "*rheumatisme de jambe gauche et neuralgie de bras droit*" and stomach problems that he reported to Marguerite Poradowska—and on the "nervous trouble" that affected him subsequently.[4] This "nervous trouble" culminated in the apparent breakdown of 1910, which began with acute symptoms of gout and laid him up in bed for three months. Jessie reported how, in this period, Conrad lived "mixed up in the scenes" and holding "converse with the characters" of *Under Western Eyes*, which lay in manuscript, uncorrected and unedited, on a table at the foot of his bed.[5]

In the second section, "Reading Medically," Bock explores various ways in which psychological medicine permeates Conrad's fiction. In *The Eternal Solitary*, Adam Gillon provided a table of Conrad's fictional characters, divided into five categories: those who are "violently killed," those who "commit suicide or sacrifice themselves," those who "die of disease or die of loneliness," those who "go through severe emotional crisis (despair or melancholy)," and those who "turn insane."[6] Bock's attention to the pervasive discourse of medical psychology within Conrad's fiction shows how many of the characters are marked by "nervousness," fear of madness, or, indeed, various forms of madness. The writing of *An Outcast of the Islands* was framed by two of Conrad's visits to Champel, and Bock makes a convincing case for Willems as a malarial neurasthenic and for Almayer as suffering a minor hystero-epileptic attack. Jim is another male hysteric; the narrator of "The Secret Sharer" suffers from "nervousness" and creeps "as near insanity as any man who has not actually gone over the border," while the characters of *The Secret Agent* constitute a catalogue of mental disorders.[7] As Bock makes abundantly clear, neurasthenia, hysteria, and "moral insanity" constantly recur in Conrad's fiction. Bock is also alert to the hysterical quality of Conrad's prose in his early fiction and to Conrad's subsequent encoding of his medical history through the metonymic tropes of restraint, seclusion, and water. His reading of "The Secret Sharer" in terms of seclusion, claustrophobia, and the fear of nervous breakdown is particularly suggestive.

If Conrad's fictions encode his medical history, they also map his anxieties: anxieties about madness, but also about gender and sexuality. As Elaine Showalter has noted, neurasthenia and hysteria were thought of, in nineteenth-century England, as female disorders.[8] Psychological medicine was rooted in and supported contemporary ideologies of gender. As Bock demonstrates, Conrad's nervous economy brought him into conflict with English nineteenth-century gender constructions, and Conrad's early work enacts his negotiation of his own "masculine" and "feminine" sides. Thus "The Return," for example, can be read as a dramatization of the tensions between male restraint and feminizing hysteria. Most interestingly, Bock argues that, after his 1910 breakdown, Conrad became reconciled to the loss of masculine restraint and was able to engage consciously, in his fiction, with constructions of gender. Thus, through the Marlow of *Chance*, Conrad undertakes an exploration of masculinity and, in *The Arrow of Gold*, explores various psycho-sexual themes while maintaining an intense focus on his characters' varying degrees of mental stress and disorder. Bock notes that Conrad publicly acknowledged his own neurasthenia only very late in life, in "The *Torrens*: A Personal Tribute" (1923); *The Arrow of Gold* similarly contains a late acknowledgment of his familiarity with hydrotherapy, even if that acknowledgment is so occluded as to have missed comment until now. More significantly, in a work that shows some familiarity with Freudian ideas about hysteria, Conrad presents hydrotherapy as an outmoded treatment. Bock also makes a strong case for "The Shadow Line" and *The Arrow of Gold* to be treated seriously as World War I fictions: his medical reading of both works in this context is compelling.

From Charlotte Perkins Gilman's response to her experience of the Weir-Mitchell rest-cure in *The Yellow Wallpaper* (1892) to Virginia Woolf's use of her treatment by Dr. Savage in *Mrs. Dalloway* (1925), the relevance of psychological medicine to women's writing in this period is well established. Martin Bock shows its relevance to the entire range of Conrad's writing: it joins adventure romance, narratives of exploration, and criminal anthropology as a constitutive element of his fictional language. Bock's use of psychological medicine to produce a medical reading of Conrad's fiction also makes a valuable contribution to the modern debate in Conrad studies about gender, masculinity, and sexuality.[9] From Conrad and Ford's experience of hydropathy through to the treatment of Wilfred Owen and Siegfried Sassoon at Craiglockhart, a hydropathic establishment which became a military hospital for shell-shocked officers, it is clear that psychological medicine is a necessary context for men's writing in this period as well, and that, as Bock shows, developments in psychological medicine provide access to changing ideas about gender and sexuality.

Acknowledgments

The McKnight Foundation and the University of Minnesota Graduate School have supported this project with Summer Fellowships, and the offices of the UM-Duluth chancellor, vice chancellor for academic administration, and the College of Liberal Arts deans have generously provided the leave time and material support necessary to complete this book.

Keith Carabine has my special thanks for welcoming me into the UK Conrad community and for his helpful commentary on early, draft portions of the manuscript. Robert Hampson urged me to write this book, knowledgeably answered my questions, and graciously provided the foreword. I wish to thank Ray Stevens for reminding me of why I began this project and, most particularly, Bruce Harkness for providing his insight and his meticulous review of the complete manuscript. Robert Evans and Dr. Emil Bock along the way offered thoughtful readings of the manuscript and helpful suggestions; Carol Bock provided valuable advice on the conclusion. Lisa Nicholetti provided me with the best of research assistance, especially on Dr. Gachet, and Megan Kingsley was an able assistant in bibliographic matters and manuscript preparation. Finally, thanks are due to Jackie McLean, my editor, for her interest in, unwavering commitment to, and sound advice on the project; to Maureen Creamer Bemko for her expert copyediting; and to Don Rude for his generous support of the project. Any infelicities that survive in this book are mine.

I owe the UMD library and its staff my gratitude for obtaining obscure materials. The Wellcome Library, London; Cornell University Library, Department of Rare Books; the Lilly Library, Indiana University; and the Brotherton Collection, Leeds University Library, have generously granted permission to publish materials housed in their collections. I wish to thank Andrew Baster for help locating records housed in Wills Library, King's College,

London; J. D. Audsley, director of Benenden Hospital, for providing me with hospital records referring to Dr. Tebb; and Michel Piller, curator of the Centre d'Iconographie Genovese, Jean-Charles Giroud, curator of the posters collections of Bibliothèque Publique et Universitaire (Geneva), and Alessia Contin, Museum für Gestaltung (Zurich), for their assistance and permission to reproduce images of Champel. Artwork for illustrations in this book was prepared by the staff of the British Library Newspaper Library, Jean-Marc Meylan, C. Poite, Dan Schlies, and Mark Summers.

Portions of this manuscript have been presented as papers at various Conrad conferences in Philadelphia, Lubbock, London, Canterbury, and Lyon and subsequently appeared in *The Conradian* and *L'Epoque Conradienne* and are forthcoming in *Conrad: Eastern and Western Perspectives*.

This book is for Carol, Nina, and Jeff, who followed me without complaint to the York Cemetery.

A Note
on the Texts

Works by Joseph Conrad are cited within the text and, with the exception of two novels, refer to the Canterbury edition of *The Complete Works of Joseph Conrad* (New York: Doubleday, Page, 1924). Quotations from *Almayer's Folly: A Story of an Eastern River,* edited by Floyd Eugene Eddelman and David Leon Higdon (Cambridge: Cambridge University Press, 1994), and *The Secret Agent: A Simple Tale,* edited by Bruce Harkness and S. W. Reid (Cambridge: Cambridge University Press, 1990), are from *The Cambridge Edition of the Works of Joseph Conrad* (Cambridge: Cambridge University Press, 1990–). In quotes from Conrad's fiction, spaced dots are Conrad's ellipses; unspaced ellipses are mine. Unless otherwise noted, letters from Joseph Conrad are cited parenthetically and are from *The Collected Letters of Joseph Conrad,* edited by Frederick R. Karl and Laurence Davies (Cambridge: Cambridge University Press, 1983–96). References to D. H. Tuke's *A Dictionary of Psychological Medicine* (London: J. & A. Churchill, 1892) likewise appear parenthetically. For convenience, Joseph Conrad is sometimes abbreviated JC.

Abbreviations

Introduction

I abhorr [*sic*] quackery.—Joseph Conrad, from a letter to
J. B. Pinker

In the summer spa season of 1907 during one of the bleakest periods of his life, Joseph Conrad wrote to John Galsworthy from Champel, Switzerland, where he was taking a cure: "I am keeping up but I feel as if a mosquito bite were enough to knock me over. Good God! If I were to get it now what would happen! As it is I don't know very well what will happen. It will be nothing good anyway— even at best. And how to face it mentally and materially is what keeps my nerves on the stretch" (*CL,* 3:454). While the letter seems irritable and overwrought, the whole Conrad family was, in fact, quite ill, and Conrad was struggling to finish the novel version of *The Secret Agent.* Borys Conrad, then nine years old, had been plagued by a series of childhood ailments for five months—adenoids, measles that relapsed, bronchitis, suspected tuberculosis—and Conrad himself was recovering from a bad spell of gout, complicated by eczema and the anxiety he felt about the health of his family. The infant John developed whooping cough, which he passed on to Borys, who then developed rheumatic fever—the effect (Conrad speculated) of an earlier bout with scarlet fever—and finally pleurisy.[1] It was, Conrad wrote to John Galsworthy, "a sort of quiet nightmare that goes on and on," in the midst of which the author would occasionally "steal an hour or two to work at preparing *The Secret Agent* for book form" (*CL,* 3:448). At the end of that novel, the ex-medical student Ossipon (nicknamed "the Doctor") ominously castigates a fellow anarchist: "'Just now you've been crying for time—time. Well! The doctors will serve you out your time—if you are good. . . . It's time that you need. You—if you met a man who could give you for certain ten years of time, you would call him your master'" (*SA,* 227).

Medical doctors were, indeed, a continuous presence in the life of Joseph Conrad, who from childhood was treated for a variety of specific or sometimes vague illnesses that were endemic to the Korzeniowski and Bobrowski families. We know from *A Personal Record* that some of Conrad's most vivid early memories focus on ill health and doctors. Conrad recalled clearly the circumstances of his mother's illness that postponed the family's political exile (*PR*, 64–67). En route to Siberia, five-year-old Conrad was successfully treated for pneumonia or meningitis by Dr. Młodzianowski of the University of Moscow, who was an acquaintance of Apollo Korzeniowski, Conrad's father. After his mother's death in 1865, Conrad, at age seven, experienced migraine, nervous fits, and symptoms of epilepsy; was diagnosed as having "gravel in the bladder"; and was treated regularly by doctors in Kiev for that and other vague illnesses during the fall and winter of 1866–67, a time when his father was becoming terminally ill.[2] From very early in his life, then, Conrad was exposed to grave and chronic family illnesses and grew accustomed to extended periods of attention from medical practitioners. In a metaphoric and literal sense, physicians thus became responsible for Conrad's life education.

After Apollo's death in May of 1869 and during his years as a ward of his uncle, Tadeusz Bobrowski, Conrad studied under the supervision of men of medicine. Conrad's primary tutor from 1870 to 1874 was Adam Marek Pulman, a medical student at Jagiellonian University, who did his best to curb the "quixotic" nature of the young Conrad.[3] After returning from political exile in 1871, Dr. Izydor Kopernicki—a well-known physician, anthropologist, and old Korzeniowski family friend—provided additional supervision of Conrad's indifferent career as a student. Dr. Kopernicki was likewise to serve as young Korzeniowski's contact in Marienbad, the Bavarian health spa, in case Tadeusz Bobrowski were delayed and unable to keep his scheduled meeting with Conrad during July of 1883.[4] In Conrad's adult life, medical doctors would continue to play an important role as admirers of his art, as close friends and confidants of Conrad's innermost fears, and as generous practitioners who provided medical maintenance for the Conrad household with its attendant afflictions: Conrad's nervous disorders, gout, and susceptibility to influenza; Jessie Conrad's emerging nervous disorders, orthopedic and coronary problems; and Borys's continual hosting of childhood diseases.

Having suffered numerous episodes of gout, depression, and premonitory minor breakdowns in 1900 and 1903, Conrad collapsed in midwinter of 1910. At the age of fifty-three, Conrad had suffered from nervous symptoms for nearly twenty years, ever since his return from the Congo. From what we know of Conrad's illnesses, he clearly displays the symptoms of neurasthenia as described by a contemporary reference tool for medical psychologists of the 1890s, D. Hack Tuke's *A Dictionary of Psychological Medicine*. Writing the entry on neurasthenia for the dictionary, Rudolf Arndt—professor of psychiatry at the University of Greifswald, Germany—outlines some of the myriad symptoms of neurasthenia that fit the Conrad medical profile: "Excitability, with a tendency to rapid fatigue and exhaustion, . . . mental excitement, . . . sense of uneasiness. . . . Hypochondriasis or melancholy develop according to the subjects with which the mind of the patient is occupied" (*DPM*, 843). Importantly, the symptoms of mental disorder are accompanied by physical symptoms: "Pains in the back and in the joints, . . . pains in the muscles, . . . peculiar and vague sensations of great fatigue, . . . principally in the legs and feet, . . . palpitation and a sense of oppression and anxiety" (844, 846). The causes of neurasthenia, listed by Arndt, read rather like Conrad's vita from the 1890s until his breakdown in 1910: "The development of neurasthenia is specially favoured by overwork, more particularly of a mental kind, by late hours, disappointment, grief and care, by unsatisfied ambition, exhaustion, long or severe illness, sexual excesses. . . . that is to say, by circumstances which, on the one hand, bring about a direct wearing out of the nervous system and, on the other, injure the general nutrition by loss of blood and strength, thus also weakening the nerves" (848).

What is more, neurasthenia was thought to "give rise to a number of other diseases representing their first symptoms. . . . Gout . . . is often preceded by it, or rather, people with a gouty diathesis [hereditary disposition] are mostly neurasthenic" (848). Conrad was thus a classic case of neurasthenia, and, since the nerve disorder was widely recognized as a gateway disease that could lead to more serious forms of mental degeneration, he increasingly feared for his mental health.

The year previous to his 1910 nervous breakdown had been personally and professionally difficult, even by the standards of an author no stranger to anxiety: he was estranged from his friend Ford Madox Ford, progress on *Under Western Eyes* had long been agonizingly slow, a bout with influenza weakened him, and an ugly row with his literary agent, Pinker, apparently precipitated his complete collapse. Jessie Conrad wrote to David Meldrum, a friend and literary advisor to Conrad, "The novel is finished, but the penalaty [*sic*] has to be paid. Months of nervous strain have ended in a complete nervous breakdown. Poor Conrad is very ill and D[r] Hackney says it will be a long time before he is fit for anything requiring mental exertion." Indeed, Conrad was apparently speaking in Polish to the characters of *Under Western Eyes* and, in more lucid moments, deeply afraid that he would be institutionalized. Jessie Conrad continues to Meldrum: "I have been up with him night and day since Sunday week and he, who is usually so depressed by illness, maintains he is not ill, and accuses the D[r] and I of trying to put him into an asylum."[5] Following Bernard Meyer's lead, many in the Conrad community have long assumed that Conrad's collapse and his odd behavior are the results of a psychotic state, induced by illness and psychological repression of various personal issues of a professional and perhaps sexual nature.[6] Conrad's admirers, of course, will never know what was *really* wrong with him. His cantankerous comment, reported by Jessie as she recalls him pouring his medicines down the kitchen drain and disparaging three loyal doctor friends who were each attending him without any knowledge of the other practitioners, only entices medical speculation: "'I know what is wrong with me,' Conrad insisted, 'but I'm not going to tell them. I'm not going to do half the dam' doctor's work for him.'"[7] Such tantalizing reports have inspired some ingenious medical sleuthing and a range of possible medical diagnoses, from mercury poisoning following calomel treatments to more exotic tropical diseases such as loiasis, whose symptoms are caused by the subcutaneous migration of newly hatched larvae deposited with the bite of the tabinid fly.[8] It is important to remember, with all due respect to the memory of Conrad, that any attempt to prove what was medically wrong with him is to diagnose posthumously his mortal remains. While we can never answer the question of what was *really* wrong with Conrad, we can pose other questions that are answerable: How would Conrad and Conrad's contemporaries have understood the medical situation that prompted his odd behavior?

To answer this question—or, put another way, to provide a side of Conrad's history that has been quite understandably neglected—we need to forgo the temptation to psychoanalyze and instead to pose an additional series of questions that will help us understand Conrad's medical identity. Why, for instance, does

Conrad exhibit a seemingly unwarranted mistrust of Jessie and Dr. Hackney? What cultural conditions, in combination with his mental excitement, may have reasonably prompted his apparently unreasonable suspicions? What did Jessie Conrad and presumably Dr. Hackney mean by a "complete nervous breakdown," and how is this breakdown related to Conrad's diagnosed neurasthenia, for which he was repeatedly treated by a recognized expert in the field? Why did Conrad wait more than thirty years to mention publicly, in *Last Essays,* that he had been diagnosed as neurasthenic?[9] The answers to these questions could again lead us to psychoanalyze Conrad. But if this distinctly twentieth-century urge can be curbed, additional new and potentially revealing questions, which may help us understand the breakdown and the artist himself, emerge. First, is the diagnosis of neurasthenia that Conrad apparently received from Dr. Ludwig at the German Hospital consistent with biographical evidence and contemporary medical discourse? If so, what would Conrad's prescribed medical treatment have been at Champel-les-Bains's Hydropathic Institute, and what *socio*psychological effects might be expected from such a cure? Given his understanding of his medical situation, what were Conrad's life prospects and how did he understand his gender and sexuality? Finally, and most importantly, what impact did these medical issues have on his fiction? How do medico-psychological issues, to appropriate Jessie Conrad's words, become "mixed up in the scenes" of his fiction?

The answers to these questions may be found in pre-Freudian medical psychology, with which Conrad probably had more than a passing familiarity, and which will be the lens through which I read his fiction.[10] As a student of Conrad, I have long believed that the most fascinating and compelling readings of Conrad's life and fiction are based on a psychology of the unconscious, but my approach in this study will be based on the supposition that the psychoanalyst often reaches conclusions—insightful, convincing, and elegant ones—that differ significantly from what Conrad knew about himself, his sexuality, and his medical and mental conditions. I make this supposition because Conrad's doctors, from the 1890s to his breakdown in 1910, were trained by or were themselves mostly pre-Freudian medical practitioners who understood nervous disorders in the context of organic pathology. To be sure, Conrad lived at the moment of the birth of modern psychoanalysis and was also treated by physicians who were proto-Freudian. Conrad's physician at Champel-les-Bains was, like Freud, a student of Dr. Jean-Martin Charcot, the French pioneer of hysteria studies who provided Freud with a point of departure for his later work on human neurosis. Thus, I do not wish not to vilify psychoanalytical readings of Conrad but to work toward an alternate understanding of Conrad's medical situation from 1891 to 1910 based on biographical materials, his medical and personal relationship with his physicians, and the pre-Freudian medical psychology in which they were trained and by which Conrad generally understood his health. As a matter of critical principle, then, I will avoid psychoanalytical interpretations of Conrad and his work, unless such observations are necessary to contextualize or elucidate the relation of psychological medicine to Conrad's life and fiction.

In part I, the first chapter of this study will focus the social history of lunacy in the nineteenth century; on various medico-psychological disorders such as neurasthenia, hysteria, and moral insanity that were mental disorders based on the anthropological paradigm of degeneration; and on how the medical discourse of the late nineteenth century provided Conrad with an understanding of his physical and emotional state after his Congo voyage. The second chapter will detail the therapy Conrad received after his Congo voyages, focusing on various aspects of the diet and water cure Conrad received in the care of Dr. Paul Glatz in Champel, Switzerland, and how the Champel treatment may have contributed to the construction of Conrad's gender identity. The third chapter will focus on Dr. A. E. Tebb, his training, and his role in Conrad's most nervous and productive years, from 1898 through and after his breakdown in 1910. Part I will also focus on the medical profile of the male neurasthenic and how he would have been perceived by the masculinist and the neuropathology-oriented medical circles of London. I wish here to disclaim either any allegiance to or present-day sense of superiority over the medical theories discussed in this study. Many of the theories and therapies are, by current medical standards or social values, inefficacious, obviously silly, or wrongheaded, and at first they are almost inevitably amusing. But when the chuckles subside, these therapies must also be seriously regarded for what they are: part of the medical reality of Conrad's day and the means by which he tried to alleviate his personal suffering.

In part II I will read Conrad medically, through the lens of psychological medicine. I will examine several formal aspects of Conrad's work, beginning with his "vivid, *nervous* descriptions" and with rhetorical or narrative strategies that represent either hysteria or the sequences of neurasthenia and thus permit Conrad to narrate his own medical history. Subsequent chapters will suggest how his fear of madness is evident in the major fictional tropes of restraint, solitude, and water—all of which were prominent issues in the medical discourse of pre-Freudian mental science. Finally, part II will examine the medical construction of nervous disorder evident in Conrad's treatment of these themes, for during Conrad's lifetime neurasthenia, hysteria, and insanity were being reconstructed as feminine diseases that might afflict either sex. The last body chapter focuses on three post-breakdown novels—*Chance, Victory,* and *The Shadow-Line*—as allegorical accounts of Conrad coming to terms with his neurasthenia and gender identity. Since the study will focus primarily on Conrad's life and work from the Congo voyage in 1890 to his nervous breakdown in 1910, it will also offer a medico-psychological reading of the achievement/decline debate that has occupied Conrad scholars on and off during the last half of the twentieth century. In the conclusion I argue that *The Arrow of Gold* marks a change in Conrad's understanding of nervous disease, and, like Virginia Woolf's *Mrs. Dalloway,* questions whether pre-Freudian medical psychology could effectively treat the neuroses of the modern world.

Part I

Lunacy, Conrad, and His Doctors

The outcry of the modern neurotic has made itself heard rather unduly of late. It is said that we are drooping with the century, a century of stress and of unsatisfied desires. . . .

If all this be true—and surely it must be true, as we are assured of it day by day—shall we wonder if the body go the way of the soul, if the fibres of our nerves be slackened, if the currents of our blood languish, if the stores in the cells of our brains decrease? . . .

If we grow morbid, over-delicate, whimsical; if we suffer from new and inscrutable degenerations, from unrest, from unnatural appetites, from quivering nerves, from hollow-ness of heart, shall we not sullenly accept realities however ugly and put off all deliriums however enticing? . . .

Among the gravest apprehensions of the moment is that the alleged increase of insanity may be true, and that, if true, it is due to a turbulent or carking mode of life which overthrows the reason or corrodes the tissues which are its instruments. . . . The only evidence of such a dispropor-tionate increase is that the number of *known* lunatics in-creases at a greater rate than the population.—Dr. T. Clifford Allbutt, Regius Professor of Physic, University of Cambridge, from "Nervous Diseases and Modern Life," *Contemporary Review,* 1895

Chapter 1
Before Freud

> Charcot, who is one of the greatest of physicians and a
> man whose common sense is touched by genius[,] is simply
> uprooting my aims and opinions. I sometimes come out of
> his lectures as though I were coming out of Notre Dame,
> with a new idea of perfection.—Sigmund Freud, from a
> letter to his fiancée

On 6 May 1910, more than four months after his nervous
breakdown, Joseph Conrad wrote to Arthur Symons, welcoming
him back to Kent and apologizing for not inviting him at once to
Aldington: "We dare not ask your wife and yourself to come
over—not just yet at any rate. We have been pigging it in 4 rooms
in a cottage looking out meantime for a farmhouse to fall empty
in this part of Kent. Our *intérieur* is not fit to be seen at present
my illness having had a generally upsetting character" (*CL*,
4:326). The next day in Oxford, Bernard Hart, lecturer in mental
diseases at University College Hospital (London), read a paper
entitled "The Psychology of Freud and His School" before the
British Psychological Society. The paper, Hart began, "endeavours
to describe, in short and summary form, the principle tenets of
[Freud's] school of psychology." True to his word, Hart then
glosses, in plain terms and examples, Freudian concepts such as
the "unconscious complex," "association," "repression/censure,"
"obsession," and dream theory.[1] Hart observed that his task was
one of "very considerable difficulty," because the material, "satisfying enough to the psychiatrist may appear forced and incomprehensible to psychologists more accustomed to the sane than
the insane."[2] Hart's sense of audience reveals a good deal about

the state of psychiatry and medical psychology at the time of Conrad's breakdown. First, the necessity for such a rudimentary lecture suggests how radical and as yet difficult Freud's theories were to the medical establishment, even though Hart delivered his paper more than a decade after the initial publication of Freud's groundbreaking work. Second, it reveals the division between psychiatrists, those few who embraced Freud's theories of the unconscious, and the recalcitrant medical psychologists in Hart's audience who were trained to understand mental disease as arising from some physiological, often neurological, disorder. Hart articulates this conflict as central both to the professional discourse of the day and to the difficulty of advancing Freud's theories: "According to the physiologically minded, when we leave phenomenal consciousness we leave psychology, and the unconscious is only to be conceived as brain-traces, brain-dispositions, and so forth. Freud claims, however, that it is possible to attempt the explanation of phenomenal consciousness not only by conceptions couched in the terms of physiology, but also by conceptions couched in the terms of psychology."[3] In short, British medical psychologists of Conrad's day found Freudian theory untenable because his work is based on the concept of the unconscious, which had no empirical basis in the medical reality of the day, that is, in the human body.

As we know from his famous dictum in the preface to *The Nigger of the "Narcissus,"* Conrad not only was comfortable with but also, as an artist, celebrated the permeability of the physical and mental worlds: "[M]y task," he insists, "is to make you *see*" (*NN,* xiv). Conrad's comment to Symons likewise recognizes the connection between phenomena and the mind: "Our *intérieur* is not fit to be seen at present my illness having had a generally upsetting character." The metaphorical significance of *"intérieur"* seems inescapable, suggesting both domestic space and, consonant with the French idiom *à l'intérieur de lui-même,* the mind, the space within the self. Clearly, Conrad here appears to anticipate the psychoanalyst. When the distinguished lecturer Hart, near the end of his paper, concludes from Freud's "demonstration . . . that the flow of phenomenal consciousness is conditioned by psychological causes of whose existence the individual is altogether unaware—a fact known implicitly to every competent novelist and historian," the intuition of the artist (and certainly that of Conrad) is elevated above the science of current psychological medicine.[4] For Conrad, as novelist and student of human nature, the mind renders the universe intelligible or, when mind fails, disordered. The mind, in this scheme, is superior to the body. But would Conrad, as medical patient, be able to see the mind as distinct from and superior to the body? Probably not, for Conrad's fear of insanity (mental disorder) was clearly pre-Freudian and, as such, was focused in his early adult years on a specific, somatic etiology: the distant threats of epilepsy and tuberculosis and his current gouty, nervous disorders as presented to him and as treated by his physicians. Despite Conrad's word play on *intérieur* and his intuitive grasp of human psychology, Conrad would have seen an intimate connection between the health of body and mind, and he apparently found Freud's psychological theories, based on the concept of the unconscious, untenable and inchoate.[5]

Similar conflicting generalizations may be observed about other literary modernists, most of whom represent the unconscious but were publicly cool to Freudian theory and its application to literature or their own medical histories. William Faulkner told an interviewer rather coyly, "Freud I'm not familiar with," but he also asserted, in affected Southern dialect, that "the writer don't have to know Freud to have written things which anyone who does know Freud can divine and reduce to symbols."[6] Virginia Woolf was more bitterly hostile to Freud. Her letters scornfully recount the failed Freudian analysis of her nephews and a distrust of Freudian symbolic interpretations, of "Germans" with their "gull-like imbecility." Nonetheless, not long after she wrote these words, the Hogarth Press published a series of psychoanalytical treatises, and by 1939 Woolf's diary entries indicate she was "gulping up Freud."[7] Chester G. Anderson suggests that James Joyce encountered Freud early, perhaps as early as 1902–4, when he was a medical student. Joyce later treated him with a superior, amused contempt—as "Viennese Tweedledee"— the kind reserved for worthy adversaries.[8]

Modernists may thus have written psychological novels or poetry about psychic disintegration and regeneration, but they did not become Freudians until, like Woolf and "H. D.," late in their careers. Like those physiologists in Professor Hart's Oxford audience, literary modernists found Freud an unwelcome competitor, working the same patch of soil but with new and different tools, challenging received notions about human motivation and behavior, but with clinical rather than narrative experimentation. Freud thus marks a fissure in the ground between the medical and literary arts of the early twentieth century. Indeed, the competition from Freud may have created a mildly reactionary response

5

in the artists to embrace the past; though self-characterized social iconoclasts, modernists such as Conrad, Woolf, and Joyce
were raised in Victorian households where moral, mental, and
general medical health were typically linked, and, in early adulthood, their illnesses were treated by physicians who, like those
men in Professor Hart's audience, were trained long before
Freud was widely accepted and who comfortably practiced pre-
Freudian medicine.

The Social History of Lunacy
in Nineteenth-Century England

Though the medical and literary communities of the early
twentieth century were slow to accept Freud's radical ideas, the
field of medical psychology was anything but dormant before
Freud. Debate about the care and treatment of the insane was an
important part of Victorian social discourse, engaging the public
as a subject in the popular journals and as a matter of government policy. Given Conrad's medical history, expressed fear of
insanity, periodical reading habits, and literary preoccupations,
Conrad was surely sensible of the extraordinary activity in the
field of mental science and what was called "the progress lunacy" during the pre-Freudian era of the 1890s. Indeed, the
whole century preceding the onset of Conrad's adult medical
problems (ca. 1790–1890) has long been regarded by medical
historians as a revolutionary time, when significant changes occurred in cultural attitudes toward mental disease and the insane,
and when medical advancements improved the understanding
and treatment of nervous disorders.[9] It is, to quote Andrew Scull,
an age that "saw the transformation of the madhouse into the
asylum into the mental hospital; of the mad-doctor into the
alienist into the psychiatrist; and of the madman (and madwoman) into the mental patient."[10] Contemporaneous assessments were no less optimistic. In 1905, the popular journal
Science proclaimed that "no greater progress has been recorded
in the history of medicine than has occurred in psychiatry during
the period that began when [Phillipe] Pinel, in the wards of the
Salpêtrière [actually the Bicêtre] first removed the chains from
the insane, and that culminated" in then-current advancements.[11]
Such appraisals and recent reinterpretations of the social history
of lunacy in nineteenth-century England often recount the almost

mythic liberation of the insane in 1792 when Pinel became chief physician at the Bicêtre, one of the four main Paris asylums.

Pinel advocated treatment that contrasted vividly with the customary treatment of the insane during the seventeenth and eighteenth centuries. According to *Madness and Civilization,* Michel Foucault's social history of madness, during the classical age the insane were popularly regarded as subhuman, lacking the rationality that distinguishes humans from other life forms. The insane were thus associated with animality as well as forbidden knowledge and mortality—all of which civilization, in the age of reason, generally sought to confine, organize, and hide away or, conversely, to exhibit before the ridiculing public, for a penny a visit.[12] The political reforms of the late eighteenth century brought with them an apparent, gradual democratization of social attitudes toward the lunatic.

The new values were the cornerstone of an asylum instituted by William Tuke, a Quaker, in 1792 and named The Retreat by his daughter-in-law Mary Marie Tuke to reflect its conception as "a place in which the unhappy might obtain a refuge; a quiet haven in which the shattered bark might find a means of reparation or of safety." It was not to resemble, in any way, the madhouses of the day, either in physical appearance, in its domestic arrangement, or in its therapeutic program. Two years after its opening, the Swiss physician Dr. de la Rive, described the house as "situated a mile from York, in the midst of a fertile and cheerful country; it presents not the idea of a prison, but rather that of a large rural farm. It is surrounded by a garden. There is no bar or grating to the windows."[13] The Retreat formulated what became known as "moral treatment" for the insane, a program that advocated individually designed treatment for each patient but whose "fundamental principles . . . should be those of kindness and consideration for the patients," as counter-distinguished either from then-standard medical therapy imposed upon the patient—the "bleeding, blisters, setons, evacuants, and many other prescriptions"—or from the brutality of standard asylum treatment.[14] The concept of moral treatment discouraged physical restraint of patients and advocated temporary seclusion in the event of a disruptive, violent incident. Drugs were administered cautiously, though "good malt liquor" was used as a nighttime sedation. The Retreat's therapeutic program offered "careful attention to the general health, and a very special use of the hot bath."[15] Recreation and agrarian occupations were encouraged for those capable of exercise or light work, such as gardening and the tending of poultry and rabbits. Finally, there was a general aim of creating an atmosphere of *"homishness"* and family life.[16]

Records of the first fifteen years of The Retreat's operation indicate an unusually high rate of restoring the insane to a state of sanity.[17] And, with the publication in 1813 of *Description of the Retreat* by Samuel Tuke, grandson of William Tuke, the conditions and program of The Retreat brought into clear, comparative focus the appalling conditions of other madhouses (especially the local York Asylum) and the need for more widespread reform.[18] Unfortunately, the existing Lunacy Law of 1774, "An Act for Regulating Mad-houses," offered an ineffective articulation of the responsibilities of madhouse proprietors and no real mechanism for enforcing the act. The official body of oversight—the College of Physicians—was *required* to issue a license to any house requesting one and had virtually no power of censure, other than a charge to post, in its own meeting place, an "animadversion" on an asylum about which the college received a complaint. It was not until the 1815–16 investigations of the Parliamentary Select Committee that the general awareness of the public was aroused. During the hearings, official visits to Bethlem and other asylums revealed squalid conditions that we today know well in our imaginations: asylum inmates chained naked in small cells covered with straw that was dampened and matted with urine and human excrement. Cells were unheated and the barred windows were often unglazed. A number of prominent asylum superintendents and their staff members were brought before the committee for questioning. The hearings further revealed that attendance of physicians was rare, sometimes as seldom as once in three months. As a result of the hearings, the efficacy of medical treatment for the insane was largely called into question, and the humane success of Tuke and Pinel's moral treatment, both in books they had authored and in institutions they administered, became increasingly apparent. In subsequent years, the superintendents of other county asylums, Dr. R. Gardiner Hill and Dr. E. P. Charlesworth in the Lincoln Asylum, for instance, and later Dr. John Conolly of the Hanwell Asylum, embraced aspects of the moral treatment. Within two decades of the publication of the Parliamentary Select Committee report, the practice of restraint was formally abolished (1837), and within three decades "An Act for the Regulation of the Care and Treatment of Lunatics" (1845) was established.[19]

The reforms of mid-nineteenth-century England—which took place while Conrad was still a child in Poland—established a system of county asylums to house local, insane paupers. John Conolly, the superintendent of the Hanwell Asylum for the Insane and author of *Familiar Views of Lunacy and Lunatic Life* (1850), described this history for the Victorian public at large. In rather emotive and sentimental terms, he urged a public accustomed to Trevelyanesque solutions to social problems to embrace a new and generous attitude toward lunatics and to adopt new treatments consistent with that attitude. Asylums were required to certify medically all consigned inmates and to keep detailed records of admission, medical treatment—incidents of restraint, seclusion, medication, other therapy—death, escape, or discharge. Asylums were subject to regular inspection by authority of the newly established Lunacy Commission.

Despite such social reforms of midcentury, abuse of the system of care for the lunatic population continued, especially in so-called "private houses" that were less subject to official intervention. In conception, private houses ensured the best possible care—more comfortable surroundings and more individual attention—for those who could afford it. But in practice such houses were often used to hide wealthy families' social stigmata. Parliamentary hearings of the 1860s, 1870s, and 1880s revealed reputed abuses of the sane by jealous or vindictive husbands and greedy relatives injured by the terms of an unfavorable inheritance, who falsely committed relatives out of revenge or even incorrigible children for convenience.[20] And since private houses operated on the principle of treatment/confinement for profit, their proprietors were often eager to admit but reluctant to discharge their patients. Reports of such gothic domestic melodrama kept the social role of the asylum in the public conscience and imagination. Ironically, the generally improved conditions in public asylums would likewise arouse public controversy in the last decade of the nineteenth century.

As Conrad was departing Europe for the Belgian Congo, the 1890 Law of Lunacy was enacted, and by the time Conrad returned, a uniform standard of care and treatment for the insane in England and Wales was in place. The law provided a detailed set of provisions governing the process of family petition, medical certification, and reception orders for committing lunatics into the asylum; rights of the lunatic including letter-writing, visitation, property rights, and leaves of absence; quality of care and treatment regarding diet, mechanical restraint, and sex of personal custodians; and removal of the incurable to workhouses or the discharge of patients.[21] Standardized procedures and judicial surveillance of the process did much to curb abuse, to improve the efficacy of treatment, and to prolong and improve the lives of the insane. Ironically, the improved conditions increased the numbers of insane persons under the official cognizance of the state and led to public alarm over this rise.

Fin-de-Siècle Medical Psychology: Degeneration, Moral Insanity, and Neurasthenia

Conrad's fear of insanity and the asylum is explicable—even rational—in light of the pervasive belief that the English people and culture were in decline, a trend validated by the paradigm of degeneration. Studies of late nineteenth-century and early twentieth-century culture have recently shown that degeneration theory served a wide range of social commentators: anthropologists, biologists, economists, social historians, political and military commentators, promoters of the bourgeoisie, and critics of modernity. Degeneration thus attained its status as a governing trope of cultural criticism due to its adaptability, versatility, and attraction to the Victorian public, who, fearing the degenerate and applying degeneration theory to the "condition of England" question, revealed in themselves a collective imaginative morbidity, attuned to the models of cultural entropy. Degeneration became, as Stephen Arata maintains, a "form of popular wisdom" that, among other things, could be used to explain the apparent rise in the incidence of insanity with the onset of modern life.[22]

Alarming the public to this rise of insanity became the life project of William Corbet, who from 1893 to 1906 published more than a dozen articles in *The Westminster Review* and the *Fortnightly Review* on "the progress of insanity." After serving more than twenty-five years as a statistician for the Irish Lunacy Department, Corbet began his career as a social commentator in 1874, reading a paper before the Statistical and Social Inquiry Society of Ireland in which he discussed "the progressive increase of insanity" in an Irish population greatly reduced by "famine, pestilence, and emigration." Corbet—who made a career of overlooking the obvious, compiling statistics, and diverting reasoned inquiry with rhetorical clichés—became a member of parliament in about 1880 and "thenceforward," in his own words, "never

10

ceased to urge the subject of the increase of insanity upon public attention both in the House of Commons and in the Press."[23] While it is difficult to adjudge the reception and impact of Corbet's project, the fact that he published so many pieces in mainstream periodicals, generated some serious responses to his work (both pro and con), and forced the sitting Lunacy Commission members to address his concerns in their annual reports, suggests that he had a genuine impact on public discourse on the epidemiology, care, and treatment of the insane.[24]

Corbet's success was the result of his tapping into a variety of popular socio-medical ideas of the late nineteenth century, especially degeneration theory and the "contagionism" of germ theory. His essays of 1893–1906—a time when Conrad suffered from continual fear for his mental stability—repeatedly invoke and synthesize the popularized themes and ideas of such writers as Charles Darwin, Benedict Augustin Morel, Sir Francis Galton, and Cesare Lombroso and are here quoted at length to elicit their tone and tactics, and the half-baked interdisciplinarity of the dilettante (all emphases are mine):

> The brain-poisoning goes on from year to year, and the authorities whose duty it is to warn the public make no sign. When the term brain-poisoning is used it will be understood as referring to the *hereditariness of insanity* with its handmaidens, crime, intemperance, and *moral depravity,* which are passed on as an *evil inheritance* from generation to generation.[25]

> The inevitable conclusion is forced upon us that not only has there been no melioration of the human species in the nineteenth century, but that we are in a state of actual *retrocession.* . . . The progressive increase in the numbers of the mentally unsound . . . tells its own sorrowful tale of *deteriorating brain-power amongst the masses,* particularly amongst the poor, from whom most of the inmates of public lunatic asylums are derived. On the other hand, the wretched physique and *stunted and misshapen forms* of the countless workers and wage-earners in our overcrowded city and town populations, coupled with the reduction of the standard height for army recruits, carry conviction as to the *physical degeneration* of the people.[26]

> Specialists, past and present, are all agreed that the virus of insanity once established in the system becomes hereditary. Broadly speaking, "like begets like" throughout nature, animate and inanimate, sound or unsound, all the world over. . . . *Darwin* (*Descent of Man,* vol. i., pp. 110, 111) says: "I have elsewhere so fully discussed the subject of inheritance that I need here hardly add

anything. A greater number of facts have been collected with respect to transmission of the most trifling as well as of the most important characters in man than in any of the lower animals,
though the facts are copious enough with respect to the latter. So
in regard to mental qualities, their transmission is manifest in our
dogs, horses, and other domestic animals. Besides special tastes
and habits, general intelligence, courage, bad and good temper,
&c., are certainly transmitted. With man we see similar facts in almost every family, and we now know, through the admirable la-
bours of Mr. *Galton,* that *genius,* which implies a wonderfully
complex combination of high faculties, *tends to be inherited;* and,
on the other hand, [Corbet's emphasis follows] *it is too certain
that insanity and deteriorated mental powers likewise run in the
same families.*[27]

Since the predisposition to mental degeneration and insanity
was, in fact, generally regarded as hereditary, Corbet often argued that the increase in insanity—metaphorically described as
an "ever-rising flood," as "advancing with rapid strides," as a
"skeleton at the feast," or simply as a "virus"—could be stopped
only by some form of genetic control, most often by compulsory
detention or a prohibition of marriage of persons with a history
of mental insanity. Sometimes he argued for more extreme mea-
sures, such as "sterilization of the insane" or even eugenic destruction of insane persons.[28]

While Corbet's tirades seem absurd to us (as indeed they did
to many of his contemporaries), they are also a product of the
germ theory that was emerging in the late nineteenth century,
combined with the spiritual and nationalist panic common in late
Victorian England.[29] Corbet's alarmist project may be read as the
reaction to a variety of then-tenable anthropological and medico-
psychological theories (especially degeneration) that arose from
and confirmed Darwinian pessimism. John W. Griffith, in *Joseph
Conrad and the Anthropological Dilemma,* has surveyed how
the health of the British Empire and Conrad's work can be understood in the context of late-nineteenth-century anthropological theories of Charles Darwin, Max Nordau, Cesare Lombroso, and others, and how such theories helped Conrad explore
the tropes of primitivism and civilization and issues such as "ac-
climatization" and tropical disease, atavism, "regression of the
cultural hybrid," and "denationalization."[30] But Conrad's interest in degeneration was focused not only on broad issues of
race, empire, and culture; it was focused on how such theories
potentially touched his own physical and mental beings. Thus,

we need to understand degeneration theory not only as a medical discourse used to critique English culture but also as the governing paradigm for pre-Freudian psychological conditions such as moral insanity, hysteria, and neurasthenia—medical issues that give rise to the central tropes of Conrad's fiction.

Degeneration theory, the most general anthropological hypothesis offering evidence of and a mechanism for the decline of the human species, was first articulated two years before the publication of Darwin's *Origin of Species* in M. Morel's *Traité des dégénérescences physiques, intellectuelles, et morales de l'espèce humaine*, a work that proved useful to late Victorians reconsidering the "condition of England" question in light of growing urbanization.[31] James Cantlie in *Degeneration amongst Londoners* (1885) and J. P. Freeman-Williams in *The Effect of Town Life on the General Health* (1890) suggested that the English race was jeopardized by the physical deterioration occasioned by urban life in an environment of poor air and water, crowded and unsanitary living conditions, and sedentary vocations out of synch with the accelerating pace of modern life. Cantlie confirmed his theory by locating a third-generation Londoner whose vital statistics were alarming: "height, 5 ft. 1 in.; age 21, chest measurement 28 in.; his head measured across from tip of ear to tip of ear, 11 in. (1 1/2 in. below the average). His aspect is pale, waxy; he is very narrow between the eyes and with a decided squint!" Freeman-Williams sounded a more ominous note: "The child of the townsman is bred too fine, it is too great an exaggeration of himself, excitable and painfully precocious in its childhood, neurotic, dyspeptic, pale and undersized in its adult state, if it ever reaches it. . . . This town type, in the third . . . generation . . . becomes more and more exaggerated. . . . A pure Londoner of the fourth generation is not capable of existing."[32] But the great popularizer of degeneration theory in England during Conrad's adult life was Max Nordau, a student of both Morel and Lombroso, whose work, *Degeneration,* was published in English translation in 1895.[33] Since the work was not only widely read but also applies the medico-psychological notion of degeneration to literature and the arts, it almost surely attracted Conrad's notice, given his inherited medical problems, chosen vocation, and subsequent references to the concept. Nordau defines degeneration—the concept of degeneration that Conrad would have known—in Morelian terms as *"a morbid deviation from an original type.* This deviation, even if, at the outset, it was ever so slight, contained transmissible elements of such a nature that anyone bearing in him the germs becomes more and more incapable of fulfilling his functions in the world; and mental progress, already checked in his own person, finds itself menaced also in his descendants."[34] Nordau saw the fin-de-siècle mood as indicating the decline of Western civilization brought about by the operation of degeneration. This decline, according to Nordau, was most evident in the mysticism of the French Symbolists and their highly personal *correspondance* between image-symbol and meaning; in the regressive, decorative medievalism of the pre-Raphaelites; in the skeptical pondering and searching of Tolstoi; in the "ego-mania" of Wagner and Nietzsche; and in the freethinking of Ibsen.[35]

The conservative moral slant of Nordau's cultural criticism was based on an inattentive reading of his "master," Cesare Lombroso, to whom he dedicated his book. In the dedication, Nordau argues that "[d]*egenerates are not always criminals, prostitutes, anarchists, and pronounced lunatics; they are often authors and artists,*" who manifest *"more or less pronounced moral insanity, imbecility, and dementia."*[36] Nordau's mentor was quick to distance himself from his disciple's work. In two columns of his review, Lombroso compliments Nordau's application of "psychiatric research to literary criticism" and for having "felt the pulse of his times" (which is not the same thing as accurately reading it).[37] But in the remaining eight columns Lombroso criticizes "Nordau's Errors," most particularly his failure to accept that degeneration is a natural bedfellow of genius: "To demonstrate that geniuses are insane is not difficult because . . . genius is a form of degenerative neurosis. . . . Degeneration, for one who follows my theories, instead of destroying, fortifies the diagnosis which proves them to be geniuses, and enlarges its range. . . . The man of genius is a man who does better than his contemporaries, and in a different way; he is therefore an abnormal being, an exception. He is different from his environment, he is not completely sane as to his intellect, he has many physiological and psychological blemishes, he is afflicted either by the delirium of persecution, or by megalomania, or . . . more often by psychic epilepsy."[38] Lombroso's criticism of Nordau focuses on the intimacy of genius and degeneration, a subject of current interest to medical psychologists that would likewise have interested Conrad, both personally and professionally, for he was then testing his own literary genius and simultaneously fearing for his mental health. Several years after his 1910 breakdown, and from a more distant perspective, Conrad's Marlow in *Chance* would refer disparagingly to "the theory of poetical

genius being allied to madness . . . in some idiotic book everybody was reading a few years ago" (*C*, 184). That book, which
Conrad probably took more seriously in the 1890s, is Lombroso's
The Man of Genius (1891), the book whose ideas Nordau
misappropriates.

Lombroso's work devotes three early chapters to "Genius and
Degeneration," "Latent Forms of *Neurosis* and Insanity in Genius," and "Genius and *Insanity*," a sequence that, as the added
emphases suggest, charts the sequence of mental decline into
madness. In the second stage of latent neurosis, Lombroso recognizes that the combined presence of genius and degeneration
may result in a "complete absence of moral sense and of sympathy," a condition known as "moral insanity."[39] The term was
made an integral part of the nosography of insanity by James
Prichard in his *A Treatise on Insanity* (1835). He defined moral
insanity as a form of "mental derangement" experienced by individuals who function in society but who suffer from "a morbid
perversion of the natural feelings, affections, inclinations, temper,
habits, moral dispositions, and natural impulses, without any remarkable disorder or defect of the intellect or knowing and reasoning faculties, and particularly without any insane illusion or
hallucination."[40] The morally insane, according to Prichard, are
persons of "a singular, wayward and eccentric character" who
are somehow "remarkable in their manners and habits" and
make the observer wonder as to whether they are entirely sane.
Such individuals have generally undergone a sudden change in
character or temperament. The altered person may have suffered
a reversal of fortune or lost a beloved relative, which has traumatized the affective life; hence, a specific form of moral insanity is
"affective insanity" (*DPM*, 56). Since this cause for insanity has
no physiological origin, Prichard suggested that moral insanity
might also arise from a "severe shock which his bodily constitution has undergone. This has been either a disorder affecting the
head, a slight attack of paralysis, a fit of epilepsy, or some febrile
or inflammatory disorder"—in other words, some lesion in the
nervous or cerebral structure.[41] Whether the etiology is emotional or somatic, the intellectual faculties of the morally insane
initially remain unaffected while the moral and affective life, at
the root of this form of mental disease, is critically altered.

Hanna Augstein suggests that Prichard's disease of the moral
faculties was inspired by his "dismay at the decline of religion in
a materialist age."[42] If her speculation is true, then "moral insanity"

may be thought of, in its inception, as a precursor of degeneration, an earlier metaphor for the acedia of modern life and the
spiritual crisis that results. Moral insanity—whether most closely
associated with a moral, spiritual, or affective degeneration—
afflicts characters pervasively in Conrad's fiction. Barbara Gates
uses Prichard's concept to discuss Kurtz, but does not acknowledge the entire range of characters who might well be diagnosed
with a similar malady.[43] Beginning with Kurtz, one might develop a list of such characters, which could include Gentleman
Brown, Plain Mr. Jones, and the Professor; the narrator of "The
Secret Sharer," Nostromo, and Razumov, who struggle to maintain their moral sanity; and, finally, the characters in *The Secret
Agent,* who may justifiably be thought a gallery of moral idiocy:
Yundt, Ossipon, Winnie-Stevie, Verloc, and even Vladimir—all
fit the medical profile. It is comically appropriate that Conrad
should divulge his medical knowledge and (perhaps) inscribe
his ideological perspective in the dying words of the notorious
Baron Stott-Wartenheim: "Unhappy Europe! Thou shalt perish by
the moral insanity of thy children!" (*SA,* 27).

If degeneration theory had any competition in the public consciousness that could similarly express the fin-de-siècle sense of
mental, spiritual, or moral decline, the alternative was nervous
disease in the forms of hysteria and neurasthenia. The nosology
of nervous diseases—especially hypochondriasis, hysteria, neurasthenia, and epilepsy—preoccupied the medical communities
of America, England, and Europe (especially France) in the
1880s and 1890s, and this process of classification and differenti-
ation, occurring early in the women's movement, sought to
codify the "interactions between medicine, disease, and gender"
that occur when cultures construct newly recognized diseases.[44]
In England, hypochondriasis and melancholia had long been
recognized as male nervous disorders that were distinguished
from their female counterpart, hysteria.[45] Challenging that gender
classification, Dr. Jean-Martin Charcot in France methodically
documented more than fifty case studies of male hysteria in the
1880s and early 1890s.[46] At the same time in America, a new disease called neurasthenia was being constructed as a cross-gender
affliction distinct from hysteria but, like hysteria, thought of as a
functional disorder that had no apparent organic cause. Skeptical of any disease that has no physiological basis, most English
mental scientists snubbed neurasthenia and, unhappy with the
linguistic contradiction of "male hysteria" but unable to question
the reputation or methodology of Charcot, construed his form of

hysteria as actually hystero-epilepsy and suggested that (female) hysteria itself was "but an important species of neurasthenia" (*DPM,* 619).[47] Conrad enters this complex medical arena as a Europe-born Englishman, diagnosed as neurasthenic by a German national, and treated in 1891 by a Swiss physician who was a student and follower of Charcot.[48]

Neurasthenia, popularly termed "nervousness" (especially in America) and in its extreme forms called "nerve prostration" or "nervous breakdown," was a disorder thought by some members of the medical profession to be one mechanism of degeneration and thus subsumed under it.[49] But nervousness was thought such a widespread disorder that it attained, in the public imagination, the independent status of an upscale, even fashionable, affliction.[50] The medical history of nervousness evolved with the career of George M. Beard, a Yale-trained physician who specialized in nervous disorders and the medical use of electricity. Practicing medicine and lecturing in New York City in the late 1860s, Beard found many of his urban patients complained of various ill-defined symptoms that had no somatic basis but produced apparently genuine anxiety, fatigue, and eccentric behavior.[51] Discerning a constellation of symptoms, Beard suggested in 1869 that his patients were afflicted with "neurasthenia" or "nervous exhaustion." As the name implies, neurasthenia was thought to be a weakening of the nervous system, the "impoverishment of nervous force. . . . 'Nervousness' is really nervelessness."[52] The pathology of the nervous system, before the concept of the neuron, was conceived as "a closed and continuous channel. A fixed quantity of nervous force, assumed to be electrical in nature, filled and coursed through this channel. It was this nervous force which carried messages from one part of the body to another, from the brain to the various organs, and, in addition, served as the raw material of conscious thought." Since the nervous system was envisioned as a closed structure with a finite amount of nervous force, stress or disease could create an imbalance or deficiency of force that could result in nervous exhaustion. But if the physiology of the nervous system was concretely envisioned, the circumstances of stress or disease left no physical lesions, and Beard would frequently rely on metaphors— dynamos, overloaded electrical circuits, overdrawn bank accounts —to describe the failure of nerve.[53] Since Beard thus defined neurasthenia as a functional disorder that had no definable pathology and whose etiology was psychological, his concept of this disorder was met with considerable skepticism by the medical community, especially in England, where the neuropathology of Henry Maudsley prevailed.[54] But during the next decade, as the number of patients showing characteristic symptoms and patterns of behavior increased, the disorder gained such acceptance in America that Beard could claim confidently that "nervous exhaustion (neurasthenia) is in this country more common than any other form of nervous disease," and, a decade later, warn that it was "the door which opens into quite a large number of diseases of the nervous system" including various forms of insanity.[55]

If current medical discourse conceived of and defined disease in terms of etiology, pathology, and treatment, Beard's neurasthenia challenged the boundaries of that model of discourse. First, the etiology of the disease was generally thought to be psychological, sociological, and cultural.[56] Neurasthenia, like its cousin degeneration, was brought on by the stress of modern, urban life: its instantaneous telegraphs, a thriving press, a rail system that invaded the tranquility of the country and increased the rapidity of transit, and the noise and relentless productivity of steam-powered, industrial society.[57] The disease spared agrarian America and was concentrated in the Northeast. If degeneration in England was often conceived as a decline led by the laboring class, American neurasthenia was a disorder of the affluent, especially the "new woman"; derailed from her traditional roles but still encouraged to be weak and sickly, she was hypereducated and her nervous system taxed beyond its limits.[58] As John Haller observes, "Neurasthenia became . . . a rationalization of America's new social order . . . a justification for the mores of the gilded age of American culture," which was increasingly turning to a brain-powered, urban culture.[59]

Neurasthenia thus became known as the "American Disease" not only by virtue of the rising diagnoses of nervousness in America but also due to its functional rather than organic nature.[60] England needed a physiological explanation for illness. While Beard suggested that the organic cause for neurasthenia would be discovered when the appropriate technology of detection was developed, English "mental scientists," as they often called themselves, required a verifiable pathology for mental disease. Indeed, when D. Hack Tuke published his groundbreaking *A Dictionary of Psychological Medicine*—just at the time when Conrad was beginning his program of medical treatments—neurasthenia was still a "foreign" disease. Of the 140 international physicians who contributed to the dictionary only six were

Americans, and the author of the entry on neurasthenia was Rudolf Arndt, a German advocate of neurasthenia as a functional disorder, who, like Freud, suspected that nervous disease might not have an organic (pathological) origin. Not surprisingly, Conrad's diagnosis of neurasthenia in 1891 was made by a German-trained physician at the German Hospital in London.

During the 1880s and 1890s, Beard and his followers focused on identifying the "sequences" of the disease: its symptoms, associated diseases, its stages, and morbidity. In 1880, C. H. Hughes, one of the leading advocates of neurasthenia, quoted Dr. E. H. Van Deusen, another pioneer in the study of American nervousness, whose summary of the causes and symptoms of neurasthenia sounds much like almost any half-year period in Conrad's life from 1890 to 1910:

> "AMONG THE CAUSES (of Neurasthenia), excessive mental labor, especially when conjoined with anxiety and deficient nourishment, ranks first. It is also traceable to depressing emotions, grief, domestic trouble, prolonged anxiety and pecuniary embarrassment; hemorrhage and debilitating diseases, following or coincident with depressing mental influences and sleeplessness. Prolonged exposure in a malarial region under certain circumstances may also induce it.
>
> "ITS LEADING SYMPTOMS are general *malaise,* impaired nutrition and assimilation; muscular atonicity, changing the expression of the countenance; uterine displacements, with consequent results, and neuralgias of debility, cerebral anaemia, with accompanying tendency to hyperaesthesia, irritability, mental depression, impaired intellection, melancholia and mania."[61]

Associated maladies include diseases of the reproductive organs, hay fever, writer's cramp, trance, paralysis, and Bright's, and such "sequences" could lead to permanent hysteria and hystero-epilepsy, neuralgia, inebriety, and various insanities, especially melancholia.[62] By 1905—when Beard's *A Practical Treatise on Nervous Exhaustion (Neurasthenia)* was in a posthumous fifth edition and when Ford Madox Ford (and Conrad) had been diagnosed with the disorder—neurasthenia could be indicated by a breathtaking list of some ninety symptoms and associated phobias, among them classical symptoms that Conrad experienced: cerebral irritation, sick headache and head pain, mental irritability, hopelessness, morbid fears (such as agoraphobia, claustrophobia, monophobia), sleeplessness, bad dreams, nervous dyspepsia, hyperesthesia, shooting pains, palpitations of the heart, spasms of muscles, convulsive movements, a feeling of profound exhaustion, vague pains and flying neuralgias, and rapid decay of teeth.[63]

The myriad symptoms were most often treated by the Weir Mitchell rest cure, a therapy program used widely on neurasthenic American women and one that had a range of socio- and psycho-medical goals that can be interpreted variously, depending on one's ideological perspective. Weir Mitchell and his followers sincerely believed the rest cure would help nervous and anemic women rebuild their supply of red blood cells and thereby restore their metabolism, appetite, energy, and mental equilibrium; in our present feminist world we realize that this program of treatment had the practical effect of restraining/imprisoning women in order to forcibly reorient them to their "natural" domestic roles. Whatever the aims or effects, the five components of the cure included rest, seclusion, diet, massage, and electric therapy.[64] Dr. George Savage, a leading medical psychologist in London from approximately 1880 to 1920 (and who had, I will argue, a once-removed but important impact on the life of Conrad), succinctly described the Weir Mitchell treatment for neurasthenia in his influential textbook, *Insanity and Allied Neuroses,* as

> [r]emoval of the patient absolutely from all friends, and the personal supervision, in all but solitary confinement, of the patient by a skilled nurse. Rest is essential, in general in bed, and in pronounced cases for weeks. Massage is performed in a way resembling shampooing, twice daily, beginning with half an hour at a time, and gradually extending to two or two and a half hours twice daily. Milk in half-pint quantities must be given every hour or two hours, and strong beef tea in similar quantities in the morning and afternoon. The muscles of the trunk and extremities must be not only individually rubbed, but also daily stimulated by electricity. Electric bath treatment and general hydrotherapeutics are useful. It will soon be found that, under this treatment, patients will develop ravenous appetites, and will take three full meat-meals daily, besides the milk and beef tea. Stimulants should be given with the meals. . . . If this treatment is to be followed, no half measures must be taken. Removal, seclusion, massage, and feeding, are the means of cure.[65]

The Weir Mitchell cure, it should be emphasized, was a rather conservative, "standard" cure for neurasthenia, and a wide variety of what today we might call "boutique" cures were also available: herbal, buttermilk, wine, and cheese cures among them. Ford Madox Ford reports seeing during his years of depression no fewer than nineteen specialists, who offered special diets ranging from grapes and dried peas to cream and fresh peaches, to pork and ice cream, and, finally, to salad with lemon dressing.[66]

The Conrad Family Medical Demons

The major biographies of Conrad have all sketched the outlines of Conrad's water cures, and Zdzisław Najder particularly attends to Conrad's neurasthenic symptoms in his youth and his later adult depression.[67] But the biographies do not specifically emphasize the Conrad family nervousness or the "cures" intended to ease the nervous symptoms and slow the ravages of tuberculosis, the disease that ended the lives of Conrad's parents. This lack of emphasis on the family's medical treatments is not surprising, for evidence about the nature of those cures is shadowy and more implied than overtly discussed. For Conrad's mother, Ewa, medical treatment available during their political exile to Vologda and later Chernikhov was inadequate to slow the progress of the disease. In the summer of 1863, she was given a medical leave from that exile to treat her poor health.[68] While the period of time and the season are consonant with some sort of cure, little can be surmised from letters about what sort of medical treatment she may have received near Nowochwastów, the site of Tadeusz Bobrowski's in-laws' estate. But a year and a half later, within two months of her death in April of 1865, Apollo Korzeniowski writes as if Ewa mistakenly understood her illness as primarily a nervous disorder: "For eighteen months the poor girl has been putting everything down to nerves; the doctors—are they doctors?—kept saying 'nothing, nothing, it will pass.' I, anxious—never having done anything for my own benefit—cringed, pleaded, begged for a year to change our place of exile so as to get a chance to find doctors deserving that name. Constantly let down and deferred, I lost hope. And a couple of months ago a sudden consuming fever, a lung condition and an inner tumor, caused by an irregular blood flow, requiring removal."[69]

It is unclear whether the attending physicians actually confused the symptoms of tuberculosis with nervousness, whether it was their bedside manner to suggest a passing affliction for a critical condition they could not cure, or whether nervousness created by that danger actually decoyed the doctors' attention. But after Ewa's death, when Apollo himself began to suffer symptoms of tuberculosis, he undertook a cure apparently prescribed to palliate both the consumption and his attendant nervousness. At age ten, Conrad witnessed his father's sheep's-whey cure in Galicia. Apollo writes to Kazimierz Kaszewski, Polish patriot and man of letters, "For ten days now I have been in a little mountain hideout at Topolnica . . . Galicia. . . I drink sheep whey with such determination that when the I[mperial] and R[oyal] police enquired as to what I was doing in Galicia, I answered with a clear conscience, 'I am drinking sheep whey.' If there is any improvement, I have not perceived it yet, but since I can drink from this source of health without any repugnance or ill-effects, the experts regard it as a proof of the restorative properties of sheep whey. The air obviously does me good."[70] While Korzeniowski was under treatment for tuberculosis by taking the mountain air, the prescription of sheep's whey is more complex and, though multifaceted, suggests that the medical community in Polish Ukraine assumed a close connection between consumption and mental health. Both William Osler, author of a standard physicians' reference work, and the *Extra Pharmacopoeia* suggest that bovine tuberculosis was long thought to be transmissible through cow's milk and through the meat of infected animals.[71] Sheep's whey may thus have been deemed a safer version of milk product, both by itself and for the production of koumiss (also kephir) that were used traditionally in the Caucasus as "a stimulant in exhaustion and in convalescence of phthisis."[72] In Conrad's adult life, whey was still recognized as a beneficial treatment for nervous disease, specifically neurasthenia.

If the comprehensive biographies of Conrad chronicle in detail Conrad's medical history of various illnesses, depression, and gout, they do not emphatically link these "family" afflictions to Conrad's extreme fear of mental insanity, a level of concern that today might be thought hypochondriacal.[73] But in Conrad's time both epilepsy and gout, like tuberculosis, were increasingly recognized as having a connection to mental insanity. Hard medical evidence that Conrad was epileptic in his childhood is scanty, and speculation about epilepsy is based on Tadeusz Bobrowski's letter to Conrad in 1891 in which he reports that Conrad's cousin, Michaś Kazimierz, may have been "suffering from the same illness as you were—anyway he had a similar fit to yours," the kind Conrad apparently suffered between the ages of nine and fourteen.[74] From this letter and other correspondence in the Korzeniowski family, Najder surmises that epilepsy was suspected and that it may have run in the family.[75] Whether this letter is sufficient evidence to conclude, as Jeffrey Meyers does, that Conrad was "pale, delicate, unstable and epileptic" and that it was his epilepsy that interrupted his education from 1864 to 1866 is problematic, to say the least; it is, however, safe to say, as biographer Frederick Karl observes, that whatever kinds of fits Conrad experienced, his later headaches and nervous disorders were consistent with a diagnosis of epilepsy.[76] The effect of such medical suspicion almost certainly had a powerful influence over Conrad, who after his Congo voyage was trying to sort out a complex and ominous medical situation, and epilepsy was increasingly recognized as linked to both neurasthenia and insanity.

Writing the entry "Epilepsy and Insanity" for Tuke's *A Dictionary of Psychological Medicine,* Dr. Savage noted that "epileptic symptoms depend upon a general nervous instability" or upon brain lesions that are either traumatic or degenerative, that is, caused either by injury or by hereditary decline. "In children of neurotic parents," Savage writes, "it is common to meet with unstable nervous systems, which seem to be ready, at the least provocation, to start into convulsions." Epilepsy was thus thought to be common in families with a nervous diathesis and was likewise regarded as "a most important factor in the production of various other forms of insanity" (*DPM,* 452). By the time of Conrad's nervous breakdown in 1910, epilepsy was recognized in its most public form of full motor seizures and also in a more insidious "masked" form (*DPM,* 454), but in either case, as Savage remarks, "The days when epilepsy was considered to be a disease apart from insanity have passed away."[77] Indeed, his "new and enlarged" fourth edition of *Insanity and Allied Neuroses* devotes a full chapter to epilepsy and insanity.

It is unlikely that Conrad had much exposure to the medical literature on epilepsy and insanity except through Lombroso, whose theories percolate through Conrad's fiction.[78] In *The Man of Genius* (1891), Lombroso devotes an entire chapter to the relationship of genius and insanity where he notes that the high incidence of epilepsy among men of genius suggests the "epileptoid nature of genius itself." Lombroso argues that in such men of genius, the convulsions that are associated with epilepsy appear only rarely during their lives. Citing Savage, Lombroso suggests that headaches are recognized as epilepsy in disguise, "causing the disappearance of every trace of pre-existing epilepsy," and, alternatively, that the intense moment of creative inspiration may well take the place of the convulsion as an outlet for nervous force. "Numerous men of genius," he notes, "have been seized by motory epilepsy or by that kind of morbid irritability which is well known to supply its place." In a catalog of examples that would have powerfully moved Conrad, Lombroso cites the coincidence of genius and epilepsy in "Napoleon, . . . Flaubert, . . . and Dostoieffsky," all influential figures mentioned in Conrad's letters.[79]

At roughly the same time that epilepsy and insanity were adjudged allied disorders, a similar consensus arose that gout and insanity were commonly associated. It had been recognized since the mid-seventeenth century that "melancholia . . . is . . . the inseparable companion of gout."[80] But Berthier, the same year Beard first ventured the case for neurasthenia, described the psychoneuroses associated or alternating with gout and observed that gout sometimes ends in insanity or is "lost" in incurable insanity. By 1881, Dr. Henry Rayner of Hanwell Asylum asserted in a paper titled "Gouty Insanity" at the Seventh International Medical Congress in London that "gout is as frequent a cause of insanity as of any other disease," and Dr. Savage pronounced himself a "convert to the belief" that gout was a cause of insanity.[81] Much later, Savage would continue to teach that there are "cases of insanity connected directly with gout . . . the disorder being co-existent and also co-extensive with gout" and would recommend as treatment "Turkish baths, saline purgatives, and change of surroundings" as "the most likely means to prevent the insanity, or to assist in the removal of depression, connected with gout."[82]

A question naturally arises here: To what extent was Conrad aware of all this? Clearly, he was aware of the theories of phrenology, moral insanity, and its relation to genius as articulated by Lombroso. References to racial degeneration in the opening pages of *An Outcast of the Islands,* written in 1894–95 and published in 1896, suggest he was aware of degeneration theory popularized by Nordau's 1895 publication of *Degeneration.* Moreover, Nordau knew Conrad's work and wrote to Conrad's friend, Cunningham Graham, in praise of *The Nigger of the "Narcissus."* Conrad's reaction, expressed to Graham's mother, is ambivalent: "I own myself surprised. There is not the slightest doubt M. N. has understood my intention. He has absolutely detected the whole idea. This to me is so startling that I do not know what to think of myself now. However I am pleased. Praise is sweet no matter whence it comes" (*CL,* 2:121). The "whole idea" of *The Nigger,* to which Nordau positively responds, is evident at the beginning of chapter 5, when the narrator reflects on the crew's relation to Jimmy: "The latent egoism of tenderness to suffering appeared in the developing anxiety not to see him die. . . . He was demoralizing. Through him we were becoming highly humanised, tender, complex, excessively decadent: we understood the subtlety of his fear, sympathized with all his repulsions, shrinkings, evasions, delusions—as though we had been over-civilised, and rotten, and without any knowledge of the meaning of life. We had the air of being initiated in some infamous mysteries" (*NN,* 139). Egoism, decadence, emotionalism, and mysticism were the great symptoms or causes of degeneration, according to Nordau. And notwithstanding Conrad's diffidence in accepting Nordau's praise, they seem to share similar preoccupations.

Just as Conrad was aware of degeneration and moral insanity, he was almost certainly cognizant of the medical theories that closely linked his family afflictions—possible epilepsy, a history of tuberculosis, and intractable gout—to serious nervous disorders that could lead to moral and mental insanity. Overtly warned by his uncle Tadeusz Bobrowski, who suffered severely from gout, not to yield to "lassitude or depression—for as you say: 'le moral réagit sur la phisique' [*sic*]."[83] Conrad learned from family not only the controlled art of suffering but the close connection between the health of the mind and the body. As I will argue in the coming pages, Conrad's attraction to a series of academically distinguished physicians suggests both his medical savoir faire and his concern about his neurasthenic tendencies. His medical history led him openly to fear for his sanity, for the health of any progeny, and for his own longevity; heredity was his curse, decline his expectation.

Chapter 2
Conrad's Water Cures

> The establishment of Champel is beautifully situated on rising ground, within twenty minutes' walk of Geneva, well shaded by fine trees, through which charming views of the surrounding country are obtained. The River Arve, on which the baths are placed, adds greatly to the beauty of the resort, and is moreover of great benefit to bathers.—B. Bradshaw, *Dictionary of Bathing Places, Climatic Health Resorts, Mineral Waters, Sea Baths, and Hydropathic Establishments,* 1900

W hen Conrad required medical attention after his Congo voyage, he was admitted to the German Hospital in Dalston, North London, where Dr. Rudolf Ludwig recommended a water cure for Conrad's various medical problems—complaints articulated in letters to Marguerite Poradowska during the winter and spring of 1891 and catalogued by biographer Frederick Karl as "legs swollen, rheumatism in left arm and neuralgia in right arm, stomach in bad condition, hands swollen, nerves disturbed, palpitations of the heart, attacks of suffocation, malarial attack, dyspepsia."[1] To Karl's list, we must add anemia (which Conrad mentions in a letter dated ?1 February 1891), a seemingly innocuous addition but a somatic disorder that was integral to his diagnosis and treatment. Unfortunately, the material evidence of Dr. Ludwig's diagnosis, a note enclosed by Adolf Kreiger in a letter to Tadeusz Bobrowski, did not survive the bombing of Warsaw in World War II.[2] But from Conrad's letters and contemporary medical discourse, it is possible to reconstruct a mutually confirming diagnosis and treatment.

The 1891 Diagnosis

Conrad's biographers often note that Conrad's admission to the German Hospital in North London is circumstantial, based on his German-national friend Adolf Kreiger's access.[3] Admitting such happenstance, I would add that Conrad also felt congenial with European medical practice, which was generally more tolerant of functional nervous disorders than were the British physiologists and which had a long tradition of advocating the kind of cures that had been a regular part of the Korzeniowski family medical history. Conrad's physician there, Dr. Ludwig, recommended that Conrad seek a cure at Bains de Champel, Switzerland, and the "prescription" for a particular spa was surely not a casual medical decision. The German Hospital offered preeminent expertise in balneotherapy and hydrotherapy in the person of Hermann Weber, M.D., also a German by birth and training and coauthor of *The Spas and Mineral Waters of Europe* (1896). Weber's text comprehensively classifies various kinds of mineral water springs as well as instructive "notes on Balneo-therapeutic management in various diseases and morbid conditions." In that text, Champel is mentioned only once, and then in passing, as a hydrotherapy spa using "plain water." But by 1901, Weber's coauthor, F. P. Weber, would recommend Champel by name as "an excellent place for hydrotherapeutic treatment."[4] The distinction here between hydrotherapy and balneotherapy is an important one, for the former involves the internal and external use of "plain," ordinary water while the latter involves stronger mineral waters with various constituents—often salts and gases—that were thought beneficial and aggressive in the treatment of specific medical problems.[5] If Conrad's list of physical problems seems to us so varied and complex as to defy an obvious diagnosis or course of treatment, the therapy recommended for Conrad is rather clearly in line with medical thought during the decade following his Congo voyage.

When we think today of Conrad's medical difficulties in Africa and upon his return, malaria and dysentery come foremost to mind. And yet, according to contemporary medical opinion, in cases of malaria, "balneo-therapeutic treatment is only of secondary importance. Pharmaceutical remedies, combined with long residence at high elevations free from malarial air, and especially near glaciers, produce in the majority of persons the most satisfactory results." Similarly, in cases of tropical diarrhea "connected with *malaria and dysentery* . . . the spa treatment can take only a small share in the management."[6] Clearly then, the two diseases typically associated with Conrad's African experience would not have indicated balneotherapy but may have suggested hydrotherapy, and Champel's proximity to glaciers would have been thought beneficial to a malarial condition. Indeed, brochures from 1887 advertising Champel list malaria as one of the "grave diseases" treated at the spa. Malaria was recognized by George M. Beard and his followers as having a close connection with neurasthenia: "Malarial poisoning frequently simulates neurasthenia, and also induces a special type of the disease which may be called *malarial neurasthenia*."[7] Further complicating the issue, Beard also warned that either affliction—malaria or neurasthenia—would have the effect of modifying virtually any other disease from which the patient might suffer. Yet another early advocate of neurasthenia, C. H. Hughes, observed that "if an individual exposed to malaria" is not in robust health, "the result is often a series of neuralgic affections and disabilities" and concludes, "when the struggle is prolonged and under circumstances of a peculiarly depressing character, the nervous system is weakened and its functions become *disordered,* the secretions are more or less deranged, digestion is enfeebled, the patient becomes irritable and depressed, and serious intellectual disturbance ensues. Thus may malaria develop the morbid condition now under consideration [neurasthenia]" (emphasis mine).[8] This connection between malaria and salient symptoms of neurasthenia is the reason that Conrad, in a letter to Poradowska, repeatedly refers to his nerves as "disordered" (*CL,* 1:77, 163) and makes what seems to the layperson a seemingly odd symptomatic connection, that he suffered from "an attack of malaria in the form of dyspepsia" (*CL,* 1:88).

Other symptoms mentioned by Conrad would not have indicated "strong" spa treatment if they were the primary dysfunction. For instance, Conrad's rheumatic complaints—"rheumatism in left leg and neuralgia in right arm" (*CL,* 1:172)—were then acute rather than chronic and would not, to Conrad's physician, have indicated "ordinary balneo-therapeutic procedures, [which] are not suitable during the first period of convalescence from acute articular rheumatism."[9] But if malarial neurasthenia were suspected, the physician might expect "multiform nervous phenomena," including "neuralgic and morbid mental manifestations, sometimes carried even to the point of maniacal excitement" and prescribe hydrotherapy.[10] Likewise, in the case of heart palpitations alone, balneotherapy was rarely prescribed, for palpitations were "regarded as a neurosis."[11] But Conrad's palpitations, as a manifestation of neurosis, would have been regarded as a "functional disorder of the nervous system" (*DPM,* 850), were consistent with the symptoms of neurasthenia, and were accompanied by other afflictions thought to be organic nervous disorders, clearly indicating hydrotherapeutic spa treatment such as that offered by Champel.[12] Conrad was both anemic and dyspeptic, conditions that are associated with, and frequently indicate, neurasthenia.[13] Dyspepsia, for instance, according to Weber and Weber, is "a manifestation of a *weak mucous membrane* . . . which . . . is intimately allied to and forms part of a weakness of the nervous system. The majority of such invalids are thin, and have little resisting power. Mental or bodily exertion is apt to produce or to aggravate the dyspeptic troubles. It often forms a prominent part of neurasthenia. No *energetic* spa treatment is suitable to such invalids, but the general management may be beneficially assisted by the simple thermal waters, . . . especially those in elevated situations."[14] Champel, with its "inactive" or simple water and its relatively high altitude was thus a suitable choice for this kind of nervous disorder comprehended under the general term "dyspeptic neurasthenia." In fact, the rest and feeding regime at Champel had a positive effect on Conrad, who wrote to Edward Garnett from Switzerland, "I live lazily and digest satisfactorily" (*CL,* 1:216).

In addition to the somatic manifestations of his nervousness, Conrad also experienced serious bouts of depression prior to his second and third cures (in 1894 and 1895) at Champel, spells that he described freely to Marguerite Poradowska. On 25 July? 1894, Conrad wrote "you've received my letter and think I am mad. I am almost so. My nervous disorder tortures me, makes me wretched, and paralyses action, thought, everything! I ask myself why I exist. It is a frightful condition" (*CL,* 1:163–64). Perhaps nine months later he writes again, "I am not at all well. To set myself up again, I am quitting my bed and going to Champel for hydrotherapy. . . . You know that when I am not well I have attacks of melancholy which paralyse my thought and will" (*CL,* 1:210–11).[15] Conrad's repeated assertion of his sense of paralysis suggests that his deepest fear may not have been malarial neurasthenia but madness, for the most comprehending disease of the nervous system is the dementia resulting from general paralysis of the insane.[16] It is difficult to determine the extent to which Conrad was playing, in his letters to Poradowska, the part of the tormented artist threatened by the specter of insanity (Corbet's "skeleton at the feast"). While the Champel treatments had at least a calming effect on Conrad, the cure was not permanent, for years later Conrad would return to this theme in letters to Edward Garnett that Bernard Meyer, as a psychotherapist, cites as evidence of Conrad's genuine fear of insanity:[17]

> [2 June 1896] I have long fits of depression, that in a lunatic asylum would be called madness. I do not know what it is. It springs from nothing. It is ghastly. It lasts for an hour or a day; and when it departs it leaves a fear. (*CL,* 1:284)

> [5 August 1896] I have been living in a little hell of my own; in a place of torment so subtle and so cruel and so unavoidable that the prospect of theological damnation in the hereafter has no more terrors for me. . . . I am paralyzed by doubt and have just sense enough to feel the agony but am powerless to invent a way out of it. . . . I knock about blindly in it till I am positively, physically sick. . . . And tomorrow . . . brings only the renewed and futile agony. I ask myself whether I am breaking up mentally. I am afraid of it. (*CL,* 1:295–96)

The mental instability in Conrad's letters to Garnett, written when Conrad was on his honeymoon in Brittany, seems genuinely linked not merely to his thematic concerns in "The Idiots" but to issues that immediately created problems in Conrad's own life. Idiocy, like lunacy, was hereditary and could (it was thought in Conrad's day) be caused by parental insanity, epilepsy, tuberculosis, and other neuroses such as "excitability" and "extreme nervousness."[18] Conrad's letters to Garnett do not appear histrionic; they are genuinely desperate.

Water Cures and Other "Humbugs of Europe"

Conrad had a clear sense that his hydropathy of 1891, 1894, and 1895 was part of the fashionable and, at times, faddish collection of cures that became popular in the late nineteenth century.[19] At the time Conrad's medical problems were organizing themselves, magazines such as *The Spectator* and *Blackwood's* published articles on Father Sabastian Kneipp (also spelled Kneip, Kniepp), a Bavarian monk who, prior to his death in 1897, attracted large numbers of followers to Wörishofen for his water and herbal cures, all freely administered. *The Spectator* describes the three-part water cure, which involves, first, "walking barefooted, either in the wet grass or snow, for a certain length of time every day. It is advisable, also, to walk bareheaded." Secondly, one must avoid wearing wool next to the skin, "but only coarse linen or cotton." Lastly, one must "never dry oneself after bathing, but . . . put on the clothes while the body is still wet."[20] This kind of cure, which sounds rather like young Stephen Dedalus mortifying his senses, explains why Conrad in 1907 would defend Champel as "a serious hydrotherapeutic establishment" (*CL,* 3:426) and preferred "Geneva now . . . [to] Davos-Platz later on where the modern Dance of Death goes on in expensive hotels" (*CL,* 3:420). Conrad's metaphor surely refers to the macabre atmosphere of the major spas of Europe, overcrowded with a mixed mob of the diseased, the pleasure-seeking, and alpine social climbers. So too, Conrad may be literally describing the long lines of tourists, snaking through the spa towns toward their mineral springs. Between Conrad's visits in the 1890s and 1907, a skeptical American journalist described the scene in Carlsbad for *Cosmopolitan* (see Fig. 1):

> The early morning scene, when the single long street is crowded over both pavements and road, from house to house, is a spectacle never to be forgotten. Photographs of bits of the crowd in front of the largest of the spring-houses seem to represent a lake or sea of human faces. The men and women, as a rule, wear their mugs or glasses at the ends of straps carried over their shoulders as tourists carry field-glasses. . . . All the shops are already open, and they present a bewildering glory of colored photographs, new hats and bonnets, jewelry, Berlin cheap knickknacks, and tens of thousands of people are babbling with the noise which is just a tone above the rythmic [*sic*] swish-swish of all their feet upon the pavements. Far down the street, a mile from the main hotel, is the Muhlbrunnen Spring, and thither go the great majority.[21]

Conrad's choice of the rather obscure Champel for his hydrotherapy was based not only on its mineral and chemical composition and the medical reputation of the institution but also on its situation: a high-altitude spa well away from the carnival atmosphere of the major spas, which he may have seen as early as his 1883 visit to the popular Marienbad spa.

During that early trip, Conrad and his Uncle Tadeusz concluded their cure with an "after-cure" at Teplice, a part of convalescence that was considered by Weber and Weber "of the greatest importance, especially after the more active waters such

Fig. 1. Typical cure fountain and the promenade at Carlsbad, *Cosmopolitan* 34 (1903): 665, 668. (University of Minnesota Duluth Library. Photo by Dan Schlies and Mark Summers)

as . . . Marienbad." Patients were advised not to return to daily life immediately but to spend perhaps two weeks in a health resort, generally in the mountains, for at this time "the nervous system and bodily functions are in a specially sensitive condition, and are easily thrown out of order . . . by nervous excitement, business worry, or bodily fatigue."[22] If the patient neglected the "after-cure," he or she would run the risk of another breakdown or losing the benefits of the primary cure. In his later trips to Champel, Conrad would not have been thought a good patient. While he did escape the burdens of daily life and improve his health during his "cures," Conrad continued to work hard during his trips to Champel: working on chapter 7 of *Almayer's Folly* in 1894 and writing as much as one-third of *An Outcast of the Islands* in 1895 (Conrad mistakenly writes 1894 in *CL,* 3:420).[23] If Conrad did not rest from his work as a novelist, neither was he in a financial condition that would allow for an after-cure, and he consequently expresses the hope his restored health will last. On two early occasions, a visit with Madame Poradowska substitutes for his after-cure, the first time with less-than-fortunate results during his Paris visit of late June 1891.

Conrad critics have, until recently, concluded from a letter Conrad wrote after this visit to Marguerite Poradowska that he disliked the Impressionist paintings that presumably hung on the walls of the consulting rooms of Dr. Gachet, Poradowska's uncle. (Gachet owned paintings by his patients Van Gogh, Cézanne, and Pissarro, and he probably displayed the art in his home in Auvers.) Gene Moore has recently corrected this assumption and established that the "nightmarish atmosphere" of the Charenton School was created by Amand Gautier's *Les Folles de la Salpêtrière (Cour des Agitées)*, a lithographic copy of which hung on Gachet's wall (see Fig. 2), and by Gachet's collectibles, such as the phrenological heads produced from death masks of guillotined criminals.[24] Gachet's *intérieur*—his pictures, electrical devices, and other medical paraphernalia used in his practice—would have created for Conrad just the sort of after-cure distress that, in the eyes of Conrad's physicians, should be avoided if the cure were to have any lasting positive effect.

Since Madame Poradowska was then Conrad's most intimate confidant, and since Conrad was at this time particularly concerned about nervous relapse, surely Dr. Gachet made a significant, negative impact on Conrad's imagination. And any complete portrait of Conrad and his doctors must include both positive and negative experiences. While there is no evidence in the

33

Fig. 2. Lithographic copy of Amand Gautier's *Les Folles de la Salpêtrière (Cour des Agitées),* 1888. (The Wellcome Library, London)

letters that Conrad ever met Dr. Gachet face to face, there is a conspicuous lack of specific reference to him. Conrad quite naturally mentions other relatives by relation and name, but Dr. Paul-Ferdinand Gachet is called impersonally, and ironically, "the doctor" (*CL,* 1:84). To Conrad, who obviously disliked Madame Poradowska staying at the doctor's *cabinet* with its pictures of madwomen, Dr. Gachet and his medical gallery are reminders of mental degeneration and the ascendancy of madness: that which threatens psychological health and endangers personal happiness and well-being. Conrad's metaphor to describe Gachet's *cabinet*—a nightmare—is a trope that later is used frequently in his letters to describe ill health, nervous strain, and the fear of mental disease as he endured the ill health of his family and underwent his 1907 cure at Champel:

> 5 June '07 [to Pinker] I come back to my paper as if out of a nightmare. (*CL,* 3:447)
> 6 June '07 [to Galsworthy] I seem to move, talk, write in a sort of quiet nightmare that goes on and on. (*CL,* 3:448)
> 3 Aug '07 [to Pinker] I long to get away from here. The place is odious to me; and the whole thing with its anxieties and expense sits on me like the memory of a nightmare. (*CL,* 3:462)

Conrad's nightmare metaphor echoes Marlow's description of Kurtz, the embodiment of illness, of moral and mental insanity.

34

To Conrad, Gachet was thus displaying professional curios from the grotesque, nightmarish world of mental instability that he abhorred. If the doctors whose help and advice Conrad sought were generally academically inclined men of professional distinction, Gachet must have existed in Conrad's mind at the other end of the professional spectrum: an eccentric and morbidly fixated quack. Later in life, Conrad would remark, "I abhorr [sic] quackery" (*CL*, 4:217), and this feeling was surely intensified by physicians whose eccentric interests and practices touched on ailments or people close to Conrad.

Throughout his career, Dr. Gachet focused on mental and nervous disease. He began his medical training in the 1850s, serving for a year under a Professor Falret at the Salpêtrière, one of the two main asylums of Paris. He completed his medical studies in 1858 with a doctoral thesis on depression entitled *Étude sur la mélancolie*. Thereafter, his medical interests were varied and quirky: phrenology, homeopathic treatment, astrology, and palmistry.[25] He was also an early experimenter in electroshock therapy for nervous disorders, the apparatus for which may have induced Madame van Gogh-Bonger (Vincent van Gogh's sister-in-law) to remark that Gachet's work room, used also as his painting and etching studio, looked like a "workshop of an alchemist of the Middle Ages."[26] Indeed, Van Gogh's first impression of Dr. Gachet, if it can be trusted, does not inspire confidence: "I have seen Dr. Gachet, who gives me the impression of being rather eccentric, but his experience as a doctor must keep him balanced enough to combat the nervous trouble from which he certainly seems to me to be suffering at least as seriously as I."[27] He was indeed a striking figure. During the years at Auvers, when Van Gogh and Conrad knew him or knew of him, Gachet was known to the locals as "Dr. Saffron"; he dyed his hair bright yellow, wore a bright blue ambulance driver's coat, and reportedly carried a green-and-white umbrella in the sunshine while advocating socialism and free love. How much Conrad knew of Gachet's eccentricities and radical political ideas is uncertain. But despite Gachet's affinities for struggling artists and his free elixir and clinical services for the poor, it is doubtful that Conrad would have approved of "the doctor."[28]

Given Conrad's medical predilections, the choice of Champel was thus quite logical and specific: Conrad could avoid quacks, the nightmare of lunacy, and the fashionable spa scene (and its high prices); he could attend a simple-water spa at a moderately high altitude, attended by a physician of high repute whose specialty was treating the specific ailments from which Conrad suffered. The reputation of Champel was established and maintained by Conrad's physician there, Dr. Paul Glatz (mistakenly identified by Tadeusz Bobrowski as Dr. Platz). Founded in 1874, the hydropathic establishment under the direction of Glatz became popularly recognized, even in contemporary travel guidebooks, for being "well managed" and, by 1891, for being "much frequented by convalescents and neurotics."[29] Like many of the physicians who attended Conrad, Dr. Glatz was a man of science who appears, at the distance of a century, to be academically distinguished. In addition to his work at Champel, Glatz was a professor of balneotherapy on the medical faculty of the University of Geneva and the author of more than twenty studies on various aspects of digestion and hydrotherapy.[30]

From Glatz's published works, we know that during the 1880s the program of therapy at Champel focused on the treatment of anemia, nervous diseases, rheumatism, gout, goiter, and digestive disorders.[31] In particular, Glatz was interested in defining a hydrotherapeutic program for individuals who were both anemic and nervous, a problematic project since the kind of therapy for each was contraindicated by the other. Traditionally, cold douches were prescribed for anemic individuals in order to invigorate the body; tepid baths were indicated for nervous individuals because of the bath's calming, sedative effects. "But," as Glatz observed, "anemia and nervousness most often exist simultaneously; and here arises a difficulty in treatment that is not always easy to surmount; what is appropriate for the one is not for the other; nevertheless we must find the means of defeating the one and the other. It is in this case that the physician must act with the greatest prudence and most discernment."[32] After his return from the Congo, Conrad was clearly the kind of patient, both anemic and nervous, that Dr. Glatz recognized as typical, symptomatically contraindicated, and therefore a likely subject for the program of treatment at Champel.

By 1889, less than two years before Conrad would arrive in Geneva, Glatz published a book on the topic of "indigestion due to weak secretion of gastric juices, especially from neurasthenic dyspepsia."[33] Given Conrad's symptoms and the academic reputation of Dr. Glatz's work and therapeutic programs, his choice of physician and institution is logical and specific. It is possible that Conrad, in these early trips to Champel, was also treated for his other related nerve problems, rheumatism and neuralgia, since neuralgia was thought to accompany neurasthenia. If so, in the early 1890s Conrad would have experienced a rather wide range of baths and procedures: cold and warm douches, variously applied as a rain shower or by moving jets, sometimes in a special bath called a "shower ring." Russian or medicinal vapor baths and Turkish or Roman steam baths were also prescribed at Champel in combination with massage. For nervous ailments, rheumatism, and neuralgia, Dr. Glatz had long advocated a treatment of baths in combination with various forms of electricity therapy.[34] While we find no direct references to such therapy in Conrad's letters, electrotherapy may explain his odd comment to Marguerite Poradowska, urging her "to be guided (for once in your life) by the light of pure reason, which, like electricity, is cold." This letter, addressed from Champel, concludes with a postscript: "cure begun two days ago, so cannot judge the results. I am bearing it well enough" (*CL,* 1:80).

What would Conrad have had to bear at Champel? Assuming he went with a diagnosis of malarial neurasthenia or neurasthenic dyspepsia, which had produced attacks of neuralgia and dyspepsia ending in anemia, Conrad would have followed the rather standard treatment at Champel, with some additional hydrotherapy. In the culminating work of his career, *Dyspepsies nerveuses et neurasthénie* (1898), Glatz describes in considerable detail the philosophy and treatment at Champel. While none of the cases Glatz cites matches the description of Conrad (who would have been from his mid- to late thirties in 1891–96), the medical profile Conrad articulates in his letters to Poradowska would have made him inconspicuous among those treated at Champel.

Glatz's therapeutic program at Champel was a modified Weir Mitchell regime, with whatever individual tailoring was indicated for a particular patient. Glatz favored the conventional Weir Mitchell rest cure only for those neurasthenics who were "depressed and very weak; to the seriously fatigued who feel the necessity of absolute and complete rest."[35] Most patients, Glatz argued, do not need absolute bed rest, which has a deleterious effect upon those who do not need the isolation, solitude, and separation from family that is recommended by Weir Mitchell. So too, Glatz curtailed the use of milk in his neurasthenic patients, among whom he had observed an aggravation of the indigestion with "an overuse of milk."[36] Glatz was particularly fond of using the *drap mouillé,* a soaked woolen sheet or blanket that is draped over the patient during vigorous massage. A typical regimen of treatment and feeding at Champel follows:

Morning at 7h.: massage with *drap mouillé* (cold water of 10–14°
C.; vigorous massage; sheet well wrung-out).
At 8h.: two saucers of porridge, two soft-boiled eggs, toast, butter.
At 9h.: total body massage for 1/2 hour to 1 hour.
At 10h.: one to two eggs, boiled in tapioca, a small cup of milk.
Noon: Roast meats, green vegetables, puréed lentils, macaroni,
rice, toast, a glass of Port or Bordeaux or Bourgogne; re-
main/lie outdoors for 3 hours.
At 4h.: Second massage, then: eggs, lentil purée or farina cooked
in milk, some tea with milk, graham (brown bread or
wholemeal bread), butter. Remain outdoors or walk from
30 to 60 minutes.
At 5h.: If necessary, faradisation of the whole body with brush or
metal brush.
At 6h.: The same meal as midday, then remain outdoors on a
chaise longue until 8:00.
At 8 1/2 h.: calming swimsuit or *drap mouillé* massage, according
to present indications.[37]

Glatz's detailed descriptions of the various methods of treatment
suggest that Conrad, given the symptoms we can glean from his
letters, surely "endured" quite a bit in this "serious" hydropathic
institute.

Since Conrad was both anemic and nervous, he would have
been given a kind of paradoxical treatment that was both stimulating and calming. For his anemia and dyspepsia he was almost
certainly given the *drap mouillé* massage, either by itself or more
likely as a preface to other kinds of bathing. Glatz summarizes
the stimulating and toning procedure:

A sheet of rough "natural" linen or wool is soaked in cold water,
then wrung hard. The bath attendant applies this sheet to the
body of the bather, taking care to roll up and hold tight the ex-
tremities. Before the application of the bath sheet, as before whatever other hydrotherapy operations (showers, swimming pool,
half-bath, etc.), one must not forget to soak the face, chest, nape
of the neck, back, the armpits of the patient, to place on the patient's face a cold compress; and finally, among the ill—who com-
plain of head pains, excitability, or the tendency to flush—it is
necessary to put the feet in warm water during the bath and to
finish the operation by a powerful jet running for several seconds
on the feet. All these precautions are necessary to prevent the
possibility of an internal congestion and above all to minimize the
extent possible, the always disagreeable first impression everyone resents when he initially receives the first jet of cold
water.[38]

Glatz suggested that the *drap mouillé,* more than any bath, was efficacious for the nervous and capable of curing mild cases of neurasthenia. In more serious cases it would have been used to prepare the patient for a full-fledged hydropathic cure.

Because of Conrad's nervousness, palpitations, and neuralgic complaints and because electrotherapy was a procedure Glatz often performed at Champel, it was probably "indicated" for Conrad: "Besides the calming and toning hydrotherapy, we have generally recourse to electric therapy," most often a weak, direct current of short duration applied to the cervix and the sympathetic nerves of the neck region. This process, Glatz observed, "produces a remarkable effect on the beating of the heart, and after employing continuous currents we have often noted a considerable reduction in the pulse."[39] Other calming procedures, such as cold-water baths, were less pleasant and riskier. Hydrotherapists in Conrad's day had found that while cold-water baths of short duration are stimulating, it was thought "incontestable that one can obtain sedative effects by using a prolonged, cold water bath." But, they recognized, it was also dangerous.[40] Therefore, such hydrotherapeutic procedures were undertaken with great care, beginning with water close to body temperature (34–28° C) and gradually cooling it to avoid stressing or shocking the patient. The prescribed order for treatment of severe cases of anemia and neurasthenia involved the progressive baths: *drap mouillé,* cool affusions, temperate swimming pool, recooled half-bath, and in certain cases, the cold swimming pool.[41]

Unfortunately, Conrad does not specifically articulate what his regime was during his stays in Champel in the early and mid-1890s. But we do know that Conrad stayed away from Champel for nine years; in 1907 Conrad returned, seeking a cure for Borys and to convalesce himself from a recent recurrence of gout. Citing the spa's salutary effects on the nerves, its altitude, and its correspondingly high repute in the medical profession, Conrad speculates to his agent Pinker that his son's predisposition to fever and high pulse rate "may be nervous phenomena" and that the Montpellier physician treating Borys, Professor Joseph Grasset, argued (in Conrad's words to Pinker) that "the best thing for us is not to take him to England yet but to proceed . . . to Switzerland—not too high up. Specifically he says Geneva lake would do for climate and altitude." Borys's program of treatment at Champel, never completed, was to include a feeding regimen that would build up the young boy, a "proper cure with special diet and so on. He wants to be fed up. The treatment will stimulate his appetite.—Those are the conclusions of the doctor" (*CL,* 3:420). The emphasis on feeding, integral to the Weir Mitchell treatment for neurasthenia, was still apparently in force at Champel though Glatz had died in 1905. Indeed, a dozen years later, after Borys's return from the war, Conrad would express worry about the return of Borys's "neurasthenic symptoms."[42] Given the strain Conrad himself experienced during the winter and spring in Montpellier, he may well have chosen Champel for himself as much as for Borys, since the two shared the same nervous constitution. Indeed, neurasthenia, like gout, was thought in Conrad's day to be hereditary. To my knowledge, this relatively private reference in a letter was one of two times Conrad admitted "publicly" that the Conrad men were neurasthenic, the last and more public instance being the admission in his essay "The *Torrens:* A Personal Tribute" that he had been diagnosed as neurasthenic more than thirty years earlier.

Chapter 3
Conrad's Breakdown

[F]or as you say: 'le moral réagit sur la phisique' [*sic*].
—Tadeusz Bobrowski, letter to Conrad

During the years following his Champel water cures of the mid-1890s, much changed in Conrad's life, the one constant being his precarious health. He gave up his bachelor life in the "hot, noisy and dissipated . . . neighbourhood" (*CL*, 1:239) of Gillingham Street in London, married, and, after a nightmarish honeymoon in Brittany, settled in the country back in England, first in Stanford-le-Hope and eventually at Pent Farm, Postling, near Hythe, where he would live for nearly a decade and produce his most nervous work.[1] Moving from the "dissipated" life of urban London, Conrad was leaving a locale of degeneration and seeking a place of solitude, congenial to a life of irritable contemplation and writing. But Conrad may also have had in mind—may have hoped for—an environment suitable to a long-range "after-cure," where he could settle permanently into a life that would give him the best chance of tolerable health to pursue his destructive profession, where, as he wrote to Ford Madox Ford, he could "preserve[] what's left of . . . [his] sanity" (*CL*, 2:93–94).

Conrad was certainly aware of the importance of the after-cure. With his Uncle Tadeusz Bobrowski, he took an after-cure at Teplitz (Teplice) following a cure in the strenuous waters of Marienbad. During Conrad's first cure at Champel, Bobrowski warns him, "You will lose all the benefit of the cure by not doing it thoroughly and by travelling immediately after."[2] Weber and

Weber stress that an after-cure is critical to complete the regimen of the patient, who should abstain from returning immediately to home or work and observe a simple diet accompanied by an "open-air life." To do otherwise is to risk relapse: "[N]eglect of the 'after-cure' may lead to disagreeable consequences, another breakdown, and the patient may lose all the good results of the treatment."[3] While Conrad could not abstain from work, his choices about where to live after his marriage follow a pattern of proximity to the sea with plenty of fresh air.

After a working "honeymoon" at Île-Grande, Côte du Nord, marred by illness and perhaps a difficult adjustment to married life, the Conrads settled in September of 1896 at Stanford-le-Hope, Essex, some dozen miles from Southend, a recognized marine bathing spa.[4] But unhappy there, within a year they had resettled at Pent Farm, Kent, in October of 1898. There are, of course, compelling explanations for their choice of the Pent. His new friend (and soon-to-be collaborator) Ford Madox Ford offered it to him; it was close to literary friends such as H. G. Wells and not far from Stephen and Cora Crane; and there he could play the role of the gentleman writer. Moreover, the Cinque Ports area—which included Sandgate and Hythe and was but a few miles from Pent Farm—was recognized as a "suitable residence after spa treatment"; the ports were especially desirable as marine spas because they were sheltered from the north and consequently warmer during the winter.[5] When Ford let the Pent to Conrad as part of their plans for literary collaboration, he was well aware of the suitability of the Hythe area as a marine spa, a place where his friend could take an extended, but working, after-cure. In *The Cinque Ports* Ford notes that "of all the watering-places on this part of the coast, Hythe is the pleasantest." He cites, perhaps too adoringly, the village's "tranquility," the lack of hurry, and "sense of leisure," where "even the tradesmen of the town remain comparatively uncontaminated by the spirit of modernity." Praising more generally the craft culture of the Cinque Ports, Ford asserts that "nothing, it seems to me, is so absolutely essential to the cure of certain mental maladies fostered by the spirit of the age as the sight of the good work . . . good craftsmanship."[6] Notwithstanding Ford's own pejorative skepticism of his style and methods in *The Cinque Ports,* the Hythe area was recognized by Ford and surely by Conrad as a locale that could help cure or fend off the modern nervousness indigenous to urban centers.[7] Indeed, Conrad's description of the Pent written to Aniela Zagorska, 18 December 1898, differs from his earlier, terse "I like Pent. It will do" (*CL,* 2:100). After three weeks' residence, Conrad's description suggests a growing attachment to the air, landscape, and sea vista:

> We are only five kilometres from the sea. The railway station is 3 kilometres and Canterbury [2]1 1/2 kilometres away. Before my window I can see the buildings of the farm, and on leaning out and looking to the right, I see the valley of the Stour, the source of which is so to speak, behind the third hedge from the farmyard. Behind the house are the hills (Kentish Downs) which slope in zigzag fashion down to the sea, like the battlements of a big fortress. . . .
> We live like a family of anchorites. From time to time a pious pilgrim belonging to *la grande fraternité des lettres* comes to pay a visit to the celebrated Joseph Conrad—and to obtain his blessing. Sometimes he gets it and sometimes he does not, for the hermit is severe and dyspeptic.[8]

Health, locale, and art are clearly linked in Conrad's imagination: the Kentish Downs were to protect him like a fortress, his art practiced in the solitude of a religious retreat, violated only by the occasional admirer and his steadfast companion, indigestion.

The first occasion when the Conrad family may have needed a local physician came at year's end, when Borys, then almost a year old, fell ill as Conrad was trying to finish the manuscript for *Heart of Darkness* (*CL,* 2:139). Perhaps H. G. Wells, newly settled in nearby Sandgate with his own health problems suggesting nervous collapse, recommended a physician.[9] In any case, the Conrads would eventually settle on the services of Dr. John Hackney, the most highly trained physician in Hythe. A graduate of University College (1865) who later took the M.D. from St. Andrews (1887), Hackney may have appealed to Conrad because of his interest in balneotherapy; in 1898, he was a member of the British Balneological and Climatological Society and by 1912 the vice president of the Balneotherapy section of the Royal Society of Medicine.[10] The senior Hackney would later relinquish his patients to his son, Clifford Hackney—"young Hackney" (*CL,* 3:25), as he was called by Conrad—who became a close friend and was Conrad's local physician until 1916–17, when he served in the British Expeditionary Forces and as medical officer of the Lympne Aerodrome. Although Clifford Hackney does not appear to have been the kind of academic physician Conrad often sought, Hackney did study mental disease at University College under William Mickle, who was England's leading expert on general paralysis of the insane.[11]

Until about 1904, the Conrads seem to have been attended primarily by local physicians, but with a growing need for specialists to treat the various medical disorders of the Conrad household, Conrad turned to London doctors as well and, in doing so, met the physician who is arguably the most influential of his life: Albert Edward Tebb. According to John Conrad, his father was slow to gain confidence in medical doctors, and Tebb was among the first Conrad consulted in England.[12] Tebb (as he was called even by his wife Bertha) was more than a medical attendant; a close personal friend of Conrad and Ford, he saw them through difficult times and ultimately helped them keep writing. In his private mental sphere, he was a knowledgeable collector of avant-garde prints and first editions, a serious violinist of apparently modest skill, and an early advocate and practitioner of socialized medicine whose patients included not only high-strung artist friends but anonymous members of the working class.[13]

Tebb steadied Conrad during the difficult spring and fall of 1904, when his wife Jessie was ill with a heart condition and suffering from a long-time knee injury. In a letter of 22 March 1904 to Alice Rothenstein, Conrad notes that "the anxiety till Dr. Tebb came was so great that I could not concentrate my thoughts upon anything whatever. The dear man has comforted me greatly" (*CL,* 3:125). Over a fortnight later, Conrad writes to William Rothenstein that "Good Dr. Tebb turned up unexpectedly to day cheering us up immensely. He's pleased with the patient's progress" (3:131). During November of 1904 the Conrads were in London to consult with Dr. Bruce Clarke, a Harley Street physician and joint specialist surgeon; Borys was ill in bed and Jessie incapacitated and upset, but Dr. Tebb, according to Conrad, was "putting them right with great success" (3:179). The specialist, it seems, botched the initial examination, finding nothing wrong with Jessie's knee, but subsequent exploratory surgery revealed displaced cartilage. The fallible expert is syntactically subordinated to Tebb, who remains, in a letter to Ford Madox Ford, above criticism, though he had initially concurred with Clarke's diagnosis: "The long and the short of it is that he [Clarke] found his mistake. The cartilage *is* displaced and must have been so for thirteen years since her first accident when she was seventeen. That no disease of the bones was set up Tebb (and also Clarke) accounts for by the large quantity of fluid always present" (3:184).[14] As Conrad had written a few days earlier, "I trust Dr. Tebb implicitly" (3:182). A week after the operation, Conrad would write that he was "anxious to have [Jessie] under Tebb's care as soon as possible" (3:188).

The only surviving correspondence between Conrad and Tebb dates from a year later and reveals a continued close relationship between the London doctor and his patients in Kent:

13th Dec 1905

My dear Tebb.

Severe in the wire was an exaggeration at the time of my gout. But after you had seen me I had it severe enough in all conscience.

Jessie has not been very well since last night. Those nervous symptoms again. She has looked very white but to night (10 pm) she seems better.

Another week wasted out of My life. Seven days without a single line.

Borys has been ordered to bed again on account of his pulse, but Batten says there's nothing to worry about.[15]

I wish we were nearer you. Your abominable journey here on Sunday lies heavy on my conscience yet.

Our friendlies[t] regards to Mrs Tebb.

Always affectionately Yours

Jph Conrad.[16]

Conrad's defensive apology for summoning Tebb from London to treat an apparently mild attack of gout suggests that Dr. Tebb was testy about Conrad's medical nervousness and that Conrad wished to please his doctor. The letter also raises a number of questions about Conrad's ongoing medical maintenance in the years leading up to his breakdown.

First, it may strike the reader as odd that in 1905, like his father in 1868, Conrad takes whey as part of a medicinal regimen. In fact, the whey treatment or some sort of dairy-product treatment may have been part of Conrad's daily routine through his 1910 breakdown, perhaps even to the end of his life. *The Extra Pharmacopoeia* of 1910, under "uses and references to Lactic Acid Bacillus Tablets and (Plain) curdled milk," suggests such milk-based products are "beneficial in migraine, neurasthenia, and allied troubles." An advertisement in *The Medical Directory* of 1910 suggests the popularity of such products as "Humanized Milk," "Lactic Acid Specialties," and "Sauermilch Whey" as sour milk treatments for dyspepsia, enterocolitis, gastric ulcer, rheumatism, and so forth. And as late as 1924, *The Extra Pharmacopoeia* still lists the lactic acid bacillus treatment as a "cholagogue in heptic congestion" and as "beneficial in migraine, neurasthenia, loss of appetite and allied disorders."[17] Conrad's digestive problems, like those of Marlow in *Chance,* who is described as having the "irritability" of someone with a "predisposition to congestion of the liver" (*C,* 32), were clearly part of the nervous disorder that culminated in his collapse. Conrad wrote to John Galsworthy two months after his 1910 breakdown that "they are treating me now exclusively with sour milk and thymionic acid all the more usual remedies having been used up in the course of these fatal ten weeks" (*CL,* 4:322). Here, quite naturally, there arise the questions of what "medicines" Conrad was taking "religiously" under Tebb's advice in 1905 and what "more usual remedies" were prescribed by Conrad's physicians—Clifford Hackney, A. E. Tebb, and Robert Mackintosh—in 1910.

Unfortunately, the material evidence is inconclusive. We know from Conrad's letter to Dr. Mackintosh of 25 July 1909 that Conrad was taking Solurol (nucleotin/phosphoric acid) to dissolve uric acid and control his gout (*CL,* 4:261, 261n). We know also that Jessie Conrad writes of a mysterious gout medication, the formula for which she knew by heart, and that John Conrad remembers his father "sparingly" taking "caffeine or phenacetin" and chlorodyne.[18] But what else, during the years leading up to his 1910 breakdown, might Conrad have taken at the advice of his physicians, under the sway of popular medical remedies, at the behest of the advertisers, or at the urging of testimonials? M. J. McLendon has argued that Conrad was poisoned by treatment with calomel, a mercury compound. But McLendon's evidence is circumstantial and his argument, as follows, is unconvincing: Calomel was a favorite purgative and tonic of the Edinburgh school of medicine, the Edinburgh school's system of medicine was widely used during Conrad's day, Conrad received medical treatment during the period for symptoms consistent with mercury poisoning; therefore, Conrad was treated with calomel and was poisoned. While I cannot subscribe to the reasoning of McLendon's argument, his conclusions are perhaps credible, but for reasons different from his line of thought.[19]

It is possible that Conrad was repeatedly prescribed calomel by numerous physicians, in several countries, for a variety of afflictions, and, in fact, calomel was a medicine used into the 1920s for nervousness and nervous debility. But *if* Conrad took calomel and suffered from symptoms of mercury poisoning, it is more likely by self-administration of the popular and easily obtainable compound than by prescription from a physician, particularly a physician like Tebb, who periodically attended Conrad from 1904 to his breakdown. Even though mercury was known by physicians to be toxic to the nervous system and cause toxic tremor, calomel persisted in the popular mind as a remedy for "the blues," as an aid to digestion, and as a kind of aperitif for more serious tonics.[20] Consider, for instance, an "infomercial" for calomel in a 1902 number of *Home Chat,* a women's penny domestic magazine that enjoyed enormous popularity; its first print run (1894) of two hundred thousand copies had to be augmented by thirty-five thousand.[21] The series "Common-Sense Treatment Talk" ran a 1902 article entitled "A Fit of the Blues," which advised that "it may sound prosaic, but the first-aid treatment [for a fit of the blues] is a 1-grain dose of calomel. Take one today, and a second dose on the third night. It is surprising how this simple remedy lightens our horizon." The same article suggested that calomel might treat indigestion, often caused by congestion of the liver:

> Digestive and liver troubles cause more depression and low spirits than any other ailments. . . . Calomel is the finest raiser and heartener of the human spirits in the whole range of the British Pharmacopoeia. . . . The owners of these clogged livers suffer terribly from "blues" and "nervous irritability," which is a polite term for bad temper. . . .
> In nine cases out of ten "depression" has its origin in the liver. Thousands of persons commit suicide for the need of a rousing dose of calomel! A huge percentage of the year's sum of suicides takes place in spring when livers are notoriously out of order. Calomel cleans out the clogged liver in the same way as a good poke clears out a cinder-clogged fire.

Finally, "Common-Sense" advocated taking calomel as conditioner for tonics, which are "admirable in their way." But a "mild dose of calomel should come first. To dose an already clogged liver with tonics. . . is to further choke the mainspring of digestive activity."[22] As the proprietor of such a congested liver, Conrad may well have been tempted both by calomel and various nerve tonics that were available and widely advertised in women's domestic magazines such as *Home Chat* and *Home Notes,* which aimed their advertisements at both female and male consumers.[23]

While one would not expect to find nerve tonics advertised in the pages of most gentlemen's magazines, advertisements for nerve tonics in women's domestic magazines were common during the 1890s and the first decade of the twentieth century. And if the targeted readership of the magazines was female and presumably remained so, the attitudes of that audience evolved as did the understanding of nervous disease. Consequently, the ads of the 1890s are aimed exclusively at women consumers and include promotions for Hood's Sarsaparilla, a blood purifier that would strengthen and steady the nerves; Guy's Tonic, which not only treated the nervous symptoms of irritability, exhaustion, and hysteria but also beautified the skin, hair, and nails; Jolly's "Duchess" Pills that cured anemia, various digestive and nervous disorders, and "female ailments"; and Hall's Coca Wine, "a marvellous restorative" for those suffering from mental and physical fatigue and general depression (see Fig. 3). But by the twentieth century, when the women's movement was gradually gaining momentum and the medical community was grudgingly recognizing that men increasingly showed signs of traditionally "feminine" nervous disorders such as neurasthenia and hysteria, women's domestic magazines began running ads for nerve tonics that were aimed at a female audience and consumer but that depicted male subjects as the patient. Most of these nerve tonics were phosphorus-based products such as Phosferine and Birley's Phosphorus, whose advertisements claimed that dyspepsia, liver complaints, nervous debility, and breakdown were due to the depletion of "Free Phosphorus" in the nervous system as a result of "the habits, occupations, incessant worry, late hours, the vices and natural modes of living, which seem to follow civilization."[24] The tonic Phosferine, coincidentally, varied its ads in *Home Chat* and *Home Notes* almost weekly in the year preceding Conrad's 1910 breakdown to reflect both male and female patients. Characteristic advertisements variously depicted "A Celebrated Beauty," "A London Journalist," "A London Businesswoman," "A Victoria Cross Hero," "A Careful Mother," "The King's Bargemaster," and so forth.[25] It is not improbable that Conrad would have seen such advertisements, some of which would have been intimately personal to him and perhaps suggestive from a literary standpoint (see Fig. 4). Given the fact that phosphorus nerve tonics were based on what was then thought to be "good science," Conrad may well have had recourse to them, given his penchant for physicians who were academically and scientifically oriented.

Conrad's choice of Dr. Glatz, a well-published hydrotherapist, and Dr. John Hackney, who had earned the highest academic credentials of the physicians practicing in Hythe, is replicated in

Fig. 3. Advertisements for Guy's Tonic, *Home Chat,* 9 May 1896, 392, and for Hood's Sarsaparilla, *Home Chat,* 24 October 1896, 284. (British Library, Newspaper Library, Colindale, England)

Advertisement for Hall's Coca Wine, *Home Chat* 1 (1895): 238. (By permission of the University of London Library)

Fig. 4. Advertisement for Phosferine, *Home Chat,* 10 October 1908, 171. (British Library, Newspaper Library, Colindale, England)

his attraction to Albert Tebb. Tebb's medical training appears unusually thorough and impressively "academic" if not academically distinguished. According to school records, Albert Edward Tebb entered Guy's Medical School at the age of seventeen, during the 1880–81 academic year.[26] Evaluative "remarks" in the hands of his various professors indicate that his attendance was regular, his performance was noted as "good" or "very good," even "v.g.i." Records in *Guy's Hospital Reports* show that he won no prizes or scholarships other than "obtaining third-class honours in Obstetric Medicine" in 1891, some fifteen years before he would use those questionable skills to deliver John Conrad.

Tebb's medical training was unusually protracted, spanning more than eleven years (1880–91). His course work at Guy's Medical School, which might typically be projected to be three to four years, extended into a fifth year; and his clinical appointments or hospital practice, generally done in the fourth and fifth years, occupied Tebb in his sixth through eleventh years of medical study. Tebb also delayed sitting for the exam for the Conjoint Diploma—Member of the Royal College of Surgeons and Licentiate of the Royal College of Physicians (M.R.C.S. and L.R.C.P.)—for many years considered the examination for general practice. With the Conjoint Diploma, Tebb could have begun his medical practice, and in fact his name makes an initial appearance in *The Medical Directory* of 1890, suggesting that he may indeed have begun seeing patients. But Tebb continued with his hospital appointments at Guy's and afterward pursued more prestigious university degrees—M.B. (1891), B.S. (1891), and M.D. (1893)—from the University of London. Finally, he studied hygiene and received his Diploma in Public Health in 1893 from University College, London. The range of clinical appointments and number of degrees is quite unusual. Even in a prestigious medical school such as Guy's, fewer than ten percent of the members of Tebb's "class" would take the M.D., and fewer than half that percentage would have the spectrum of Guy's hospital appointments and academic degrees completed by Tebb.

The correspondence that survives from Tebb's years as a medical student and young practitioner does not reveal the reasons for the length of his medical training unless, perhaps, indirectly. Only two of the fourteen letters in the Tebb Autographs housed in the Brotherton Collection, Leeds University Library, refer to medical matters at all. The autograph letters from this time (1880–95) that Tebb preserved and presumably valued are generally from correspondents involved in the arts: musicians, print dealers, publishers and men of letters, among them Arthur Symons.[27] Tebb's interest in the arts and his rigorous academic training may well be what attracted Conrad to his practice in Hampstead at 226 Finchley Road, the residence where Conrad would have known Tebb and where Ford, whom Conrad steered to Tebb's practice, recuperated in 1905 from his neurasthenic breakdown. Tebb's later residences in Hampstead are conspicuous for their proximity to homes of the noteworthy in the arts community. The Grove Cottages, where Tebb and his family lived for most of the second decade of the twentieth century, were within one hundred yards of four famous houses: Abernethy House, where Robert Louis Stevenson once resided with Sidney Colvin; Fenton House, once inhabited by the musical and literary Burney family; the home of George du Maurier, the famous London actor and stage manager; and the so-called Admiral's House of local Hampstead lore, on whose roof Admiral Matthew Barton periodically emerged from retirement to fire two cannon, mounted there to mark occasions of public rejoicing, especially those prompted by great naval victories.[28] (It is speculated that Dickens got wind of this Wemmickean ritual.)

Even if Tebb was attracted to Hampstead for its historical and artistic significance, he developed close friendships with the contemporary writers and artists who lived there. In addition to his connections with Conrad and Ford, Tebb was well known to other members of the Conrad circle and the arts community. Olive Garnett, in her unpublished autobiography "A Bloomsbury Girlhood," mentions Dr. Tebb numerous times, not only in his capacity as a physician but also in his social roles as a member of a luncheon party or as a playgoer. And, though he is not remembered in William Rothenstein's voluminous *Men and Memories,* Tebb was a close mutual friend of both Conrad and the portrait painter. Before Conrad offered The Pent to Rothenstein in the summer of 1906, he had offered the farm first to the Tebbs, who could not accept his offer. So too, one of Will Rothenstein's closest companions at this time was likewise a mutual friend of Tebb's, George Calderon, with whom Rothenstein would often walk on the Heath. Like Rothenstein, Calderon also opened his home—Heathland Lodge in the Vale of Health—as a gathering place for artists. And like Tebb, Calderon had wide-ranging interests but seemed to move on the fringe of greatness.[29] Tebb was thus a figure who was connected to several intersecting artistic circles.

Both Conrad and Ford would become "dependent" on Tebb.[30] Although "queer" and "quack-like" in appearance, he inspired confidence in Conrad and Ford with his reputation for curing his patients—qualities recognized by Violet Hunt in her memoirs.[31] Hunt confirms the sense that Tebb was quite scientific in his approach to medications, often responding to his patients' medical problems with some new wonder drug. Tebb was thus more cautious prescribing drugs for his patients than he was for himself, since Tebb became addicted to painkillers after twenty years of treatment for rheumatoid arthritis. When Ford became dependent on the tranquilizer Adalin, Tebb administered placebos (bread pills) to wean Ford from the medication.[32] One presumes, then, that Tebb would have been wary of the mercury-based calomel, and reluctant to overprescribe bromides, a class of sedatives that were often administered to neurasthenics. The fact that Conrad remarks in his 1905 letter to Tebb that in the absence of pain he expected to sleep suggests that he was frequently bothered by pain but not accustomed to sedation. Ironically, Tebb himself became a kind of addiction for Conrad and Ford because he was medically comfortable with the concept of male neurasthenia and probably treated it in his literary patients without exhibiting the moral condemnation that many English doctors would have barely suppressed at the mention of male neurasthenia.

Conrad, Ford, London Physicians, and Neurasthenia

As much as Conrad voiced his medical complaints to family and friends, he was also absolutely tight-lipped about his deepest personal fears, except perhaps with Ford. Prior to his 1910 breakdown, Conrad never shares a diagnosis or suspicion of neurasthenia in any letters, largely, one suspects, because of the pre–World War I stigma attached to men who may have shown the symptoms from which Conrad suffered. If we are to believe Ford's assertion that he lived and collaborated with Conrad in a most intimate way, it is likely that some of those intimacies included discussions touching upon sexuality, marriage, personal health—a constellation of issues that are all related to the medical problem of neurasthenia.[33] Moreover, Conrad and Ford's attraction to and "sharing" of Dr. Tebb may have been due to Tebb's medical acceptance of male neurasthenia.[34] Tebb's medical training at Guy's would not have encouraged the facile diagnosis of the disorder, though his training necessarily culminated in the study of mental disease, which was the specific focus of the exams leading to the M.D. degree. Tebb could have earned the M.D. in 1893 from the University of London, either by thesis or by examination. Tebb passed the exams, which were read by the leading medical psychologist of the day, D. Hack Tuke, the editor of *A Dictionary of Psychological Medicine* (1892), a text frequently quoted in this study. And, it is likely, Tebb prepared for the exam directly or indirectly under the instruction of Sir George Savage, London's leading expert in mental disease. The subjects of the exam were "Mental physiology, especially in its relations to Mental Disorder" and "Medicine."[35] The term "medicine" here may be generally understood as both the application of anatomy to medicine and the methods of medical diagnosis. At the time Tebb pursued his studies at Guy's Medical School, a course in mental disease was not yet part of the required curriculum. Indeed, Tebb took his M.D. just at the time Guy's recognized this need and was adding faculty to teach such courses. Thus, the *Guy's Hospital Pupils' Returns, 1881,* which records Tebb's course of study, has no designated space (after the space designated for listing the completion of course work required for examination for the Conjoint Diploma) to enter and list lectures Tebb may have attended on mental disease as he prepared for the M.D. examination. But we do know that at the time Tebb was sitting for the degree, a new course was being instituted at Guy's in "Mental Physiology, and Pathology and Experimental Psychology," designed and "adapted to the requirements of candidates preparing for the examinations of M.D. or M.S. in the University of London." While this course, taught by Dr. George Savage and Dr. W. H. R. Rivers, was not apparently available to Tebb, Dr. Savage had long been a distinguished lecturer at Guy's in "Mental Diseases." And since Tebb would have been eligible for the privilege of "Perpetual Studentship of the Hospital," Dr. Savage's "Mental Disease" course was available to him as he prepared for the M.D. examination.[36]

Guy's curriculum in mental disease was, not surprisingly, rather conservative. The new course of 1894–95 seems to emphasize physiology over "experimental psychology," but the fact that it covered "experimental psychology" at all is impressive. (Indeed, Dr. Rivers would become one of England's early Freudians and would go on to treat Siegfried Sassoon.) Savage's long-standing course "Mental Disease" was clearly partial toward medical psychology and comprised: "An introductory Lecture.

Lectures on the general causes of and predisposition to Insanity. Classification of Insanity. Forms of Mental Disorder. Melancholia. Mania. States of Stupor. Mental weakness (Chronic Mania and Dementia). Monomania, and Delusional Insanity. General or Progressive Paralysis of the Insane. Epilepsy and its relations to Insanity. Relations of Insanity to Phthisis, Rheumatism, Gout, Syphilis, &c. Idiocy. Legal relations."[37] Conspicuously absent from the course outline is any recognition of neurasthenia in relation to mental disease, even though it was thought of in America and on the continent as the most widespread modern nervous condition and a potential gateway to insanity, but this omission is not surprising given the privileging of physiology among English neurologists and medical psychologists, who shunned neurasthenia as a "functional," psychological, and therefore spurious disorder.

During the 1890s and early part of the twentieth century, the influence of Sir George Savage on psychological medicine was rather pervasive, indeed at times disturbingly so. The distinguished lecturer in mental diseases at Guy's Hospital was also a physician and superintendent of Bethlem Royal Hospital for the insane (where he worked with Rivers), coeditor of the *Journal of Mental Science,* and president of the Medico-Psychological Association of Great Britain. But his most far-reaching influence lay in the text he authored, the most widely used by students and practitioners alike during the 1890s, entitled *Insanity and Allied Neuroses: A Practical and Clinical Manual.* First published in 1884, the text gave him preeminent power and prestige. A 1908 review of the fourth edition published in the *British Journal of Psychology* remarks, "Savage's *Manual* has been a household word with the English student and practitioner for the last twenty-three years" and predicts, despite the rapidly changing field of psychology, that it "will hold its pride of place for several generations of students." (And, in fact, the table of contents of the 1907 edition is very similar to the 1894–95 syllabus for his Guy's Medical School lectures on mental disease.) The review continues, praising "his singular sagacity and clearness of judgement [that] give all his opinions a power and weight rarely to be found in the utterances of the specialist. He is one of those few writers who 'see life steadily and see it whole.'"[38] The reviewer's Arnoldian phrase captures the Victorian tone and ideology inscribed in Savage's text. Among his many accomplishments, Sir George Savage was the family physician of Sir Leslie Stephen, one of Virginia

Woolf's physicians during the nervous breakdown she suffered following her father's death in 1904, and the physician attending Thoby and Virginia Stephen in 1906 during his misdiagnosed and fatal case of typhus and during her various episodes of nervous exhaustion. Woolf's sense of that doctor-patient relationship has been recorded in biography and diaries—Woolf thought Savage "tyrannical" and "short-sighted"—and the physician himself was one of three models for Woolf's Dr. Bradshaw in *Mrs. Dalloway*.[39] Both Woolf and her apologist Stephen Trombley focus on the heavy moral tone of Savage/Bradshaw's steady vision of life: in a word—Woolf's word—"proportion."

Dr. Savage's moral vision, which seems almost to parody Victorian moral earnestness, is evident throughout his medical textbook. The representative passages quoted below that define the "border-land" between "normal" eccentricity and insanity illustrate Woolf's metaphor of "proportion" and the Conradian trope, restraint: "Most persons," Savage notes, "have their own idiosyncrasies of temperament. . . . If these are not duly restrained and checked, a habit is in process of development which may influence for evil the whole life of the individual." Savage admits that most sane people may be suspicious, jealous, or vengeful, "but if left unrestrained, or stimulated in growth by foolish encouragement, their tendency is to make men, in the first place, eccentric, and afterwards possibly to form the groundwork of an attack of insanity."[40] The tone of moral seriousness is pervasive in a wide range of Savage's work, dating back to his first publication in the early 1880s, which fittingly focused on "moral insanity."[41]

During the years that Conrad was being treated at Champel for neurasthenic dyspepsia, malarial neurasthenia, and later perhaps gout (1891, 1894–5, 1907), Dr. Savage's pronouncements on neurasthenia in his text are brief (under two pages), masculinist, and morally contemptuous. In discussing the Weir Mitchell treatment of "so-called neurasthenic cases," Savage admits that "[p]atients who have slowly become chronic invalids have been by this method brought back not only to life but to active *usefulness*" (emphasis mine). His discussion comes at the end of a chapter entitled "Hysteria and Its Relationships" and thus explicitly classifies neurasthenia as a condition common to women or connected with femininity. Indeed, the typical history and case he cites describes "[a] woman, generally single, or in some way not in a condition for performing her reproductive function, having suffered from some real or imagined trouble, or having passed through a phase of hypochondriasis of sexual character, and often being of a highly nervous stock, becomes the interesting invalid. She is surrounded by good and generally religious and sympathetic friends. She is pampered in every way. She may have lost her voice or the power of one limb. . . . In the end the patient becomes bedridden, often refuses her food, or is capricious about it. . . . The body wastes, and the face has a thin anxious look, not unlike that represented by Rossetti in many of his pictures of women."[42]

While there was an open discussion and disagreement in professional circles as to whether neurasthenia was solely a woman's disease, there was general agreement among medical professionals before World War I that neurasthenia was primarily a disease of women.[43] Is it any wonder Conrad and Ford said little, by name, about their affliction? Even Ford's friend and confidant, Douglas Goldring, recounting Ford's neurasthenia, speaks condescendingly as a man about Ford's nervous collapse: "The incident establishes the fact that Ford was a sufferer from neurasthenia in its most advanced form and needed treatment similar to the smart box on the ears or bucket of cold water which is sometimes administered to hysterical females."[44]

The incident to which Goldring refers is described by Ford in "Some Cures," a chapter in *Return to Yesterday*. Published almost three decades after his three-year illness of 1904–6, Ford's memoir testifies both to the medical biases of the early twentieth century and to cultural attitudes toward neurasthenia. During those years, Ford experienced the "uninterrupted mental agony" attendant to "agoraphobia and intense depression" and reports that he consulted some nineteen specialists, who offered various spa "nerve-cures" in England and five other European countries, ranging from a pork and ice cream cure in Germany to a dried pea and grape cure on the Lake of Constance on the Swiss-German border. Ford attributes his actual "cure" to Dr. Tebb, a medical interview he narrates in histrionic detail.[45]

Ford describes Tebb as "the most mournful looking man I have ever imagined. He was thinner than seemed possible—thinner than myself! He wore extremely powerful glasses that dilated his eyes to extravagant dimensions."[46] The description of Tebb's "medical" cure of Ford is not only improbably fictionalized, consciously arranged, and dramatized, but it also presents concrete insight into the neurasthenic state and how Tebb, Ford and Conrad's doctor, treats it:

He came into the room where I lay. . . . Tebb with his stethoscope in his top hat was like a ghost.

He sat beside me for more than two hours. He hardly spoke at all. Now and then he asked a question. It was as if his voice came from a tomb. . . .

After Tebb had been silent for an hour and a half, I said: "Doctor, I know I am going to die. Mayn't I finish a book I have begun?"

"What book?" he asked cavernously. I said it was a life of Holbein.

Half an hour afterwards he said:

"Yes, you may as well finish your life of Holbein if you have time. You will be dead in a month." He said it with a hollow and mournful vindictiveness that still rings in my ears. He told me to go to Winchelsea to do that work. If I was alive at the end of a month I could come and see him again. He went away, leaving no prescription.

As soon as he was gone I jumped up, dressed myself and all alone took a hansom to Piccadilly Circus. You are to remember that my chief trouble was that I imagined that I could not walk. Well, I walked backwards and forwards across the Circus for an hour and a half. I kept saying: "Damn that brute, I will not be dead in a month." . . .

At the end of the month, I saw Tebb again. I said triumphantly: "You see, I am not dead."

He answered as mournfully and hollowly as if here were in despair at the falsification of his prophecy:

"If I hadn't told you you would be dead, you would have been dead."[47] He was no doubt right.

At a distance of more than a quarter century, Ford seems to play with the representation of pre-Raphaelite decadence bringing him to the brink of physical and mental degeneration. Reclining on the sofa upon which Shelley spent his last night, Ford confirms Dr. Savage's description of the neurasthenic as a "decadent" type who withers away: "In the end the patient becomes bedridden, often refuses her food. . . . The body wastes, and the face has a thin anxious look, not unlike that represented by Rossetti in many of his pictures."[48] Tebb is represented as befuddled but as an unyielding and unforgiving voice that will neither validate the illness nor excuse the moral feebleness. Ford scholars have long questioned whether Tebb's "cure" of Ford has any basis in fact. I believe it does, for Tebb's appearance as a "prophet of death" figure and his stern bedside manner apparently follow the advice of the famous teacher from his alma mater: "In such cases the patients must not be accused of malingering when they say they cannot walk or sit up. If not vigorously treated they will die."[49] Tebb's matter-of-fact "vigorous" treatment, informing Ford that he would die, was apparently just the sort of reverse psychological pampering needed to get his patient back on his feet. As Douglas Goldring remarked in his memoir *South Lodge,* Tebb was "infinitely wise about the ailments of artists."[50]

Conrad's ailments as he approached his own collapse were not, as Ford recollects his, "purely imaginary." Nor was Conrad ever able to recollect his illnesses from the amused perspective of good health. His collapse of January 1910, the culmination of months of psychological strain and a recent bout with influenza, is narrated by Jessie Conrad in *Joseph Conrad and His Circle*. In the days preceding his breakdown, Conrad is described by Jessie as experiencing "extreme agitation. . . . He was very irritable and I felt sure this was a forerunner of an attack of gout, . . . his nerves already frayed to tatters" when he visited his agent, Pinker. There, Jessie Conrad continues, "his irritability increased out of control. At such times he did not know his own nervous strength. In the course of that heated argument, he placed his elbows against the arms of the big leather arm-chair and pushed the sides out." That night, no doubt trying the hospitality of his friend John Galsworthy, he "pushed the foot out of the bed in an excess of nervous strength."[51] The nervous collapse occurred the next day, and Conrad did not regain his strength until the late spring, though as Keith Carabine has shown, he heavily revised the typescript of *Under Western Eyes* beginning in April.[52]

Jessie's repeated use of the term "irritability" is consistent with medical usage: "mental restlessness, agitation and impatience, resulting from a loss of inhibitory power consequent on nervous exhaustion" (*DPM,* 715). In other words, the weakened and exhausted Conrad was losing his restraint. The apparent excitability and nervous strength exhibited by the destruction of furniture is actually consonant with "nerve storms" leading up to and culminating in a complete breakdown:

> According to the law of stimulation of a fatigued or degenerating nerve, the nervous excitability as such is decreased, but nevertheless appears at first increased on account of the greater capacity of conduction consequence of the decreased resistance; this exaggerated excitability still increases, at first rapidly, thereby producing painful and spasmodic symptoms, which are far from being proportionate to the stimulation. . . . The increased excitability being produced by a decrease of the normal resistance, which naturally is followed by a decrease of nutrition and consequently by a condition of weakness, which a degenerating nerve

at first presents, cannot last long, and that soon decreased excitability, bluntness, paresis, or whatever we call fatigue and exhaustion, must take its place. Excitability, with a tendency to
rapid fatigue or exhaustion, is therefore a characteristic of neurasthenia. (*DPM*, 842–3)

This apparent rise of nervous force followed by actual nervous
exhaustion is typical of the "sequences of neurasthenia" and
Conrad's composition process that he describes in a letter to H. G.
Wells: "As to working regularly in a decent and orderly and in-
dustrious manner I've given that up from sheer impossibility.
The damned stuff comes out only by a kind of mental convulsion
lasting two/three or more days—up to a fortnight—which leaves
me perfectly limp and not very happy, exhausted emotionally to
all appearance but secretly irritable to the point of savagery" (*CL,*
3:288). Such nerve storms accompanying or replicating the creative process would lead, as Conrad approached the completion
of *Under Western Eyes,* to a complete nervous breakdown.

The effect of this collapse on Conrad's career has been debated since Thomas Moser argued that Conrad wrote his best fiction before his breakdown—in contemporary medical terms,
when he was at the height of the nervous irritability that Conrad
continually struggled to restrain.[53] I can only guess that, with his
history of neurasthenia, so closely associated with female hysteria, Conrad felt his life as a masculine writer of adventure fiction in grave danger as he felt himself slipping into nervous exhaustion, in Jessie's words, "rambling off into evident delirium."
As Conrad's neck swelled in an accompanying attack of gout, the
last coherent words before his delirium (as recorded by Jessie
Conrad) were: "[G]ive me a looking glass. I must look a pretty
guy, with all this beard." Then she notes, "[H]is voice ended almost in a sob."[54]

Part II

Reading Medically

[W]hen writing *Lord Jim* in ten months or less I had been feeling always on the brink of the grave. Explain it who may. And perhaps true literature (when you 'get it') is something like a disease which one feels in one's bones, sinews, and joints.—Joseph Conrad, from letter to David Meldrum

Chapter 4
The Vivid, Nervous Descriptions of Conrad's Fiction

> [F]or me, writing—*the only possible writing*—is just simply the conversion of nervous force into phrases. . . . But the fact remains that when the nervous force is exhausted the phrases don't come:—and no tension of will can help.
> —Joseph Conrad, from a letter to H. G. Wells

Conrad dedicated *An Outcast of the Islands* to Ted Sanderson, a passenger on the *Torrens* where Conrad berthed as first mate from 1891 to 1893, a period, in Conrad's words, "not so long since I had been neurasthenic."[1] Conrad writes about his neurasthenia rather casually in "The *Torrens:* A Personal Tribute," composed in 1923, but only after keeping the illness from public view for some thirty years; he confesses in the context of describing a troublesome neurasthenic passenger who experienced a morbid fear of the sea several days into the voyage but in whom the ship's doctor "could not find the slightest evidence of organic disease of any sort."[2] Whether or not Conrad and Sanderson discussed the passenger's affliction or Conrad told Ted Sanderson of his own bout with neurasthenia in 1891, they would develop a close friendship that included discussions of personal health.[3] When Helen Sanderson received the copy of *An Outcast of the Islands* Conrad sent the couple, she wrote back immediately, praising the novel using popular medical terminology: "I have been greatly fascinated in reading again sundry amazing passages already." She commends especially "yʳ marvellous [*sic*] introduction of yʳ scoundrel. . . . One does not tire at all ever—of yʳ. vivid, *nervous* descriptions."[4]

What Helen Sanderson meant by "vivid, *nervous* descriptions" is problematic, but the combined possibilities mirror not only Conrad's medical situation but the cultural construction of language as well. "Nervous," as a critical descriptor "of writing, arguments, etc." traditionally meant "vigorous, powerful, forcible; free from weakness and diffuseness" and is specifically associated in the eighteenth century with sinewy muscularity and masculinity. The last historical example of this usage in the *Oxford English Dictionary* is, coincidentally, 1896, the year Conrad published *An Outcast of the Islands*. In the nineteenth century, the word "nervous" increasingly assumed medical nuances and, as a descriptor "of persons" came to mean "suffering from disorder of the nerves; also excitable, easily agitated, timid."[5] The two meanings of the word thus seem to carry conventional gender associations at odds with each other, especially if "nervous" lost its masculine connotation in late-nineteenth-century rhetorical criticism due to the increasing medical association of nervousness with femininity. But in fact, the so-called "sequences" of neurasthenia comprehend both meanings, for they imply the increase of nervous strength followed by nervous weakness; when this pattern of alternating nervous force and weakness repeats itself, it could lead to increased irritability, "nerve storms," and finally to nervous breakdown. Hence, "yʳ. vivid, *nervous* descriptions" is a perfectly apt characterization of Conrad's prose style as defined by gender stereotypes of the day: both vividly powerful in its evocation of scene and somewhat tremulous and ephemeral in meaning.

In the author's note written in 1919 for a new edition of *An Outcast of the Island,* Conrad reflects that the novel was composed at a time of his life when he suffered from a sense of personal conflict and paralysis. "I was the victim," Conrad confesses, "of contrary stresses which produced a state of immobility" (*OI,* xliii).[6] The immediate context of the passage implies that the contrary stresses are the competing calls of the sea and the pen, for Conrad at that time was torn between the two professions. But the fact that Conrad produced his second novel in a little more than thirteen months suggests that the state of immobility to which Conrad refers does not apply to his career as a novelist. *An Outcast* was begun as a short story called "Two Vagabonds" at Champel-les-Bains on 16 August 1894 (*CL,*1:171) and finished 16 September 1895 (1:245), several months after Conrad returned from yet another trip, his third, for hydrotherapy. Champel water cures thus frame Conrad's composition of the novel, perhaps a third of which was written while Conrad underwent therapy for what he called "attacks of melancholy which paralyze my thought and will" (1:11). Clearly the immobility of which Conrad speaks was more than the competition between the vocations of sailor and author but was intimately related to Conrad's mental health and physical well-being.

The Allure of Champel

An early Freudian might observe that the sea and pen can be taken to symbolize female and male sexuality and that Conrad may have been mindful of such "contrary stresses" in himself. He would certainly have been aware of such differences at Champel. Although the sexes were traditionally segregated at the hydropathic institute, Conrad would have been aware of sexual difference because Champel apparently catered to a predominantly female clientele in its therapeutic program but appealed to both sexes in its advertising strategies.[7] Extant promotional brochures, various postcards, and a poster that advertises Champel-les-Bains (see Fig. 5) each seem conceived to appeal to a specific sexualized viewer. An early advertisement of Champel, for instance, published in 1887 by the Association of Commercial and Industrial Interests, serves as a twelve-page introduction to the *Illustrated Guide to Geneva* and was presumably aimed at a male businessman who might visit Geneva and arrange for his wife to take a cure at the hydropathic institute or who might have a more sexually predatory design. The description of Champel is prefaced with an illustration of a bare-breasted woman, lounging in an attitude of repose at water's edge as an attendant bathes her feet in the Arve River (see Fig. 6). One presumes that few men are on the institute grounds, that the women are ostensibly secluded and pampered, and that a businessman might take mild erotic pleasure in imagining his wife, with other scantily clad women, in such sensuous activity. But the reality may well have been different.

Guy de Maupassant, who sought the *"douche à la Charcot"* of Champel's therapy program a few weeks after Conrad's visit to Champel in the summer of 1891, reportedly boasted about amorous encounters at Champel. Under treatment for nervousness,

Fig. 5. Poster of Champel-les-Bains, Museum für Gestaltung, Zurich, Switzerland. The Champel complex consisted of the Hydropathic Institute (below the *B* of *Bains*), the Hôtel Beau-Séjour (spread out below the word *Champel*), and the Pension La Roseraie, where Conrad lodged (below the last two letters of *Bains*).

LA ROSERAIE

Fig. 6. Postcards of Champel-les-Bains: Hôtel-Pension La Roseraie, Champel, Switzerland; woman bather at Hydropathic Institute. (Bibliothèque publique et universitaire, Genève. Photo by C. Poite)

perhaps sexual neurasthenia, and the later stages of syphilis, Maupassant claims to have seduced a *"petite femme"* during a medical excursion to Geneva. Maupassant's exploits and treatment at Champel remain rather shadowy. In June of 1891, after a disagreeable cure (probably for "constitutional syphilis") in the sulfurous waters of Bagnères-de-Luchon, he took a water cure at Divonne-les-Bains not far from Geneva, perhaps twenty miles by train.[8] But unable to enjoy his favorite Champel shower, *"'la douche à la Charcot'* that had a powerful jet, so powerful that only the toughest kind of men could stand it," Maupassant apparently traveled to Geneva, where Dr. Glatz, a follower of Charcot, offered the treatment.[9] (Conrad likewise surely refers to *"la douche à la Charcot"* when he speaks of the "active fire hose" [*CL*,1:212].) Once, when returning from Geneva, Maupassant bragged of his sexual exploits, claiming amorous brilliance and that he was cured even though Dr. Glatz at this time apparently described Maupassant as a "candidate for general paralysis."[10] This description indicates that Maupassant was not only a "victim" of so-called sexual neurasthenia—the loss of sexual potency due to chronic overindulgence, masturbation, and so on—but also syphilitic.[11]

The sensuousness of the 1887 Champel brochure is probably aimed at a male audience, perhaps sexually adventuresome if not as highly sexed as Maupassant, reading a business-oriented guide to Geneva. The appeal to this kind of masculine audience disappears from extant publications during the next decade. A later brochure cover (Fig. 7), postdating Conrad's 1894 and 1895 visits and perhaps from around the turn of the twentieth century, portrays a delicate, demure woman sitting on the grass in a flouncy sundress, eyes downcast, picking flowers for her basket.[12] Shades of pastel green and pink predominate, and, unlike the earlier black-and-white advertisement, these images seem aimed at a female consumer. An illustration from this brochure of Hôtel-Pension La Roseraie depicts the hotel, six women, four children, one man, and a large dog (see Fig. 6). The only illustration of a male patient presents an image of what the malnourished neurasthenic patron hopes to feel like after his cure and may well fit the Victorian stereotype of the male hysteric.[13] The depicted male patient under a douche shower is chubby, smiles as if tickled by the shower, and modestly hides his bare chest as he giggles (see Fig. 8). He is neither conventionally masculine nor does he appear as we might imagine the anemic, depressed, and pain-racked Conrad. The specific afflictions treated at

Fig. 7. Cover of commercial brochure for Champel-les-Bains (Geneva: Société d'Affiches artistiques, n.d.). (Bibliothèque publique et universitaire, Genève. Photo by Jean Marc Meylan)

Fig. 8. Male patient in shower douche, Champel-les-Bains (Geneva: Société d'Affiches artistiques, n.d.), 5. (Bibliothèque publique et universitaire, Genève. Photo by Jean Marc Meylan)

Champel, listed on the first page of text and here translated and also reproduced (see Fig. 9), likewise seem to focus on female disorders or disorders of the feminized male:

1.—Particular Ailments Treated at Champel

THE INSTITUTE brings together everything that modern science has discovered and perfected for the treatment of the following afflictions:

Maladies of the nervous system: NEURASTHENIA, Hysteria, Hypochondria, Insomnia, St. Vitus's Dance, Epilepsy, Illnesses of the Spinal Cord (Locomotor Ataxy, Infantile Paralysis, etc.)
Nervous exhaustion (following excessive intellectual work or from physical overtaxing), Nervous troubles consequent upon infectious illness, and from alcoholism or the abuse of morphine.
Anemia and Chlorosis (paleness). Tubercular diathesis (Hydrotherapy and aerotherapy).
Neurasthenia.
Rheumatism and Neuralgias. Sciatic Neuralgia.
Diabetes and Albuminuria (nutritional disorders).
Weakness of the Sexual Organs. Sterility.
Uterine Ailments: Troubles from menstruation. Amenorrhea (suppression or absence of menstruation), Dysmenorrhea (difficult or painful menstruation), Fibrous tumors of the Uterus (Electricity and Hydrotherapy).
Exophthalmic Goiter, Syphilis.
Ailments of the digestive route. **Nervous Dyspepsia.**
Neurosis and Dilation of the Stomach and Intestine.
Convalescence from Grave Illnesses (Typhus, Scarlet Fever, Malaria, Influenza, etc.).

Most of the illnesses described, with the obvious exception of the uterine ailments, were afflictions that could strike both men and women. But the attention to nervous disorders, especially neurasthenia brought on by intellectual work and hysteria, and the less sexualized feminine appeal of the later advertisements, suggest that between 1887 and the turn of the twentieth century the advertising strategy shifted from an appeal to a consumer businessman who might "target" women patients toward a targeted female consumer audience and a more feminized male patient. This shift occurred even though the medical specialty of the Champel—the treatment of nervous disorders—remained the same.

The predominance of, and increased catering to, a female clientele may explain why Conrad, in an 1895 letter to Marguerite Poradowska written from Champel, ends his description of the inception of *An Outcast of the Islands* with a questioning

I. — Affections spécialement traitées à Champel.

ÉTABLISSEMENT réunit tout ce que la science moderne a découvert et perfectionné pour le traitement des affections suivantes :

Maladies du système nerveux : NEURASTHENIE. Hystérie, Hypocondrie, Insomnie, Chorée ou Danse de St-Guy, Epilepsie, Maladies de la Moëlle épinière (Ataxie locomotrice, Paralysie infantile, etc.). **Epuisement nerveux** (suite de travail intellectuel exagéré ou de surmenage physique), Troubles nerveux consécutifs aux maladies infectieuses et à l'alcoolisme, ou à l'abus de la morphine.

Anémie et Chlorose (pâles couleurs). Disposition à la Phtisie (Hydrothérapie et Aérothérapie).

Neurasthénie.

Rhumatismes et Névralgies. Névralgie sciatique.

Diabète et Albuminurie (Maladies de la nutrition).

Affaiblissement des organes sexuels. Stérilité.

Affections utérines : Troubles de la menstruation. Aménorrhée (suppression ou absence de la menstruation), Dysménorrhée (menstruation difficile et douloureuse), Tumeurs fibreuses de l'utérus (Electricité et Hydrothérapie).

Goitre exophtalmique, Syphilis

Affections des voies digestives. **Dyspepsies nerveuses.**

Névroses et dilatation de l'estomac et de l'intestin.

Fig. 9. Champel program of treatment, Champel-les-Bains (Geneva: Société d'Affiches artistiques, n.d.), 3. (Bibliothèque publique et universitaire, Genève. Photo by Jean Marc Meylan)

exclamation for Poradowska: "Do you think one can make something interesting without any women?!" (*CL*,1:171). Conrad, I think, felt outnumbered. In finished form, *An Outcast* would mirror the ambiguity of Conrad's question/exclamation, which can imply that women are indispensable to the form of the novel or suggest that it would be nice if women could be eliminated from it altogether. The novel, accordingly, can be read in one of two competing ways: as the conventional story of a man and woman whose love is doomed to fail due to differences in race and culture, or as an equally conventional psychodrama of nervous collapse, in which the woman is less a human being than a reflection of the moral insanity of the male protagonist who operates in a landscape that, like Aïssa, mirrors his degeneration. The "vivid, *nervous* descriptions" that Helen Sanderson detects may thus be thought the product of Conrad's nervous constitution in combination with sexual stereotypes of fin-de-siècle English culture, which conventionally portrayed insanity in feminine terms and exotic places as both a threat to civilization and a challenge or "self-same complement" to empire.[14] This combination of nervousness and gender stereotypes, I think, accounts for Conrad's confession in the 1919 author's note: "The mere scenery got a great hold on me as I went on, perhaps because (I may as well confess that) the story itself was never very near my heart" (*OI,* ix). Nearer to Conrad's heart is the narrating of his own medical history: the evocation of nervousness through narrative form and the exploration of his own fears and gender confusion in the process of tale telling.

Conrad's question to Marguerite Poradowska is thus quite serious. Representing fin-de-siècle nervousness and the threat of madness, the feminine principle was something Conrad feared and yet recognized as somehow essential to the nervous power of his fiction. This feminine nervousness, perceived as inseparable from his sensitivity as an artist, was identified by Edward Garnett as one of Conrad's defining characteristics that he remembered vividly from their first meeting in the office of T. Fisher Unwin, Conrad's first English publisher:

> My memory is of seeing a dark-haired man, short but extremely graceful in his nervous gestures, with brilliant eyes, now narrowed and penetrating, now soft and warm, with a manner alert yet caressing, whose speech was ingratiating, guarded, and brusque turn by turn. I had never seen a man so masculinely keen yet so femininely sensitive. The conversation between our host and Conrad for some time was halting and jerky. . . . Conrad, extremely polite, grew nervously brusque in his responses, and kept shifting his feet one over the other, so that I became fascinated in watching the flash of his pointed patent leather shoes. The climax came unexpectedly when in answer to Mr. Unwin's casual but significant reference to "your next book," Conrad threw himself back on the broad leather lounge and in a tone that put a clear cold space between himself and his hearers, said "I don't expect to write again. It is likely I shall soon be going to sea." A silence fell.[15]

While some of the femininity Garnett perceives may be Conrad's Polish manner and aristocratic demeanor, such differences or the perception of such differences were often painful to Conrad. But conversely, if Conrad's nervousness and the various neurasthenic symptoms were a source of torment to him, Conrad and his friends recognized them as essential to his sensitive nature and therefore to his function as an artist. Constance Garnett would write to Conrad that "the artist is more than half feminine," and to Helen Sanderson, at about the same time, Conrad would write that "women have a more penetrating vision"

(*CL,*1:334).[16] As Susan Jones has convincingly demonstrated, these compliments to the female sex are not patronizing but as genuine as Conrad's sustained intimacy with Marguerite Poradowska, a woman novelist with whom Conrad shared, in the formative years, both his histrionic postures and his deepest fears about madness as he began writing his "vivid, *nervous"* fiction.[17]

Neurasthenia, Gender, and Medical Discourse

Feminist scholars and critics have demonstrated that English culture constructed insanity or particular versions of insanity as a "female malady," despite the data gathered by male physicians of the day, which indicated that there was no statistically significant difference between male and female admissions to lunatic asylums in the later part of the nineteenth century (*DPM,* 1202–3).[18] The persistent cultural association between women and insanity may have extended from the growing number of nervous women and the attention paid to them in popular journals during the early twentieth century, especially in America. *Good Housekeeping, Harper's Bazaar,* and the *Ladies' Home Journal* ran articles on nervous breakdown, and, in England, women's penny domestic magazines such as *Home Chat* and *Home Notes* advertised products to strengthen and purify the nerves and blood.[19] Yet in English medical circles, there was still reluctance to accept the popular social disorder as a verifiable medical condition. William Ireland, reviewing a translation of Adrien Proust and Gilbert Ballet's *The Treatment of Neurasthenia,* asserts that "neurasthenia, a plant of American growth, has not taken its root in Britain. . . . On the continent, this disease gets wider recognition."[20] The grudging reluctance to recognize neurasthenia is still present in Sir George Savage, who as late as 1910 speaks skeptically of the "treatment of so-called neurasthenic cases which Dr. Playfair so fully introduced into England," and in William Osler, who complains the disease "covers an ill-defined, motley group of symptoms."[21] Indeed, by the time of Conrad's 1910 breakdown, neurasthenia was generally becoming a less fashionable diagnosis, attacked by conservative physiologists like Savage on the one hand, and by the revolutionary Freud on the other, who advocated in 1909 the replacement of "neurasthenia" with various, more specific, anxiety neuroses.[22] While professional disagreement was due in part to parochial national systems of medicine—medical opinions in England, America, and Europe were often at odds with each other—it was difficult, even within a given medical community, to find consensus among the experts about the symptoms, diagnosis, and classification of nervous disorders and their relative incidence in the male and female sexes. The issue of sexing or gendering the closely related diseases of hysteria and neurasthenia was a particularly nationalist medical practice.

In America, where Beard "introduced" neurasthenia in 1879 to the scientific community, he acknowledged its longstanding, vague recognition and its similarity to hysteria, but he also counterdistinguished the two disorders. The hysterical state, he argued, occurs in the presence of "convulsions or paroxysms" and "is found usually in individuals whose emotional natures greatly predominate. Hence, relatively to neurasthenia, it is far more common in females than in males." Neurasthenia, on the other hand, was sexually if not socioeconomically more democratic: "[A]lthough more frequent in women, [neurasthenia] is yet found in great abundance in both sexes, and in both men and women of intellect, education, and well-balanced mental organizations."[23] Still clinging to traditional linguistic classifications in the 1890s, C. H. Hughes, generally an American disciple of Beard, maintained that "the most typical forms of neurasthenia are found in men, while as its name implies, hysteria is chiefly found in women."[24] In France, as noted in chapter 2 of this book, the work of Charcot challenged the sexing of hysteria as a woman's disease. In England, the medical community responded to this French novelty with the straight-faced assertion that the difference between the incidence of French and English male hysteria could be attributed to "racial and social differences."[25] Similarly, when neurasthenia was recognized and discussed in English medical texts, the typical case was "a woman" because "it is natural that the female sex, being more sensitive, should be more subject to [neurasthenia]" (*DPM,* 848). Dr. Guthrie Rankin, writing on neurasthenia in the *Contemporary Review* (1906), argued that women were "sufferers more frequently than men" and that the disease appeared both among the poor due to "poverty, imperfect hygiene and squalor" and among the wealthy due to "indolence, over-indulgence and unwholesome excitement."[26] The moral tone of this particular essayist—a Harley Street physician—shifts to an ideological and political admonition: "'Break-down of the nervous system' is no mere society craze which is fashionable to suffer from, but is becoming a national calamity which bids fair to rob our descendants of many of those qualities which have done so much to make this empire what it is. . . . In so far as social customs and personal habits are contributing to the increase of nerve-instability, they must be altered if we are to escape that downfall of our supremacy which other great nations before us have experienced."[27] This connection between the breakdown of the human nervous system and the health of the empire is a theme that Conrad develops in early works such as *Almayer's Folly, An Outcast of the Islands,* and *Tales of Unrest,* but throughout those early works, the deeply felt need to narrate his medical history and register his personal fear of mental degeneration is a contrapuntal text that admixes with, runs counter to, and perhaps even dominates the more public, historical themes.

While the politics of gender are clear in Rankin's essay—if the empire is to remain robust, then gender roles must remain distinct and inviolable—they are not so clear in Conrad. Conrad's fiction makes problematic the loss of male restraint and the ascendancy of feminizing nervousness in his male characters. This preoccupation is explicable and reasonable given Conrad's sense of his feminized self and the sociohistorical context of his post-Congo medical problems, which evolved at a moment when the institutions of English culture were redefining themselves.[28] Eve Kosofsky Sedgwick specifically cites 1891 (the year following Conrad's voyage) as "a good moment to which to look for a cross-section of the inaugural discourses of modern homo/heterosexuality—in medicine and psychiatry, in language and law, in the crisis of female status, in the career of imperialism."[29] In medicine and psychiatry—or more appropriately, medical psychology—"sexual inversion" was beginning to be recognized as a distinct pattern of sexual behaviors, evident as a "class" of people. And while the male homosexual was being socially constructed and ostracized, his medical profile had a distinct connection to nervous disease and insanity. The entry on "sexual perversion" in Tuke's *A Dictionary of Psychological Medicine* (1892), for instance, suggests that "such persons often spring from neurotic families—are themselves neurasthenic, and frequently exhibit temporary or permanent conditions of degenerative mental disturbance" (*DPM*, 1156). Since the extent to which Conrad was conscious of homosexuality, either in his life or fiction, is ultimately an unknown, Sedgwick's concept of the continuum of male homosocial desire is useful, for it is less a finite measure than a broad spectrum from homosocial to homo-erotic.[30] Wherever Conrad or his characters may lie on the con-tinuum, homosocial desire, heterosexual irritability, and neuras-thenic enervation were defining conflicts in his life and would inform every layer of his fiction: the imagery, narrative style and strategies, and the major tropes.

Imagery, Narrative Style, and Theme

The imagery of Conrad's "vivid, *nervous* descriptions" should thus be understood as cutting across gender lines and to include images of both vital force and enervation. The images of vital force in Conrad's early fiction represent such valuations as power, increase, movement, and light; the nervous descriptions are completed by opposing images that suggest degeneration—ruin, decay, entropy, and darkness—and images representing neurasthenic weakness, attenuation, and lassitude. When Helen Sanderson praised Conrad's descriptions, she referred specifi-cally to the introduction of Willems in "those first pages." She means, I suspect, the kind of passage that occurs on the second page of the novel, where Willems surveys the locale of Macassar and its inhabitants, a passage Edward Garnett calls a "brilliant opening."[31] It reads:

> They were a *numerous* and an *unclean* crowd, living in *ruined* bamboo houses, surrounded by *neglected* compounds, on the outskirts of Macassar. He kept them at an arm's length and even further off, perhaps, having no illusions as to their worth. They were a *half-caste, lazy lot,* and he saw them as they were—*ragged, lean, unwashed, undersized* men of various ages, *shuf-fling* about *aimlessly* in slippers; *motionless old women* who looked like *monstrous bags* of pink calico stuffed with *shapeless lumps* of fat, and deposited *askew* upon *decaying* rattan chairs in shady corners of dusty verandahs; young women, *slim and yellow, big-eyed, long-haired,* moving *languidly* amongst the *dirt and rubbish* of their dwellings *as if every step they took was going to be their very last.* He heard their shrill quarrellings, the squalling of their children, the grunting of their pigs; he smelt the *odours of the heaps of garbage* in their courtyards: and he was greatly dis-gusted. But he fed and clothed that *shabby multitude;* those *de-generate* descendants of Portuguese conquerors. (*OI,* 4; emphasis added)

Taken as a whole, the passage is a powerfully vivid evocation of sight, sound, and smell. Discrete images and objects in the scene are also, when decontextualized, vivid and powerful. The crowd is "numerous"; the older women are "fat," even "monstrous," in size; and the "young women" are "big-eyed, long-haired" and quarrel shrilly in vocal competition with their "squalling" progeny. Although not attractive, the images suggest vital power and biological increase. Yet they are virtually blotted out by images of degeneration and enervation: the old women are "shapeless" and "motionless," and the young women are neurasthenically "slim" and move "languidly . . . as if every step they took was going to be their very last." Images of ruin and decay abound. Combined, these "contrary stresses" (to take Conrad's words), create the "vivid, *nervous* descriptions" to which Helen Sanderson alludes.

There are numerous passages in the novel that show such competing images of vitality and enervation. Take, for instance, the evocative beginning of part IV: "The night was very dark. For the first time in many months the East Coast slept unseen by the stars under a veil of *motionless* cloud that, *driven* before the first breath of the rainy monsoon, had *drifted slowly* from the eastward all the afternoon; *pursuing the declining sun* with its masses of *black and grey* that seemed to *chase the light* with wicked intent, and with an ominous and *gloomy steadiness,* as though conscious of the message of *violence and turmoil* they carried" (*OI,* 213; emphasis added). The veil of cloud is "motionless" but "driven"; the veil also "drifted slowly" as it is "pursuing" the "declining sun" with "gloomy steadiness" and a message of "violence and turmoil" (213). Although Helen Sanderson wrote to Conrad that she "never tired" of such descriptions, they are the kind of heavily written, purple passages that Max Beerbohm would imitate so hilariously in his parody of "The Lagoon." But it is the very nature of this overwritten, heavily vocalized style that creates the hysterical quality of Conrad's prose, a quality most gaudily apparent in his early fiction.

Conrad was known, by his friends, to write hysterical personal letters. William Rothenstein, corresponding with Edmund Gosse (both men had been instrumental in securing for Conrad a grant of five hundred pounds from the Royal Bounty Special Service Fund [*CL,* 3, 226–27]), apologized for Conrad's reaction to restrictions on the grant's disbursement: "Dr. Mr Gosse," writes Rothenstein, "I am sorry you should have had any further trouble in the matter of Conrad, & that he should have written you in a similar strain that in which he often writes me. Of course he is terribly hysterical—indeed last year I feared for his reason—that was the beginning of my wish to remove at least one weight from his morbid & excitable mind."[32] The letter of 16 May 1905 (*CL,* 3, 246–8) to which Rothenstein refers is indeed an excited profusion of words. Rothenstein's disdain, real or affected for Conrad's sake, reminds one of Goldring's intentionally demeaning comment, quoted earlier, that Ford occasionally became like a hysterical woman in need of a bucket of cold water.[33] More to the point, does such effusive emotionality have a rhetorical analogy in Conrad's fiction, apparent in the early works and refined in the later ones?

Avrom Fleishman long ago recognized what he aptly calls "The Landscape of Hysteria" in *The Secret Agent.* This landscape is characterized by an ability to "break down the strict demarcations of subjectivity and objectivity" or an "alternating of omniscient and focalized narration, the mingling of figurative and literal stylistic modes, the juxtaposing of the horrors of hysterical neurosis and the sometimes greater horrors of the historical world."[34] In other words, it is a permeability between "contrary stresses" that characterizes both Conrad's conflicted inner world and the intersection of that inner world with the outer world. More recently, Michael Finn has suggested that the work of Marcel Proust, who was also diagnosed as neurasthenic and perhaps hysteric, sometimes exhibits a "flawed narrative mode that threatens to substitute itself for writing. The inner voice, a hysterically active one, constantly tries to cover over silence and short-circuit the process of reflection."[35] This hysterical voice is likewise at work in Conrad's heavily written passages that seek to "cover over silence" with thick layers of description, the compounding of adjectives, and the stacking of phrases. It came to Conrad during the early years of his own psychological vicissitudes and is balanced, I would argue, by a voice of enervation that is characterized by hesitation, stuttering, ellipses, and silence.[36] The rhetoric of Conrad's narrative style may thus be thought to replicate the sequences of neurasthenia: nervous force followed by nervous weakness. But it also simply replicates Conrad's actual human voice, his speech, which was, to recall Garnett, "ingratiating, guarded, and brusque turn by turn. . . . The conversation between our host and Conrad for some time was halting and jerky."[37] The narrative technique of Conrad's early fiction, which involves the juxtaposition of "contrary stresses" or vocalizations of the hysteric and the enervated, simply mimics Conrad's own nervous speech pattern.

This pattern is evident in chapter 3 of part IV of *An Outcast of the Islands,* which describes the developing confrontation between Lingard and the agitated Aïssa, who hopes to prevent Lingard from taking Willems away. The chapter begins with rather typical nervous descriptions of Aïssa's mother then quickly shifts to Aïssa herself, who is described throughout the chapter as a series of contradictions: "defiant yet shrinking," "a voice trembling but distinct" (*OI,* 244), a "being savage and tender, strong and delicate, fearful and resolute" (249). The hysterical narrative building of oppositions moves toward a verbal storm: "Her anxious eyes saw some shade of expression pass on her listener's face that made her hold her breath for a second, and then explode into pained fury so violent that it drove Lingard back a pace, like an unexpected blast of wind" (251). The speech that follows is clearly meant to be taken as hysterical, filling the Jungle/Book's silences with an effusive flow of words: "I tell you I was all that to him. I know it! I saw it! . . . There are times when even you white men speak the truth. I saw his eyes. I felt his eyes, I tell you! I saw him tremble when I came near—when I spoke—when I touched him. Look at me! You have been young. Look at me. Look, Rajah Laut!" (251). This is, I suppose, rather bad stuff, in Finn's terms the "flawed narrative mode that substitutes for writing," where vocality itself replaces reflective prose, or in this case, reflective speech. Thus, when Aïssa asks, "Tell me, Rajah Laut, do you know the fear without voice—the fear of silence—the fear that comes when there is no one near?" she is referring literally to the solitary life without Willems, but she is also registering a hysterical vocality that is Conrad's, which bespeaks the writer's fear about silence, the blank page, and, more generally, the fear of a soul who feels the threat of solitude and madness.

Aïssa is, in fact, likened to a lunatic as she tries to defend her enclosure from the advancing Lingard. The hysterical narrative description typifies what Finn calls the "habit of verbal embellishment—overloading objects of observation with epithet and metaphor—[which] is a further connection between the oral and the literary register."[38] Aïssa "came close up to Lingard, with the wild and stealthy aspect of a lunatic longing to whisper out an insane secret—one of those misshapen, heart-rending, and ludicrous secrets; one of those thoughts that, like monsters—cruel, fantastic, and mournful, wander about terrible and unceasing in the night of madness" (*OI,* 253). The object of observation here is simply Aïssa. She is embellished by the description of her manner—that of a lunatic consumed by the longing to whisper a secret. The nonexistent secret is itself described by three adjectives and amplified by an appositive—"one of those thoughts"—that, in turn, is described by a simile—"like monsters"—itself described by five adjectives. This hysterical vocality leads, as is typical of Conrad, to an opposing diminution of force. As the narrative builds to verbal effusion, Aïssa stutters to a verbal breakdown, illustrating the rhetoric of enervation, approaching momentarily what is known in medical parlance as aphasia or "hysterical mutism" (*DPM,* 636): "He is all! Everything. He is my breath, my light, my heart. . . . Go away . . . . Forget him. . . . He has no courage and no wisdom any more . . . and I have lost my power. . . . Go away and forget. There are other enemies. . . . Leave him to me. He had been a man once. . . . You are too great. Nobody can withstand you. . . . I tried. . . . I know now. . . ." (*OI,* 253). The language of enervation that completes the sequences of "vivid, *nervous* description" is speech that degenerates into hesitant ellipses and eventual silence, a language that mimics the movement toward the fragmented vocality and final aphasia of the general paralytic (*DPM,* 526–7).

Evidence in Conrad's early fiction of his interest in the medical symptomatology of hysteria and neurasthenia is transparent, if not entirely accurate in its medical particulars. In *An Outcast,* Almayer is depicted as having a minor hysterical or hystero-epileptic attack (*DPM,* 622, 630–1), which was, in Conrad's day, a symptom thought to distinguish hysteria from neurasthenia: "He fell back in the chair and his face became purple. A little white foam appeared on his lips and trickled down his chin, while he lay back, showing the whites of his eyes" (*OI,* 174). In a convulsive hysterical attack, respiration was thought to be suspended (*DPM,* 630), which is apparently why Almayer "gasped" when he regained consciousness. Similarly, the medical condition of Willems is conspicuous and strikingly similar to Conrad's own in 1891, when his symptoms and prescribed treatment suggest a probable diagnosis of malarial neurasthenia: "[Willems] felt very weak. He held up his arm before his eyes and watched for a little while the trembling of the lean limb. Skin and bone, by God! How thin he was! . . . He had suffered from fever a good deal, and now he thought with tearful dismay that Lingard, although he had sent him food ... had not sent him any medicine. ... [Willems concludes,] Did the old savage think that he was like the wild beasts that are never ill? He wanted quinine" (*OI,* 341). The description of Willems as a malarial neurasthenic is followed by passages that suggest the paralysis of the insane: "The approaching end of all things in the destruction of his own personality filled him with paralyzing awe. ... He remained motionless, huddled up on his seat: terrified and still" (342). His illness is real. When Aïssa approaches him, "she perceived suddenly a kind of a dried-up, yellow corpse, sitting very stiff on a bench in the shade" (343). Conrad invested himself in both the feminine principle, Aïssa, who fears solitude and silence, and in the masculine principle, Willems, who shares the bodily diseases from which Conrad suffered. And the various forms of nervous disease from which Conrad suffered or which he feared are reflected in his descriptive style and narrative technique. Conrad's fear that such disorders could progress to full-blown madness is revealed in "The Idiots."

The important psychoanalytical biographers of Conrad have all commented on the unusual circumstances of Conrad's courtship, marriage, and illness-plagued honeymoon in France, where he wrote "The Idiots."[39] All concur with Meyer's influential assumption that Conrad may have been "disturbed by the sexual aspects of marriage."[40] This psychoanalytical approach to Conrad's actions tends to mystify events that, when viewed through the lens of a pre-Freudian medical psychology, are not only easily explicable but also readily understandable and corroborated by the fiction Conrad was writing. Conrad's wife Jessie narrates the circumstances of Conrad's "strange proposal of marriage. He had begun by announcing the he had not very long to live and no intention of having children; but such as his life was (his shrug was very characteristic), he thought we might spend a few happy years together."[41] Meyer asserts that "there was not the least evidence" to support Conrad's claims.[42] But Conrad had a nervous father, both parents died of tuberculosis, epilepsy was suspected in his youth, and he was diagnosed with neurasthenia. Any of these inherited disorders, it was thought in Conrad's day, could lead to mental degeneration, lunacy, and general paralysis of the insane. Given the public discussion of the "progress of lunacy"—the rapid rise of the incidence of cases of insanity reported in England—it is not at all strange that Conrad felt unsure about how long he might live and that he might want to live abroad. And if Conrad was worried about his mental health, to which his letters vividly attest, it is little wonder he would propose to Jessie George and discourage any thought of children. If during 1895 Conrad had three women friends with whom he shared varying degrees of intimacy and with whom he might potentially marry—Marguerite Poradowska, Émilie Briquel, and Jessie George—Jessie George was the most suitable, given Conrad's temperament and medical situation. Though Conrad was more intimate and compatible with Marguerite Poradowska, that very compatibility made them an unwise match, for she was, like Conrad, prone to self-doubt, illness, depression, and nervous disorder. Émilie Briquel was a less interesting intellectual companion but still posed a potentially dangerous medical match, for during their acquaintance her mother was apparently prone to illness and was taking a Carlsbad cure (*CL*, 1:232–3). Jessie George was attractive to Conrad, and if she did not prove flawless in reading from his work, she was sensible, composed, and perhaps even a bit stolid—a suitable domestic antidote to Conrad's nervous irritability.[43] Edward Garnett observed that "Conrad's ultra nervous organization appeared to make matrimony extremely hazardous, but his instinct proved right, and Jessie Conrad's temperament was perfect; calming him and taking the daily trials and rubs of life off his shoulders."[44] Clearly, Conrad did not wish to pass on his nervousness or to accelerate the process of his own possible degeneration. Accordingly, he married a healthy typist, planned no children, and left England with its apparently rising number of lunatics. Unfortunately, in Brittany mental degeneration would haunt the newlyweds' honeymoon, like Corbet's "skeleton at the feast," in the form of the Lannion village idiots. Conrad's composition of "The Idiots" suggests that this fear of mental degeneration was quite real to him, for it is revealed near the story's end that Susan Bacadou—who bears four idiot children, murders her husband, and goes "unquestionably insane" (*TU*, 85) before she commits suicide—is herself the offspring of a father who had been "'deranged in his head' for a few years before he died" (74). It is for this reason that Conrad writes to Garnett from Île-Grande, fearing "the treachery of disease" (*CL*, 1:300) and complaining of his "long fits of depression, that in a lunatic asylum would be called madness" (*CL*, 1:284), those epistolary themes close to his "innermost being."

From his illness in the early 1890s to his nervous breakdown in January of 1910, Conrad suffered from a variety of nervous disorders—neurasthenia (probably diagnosed as malarial neurasthenia), simple nervous irritability, various neuralgias, nervous dyspepsia, and possible episodes of hysteria then called hysterotraumatic paralysis. In a medical era when such disorders were associated with femininity and madness, Conrad's nervous economy was a constant source of personal worry—involving gender identity, sexuality, creative temperament, and the threat of madness—but, at the same time, his nervousness was the wellspring of what were arguably his most productive and imaginative years. Conrad may thus be thought to amend or complicate the cultural construction of madness as feminine with a positive adumbration: linking femininity not simply with madness but with the genius of the nervous writer as well.

The challenge to Conrad's writing genius was to transform the blunt characterizations we see in *An Outcast*, the transparent themes in a story like "The Idiots," and the hysterically bad writing of his early fiction into the shimmering, nervous prose of his mature career. To accomplish this transformation and to narrate the history of his medical life, Conrad developed the metonymic tropes of restraint, seclusion, and water, all of which are important treatments or disciplines for nervous disorders and lunacy in Conrad's day. Each of the remaining chapters in part II will read Conrad medically and show how Conrad narrates his innermost fears of nervous disorder and madness. To do this, the chapters will follow a flexible pattern: I will introduce the trope through illustrative passages from the fiction, draw lines of convergence between Conrad's fiction and the medical and popular discourse on the trope, and demonstrate how the trope is itself nervous, oscillating between "contrary stresses." For example, Conrad will be shown to develop the trope of restraint through the competing themes of savagery and civilization, anarchy and duty, cannibalism and restraint. The trope of seclusion is developed through the opposing views of romantic and existential solitude, and the contrary phobias of agoraphobia and claustrophobia. Finally, the trope of water—the elemental force that is both destructive and restorative—is evident in competing experiences characterized by rest and unrest. Each of these tropes contributes to the rhetorical voice that narrates Conrad's mental history, that tells the story of his struggle to maintain his mental calm. The study of Conrad's fiction will conclude with a reading of several post-breakdown fictions as allegorical accounts of his reconciliation with nervous disease.

Chapter 5
Restraint

I . . . hav[e] an instinctive horror of losing my sense of full
self-possession.—Joseph Conrad, *A Personal Record*

W hile treatment of the insane improved during the nineteenth century, the debate surrounding the use of mechanical restraint was revived by century's end. Pinel's liberation of the
inmates of the Bicêtre asylum, Tuke's development of moral
treatment at the York Retreat, and Conolly's advocacy of an or-
dering "system of regularity" for the care and management of the
insane did not eliminate the need to mechanically restrain some
patients with mental disease.[1] As early as 1875, conservative and
querulous voices in the *Journal of Psychological Medicine and
Mental Pathology* criticized Conollyism as "do-nothingism"
based on a "humanitarian sentimentalism" that conflicted with
"professional duty."[2] In the years around the onset of Conrad's
adult medical problems, mainstream figures like Savage would
"accept as axiomatic that theoretically 'non-restraint' is desirable,
though in practice cases may possibly arise in which some mode
of restraint has to be followed."[3] And, with a certain familial reluctance, a descendant of the founder of the York Retreat, D.
Hack Tuke, admitted that "it has thus come to pass that the
whole question of mechanical restraint has been re-discussed in
these latter days, and there has been undoubtedly a certain reaction against the iron rule to which the superintendents of asylums had been subjected since the triumph of Conollyism"
(*DPM,* 1318). Thus, as Conrad began his career as a novelist and
took water cures to combat nervousness and mental depression,

asylum physicians openly discussed the uses, limitations, and benefits of mechanical restraint, even as they investigated "the breaking strain of the ribs of the insane."[4]

The early critics of Conollyism charged that advocating a "system of regularity" in place of "camisoles" (straitjackets or "side-dresses") amounted to little more than trading mechanical restraint for moral restraint: "the no-restraint of the English (surveillance and repression by the keepers, and constant isolation in cells) is only physical restraint in disguise."[5] Foucault elaborates on these ideas in his works on cultural surveillance and the social history of madness, noting that in the nineteenth century the cultural exercise of power over the criminal and the lunatic shifted from the use of physical oppression to the exercise of psychological power in the form of surveillance, which developed in the inmate a culturally constructed moral self-consciousness and guilt.[6] The surveillance of moral treatment was, in effect, "restraint in disguise." This internalized restraint, developed by the general populace to avoid imprisonment and by inmates to avoid further punishment such as mechanical restraint, requires the exercise of human will, a faculty that was recognized on both sides of the Atlantic as the moral mechanism that checks the progress of nervous disease. Consider, for instance, Dr. J. J. Putnam, an American, who viewed nervous breakdown "not so much a real failure of the nervous strength as a sort of abandonment of nervous control," a kind of moral failure of will: "The man who feels himself—as everyone should feel—under bonds of loyalty to his own standards, to the needs of the community, large or small, in which he lives, and to the cause in which he is engaged, should, to avoid the dangers of nervous breakdown, organize himself on more stable lines[:] . . . by a systematic development, under due precautions, of the powers of mental and of physical endurance, by a study of the means for making the body 'the ready servant of the will.'"[7] In England, Dr. Guthrie Rankin criticized the "vast multitude of neurasthenics and neurotics who are tottering on the brink of self-control," especially women "who allow themselves to become neurasthenic."[8] The sense that nervous breakdown resulted from a failure of will—that is, self-restraint—is implicit in Conrad's post-breakdown comment to William Rothenstein: "I am keeping a tight hand on myself for fear my nerves go to pieces" (*CL,* 4:332).

The medical discourse of Conrad's day that engaged the theory of the will sought to distinguish its medical conception from the nineteenth-century metaphysical or philosophical notions of human will, in particular, the exercise of "free will," which was a medical oxymoron. D. Hack Tuke, in his essay "Philosophy of Mind," which introduces his influential *A Dictionary of Psychological Medicine,* defined will as "the act of striving to procure a pleasure or to suppress a pain. It is well never to lose sight of this definition, for much of the perplexity of the present subject arises from widening the notion" (*DPM,* 41). Although Tuke's definition sought to avoid Victorian philosophical thought and seems to anticipate Freud's theory of the pleasure principle, his ideas are clearly an outgrowth of Victorian utilitarianism and enlightened self-interest, for an individual's strength of will and "prudential self-control allows the greatest sway to the idea of the individual's most durable interests, and moral self-control is action in conformity with the idea of the good of all" (42). But Tuke's insistence on the narrowness of his definition was also intended to link pleasure and pain, in their most basic forms, to the functions of the nervous and muscular systems. The medical argument defining the will in materialist terms is articulated most fully in Henry Maudsley's *Body and Will: Being an Essay Concerning Will in Its Metaphysical, Physiological, and Pathological Aspects* (1884). Maudsley begins his argument rejecting both the "bad theological fashion of despising the body" and the presumption that the cause of human will is really "the will of God, inciting or restraining." Maudsley insists on a physiological basis for will, proclaiming in an oddly Whitmanesque/anti-Whitmanesque fashion, "'Tis 'I,' compact of nerve, muscle, gland, bone, who choose to resolve to do or not to do on each occasion, not any part of detached principle or sublimed essence."[9]

Though the body and will are self-contained in his view, Maudsley, like Tuke, recognizes the interdependence of human will and social organization, an interaction that creates the logocentrism of a culture: common language, law, reason, and understanding. "It is the common mind of the race in me," Maudsley writes, "which belongs to me as one of my kind—the common sense of mankind, if you will. Because the *kind* is in me and I am a living element of it, I cannot help consciously or unconsciously appealing to and silently acknowledging its rules and sanctions." Maudsley's theory of the individual and society offers a cultural relativism that at first glance seems rather progressive. He argues that "there is no rule to distinguish between true and false but the common judgment of mankind, no rule to distinguish between virtue and vice but the common feeling of mankind. Wherefore the truth of one age is the fable of the next, the virtue of one epoch or nation the vice of another epoch or nation." But he concludes monolithically that "the individual whose judgment is deranged has his private truth-standard that is utterly false."[10] While Maudsley does not deny the "categorical moral imperative," he recognizes the process by which social custom is naturalized, even if his hierarchical conclusions seem to belie that recognition: "It is because mankind has felt dimly and vaguely the inward imperative, because it has been un-awares under that constraint, and because it has *not* been free to go its own way, that it has made the progress which it has made from its lower to its higher stages of being. The implicate of the moral imperative is not liberty but constraint."[11] Civilization and constraint/restraint are indivisible except for the "deranged" or diseased individual whose will has degenerated in association with mental or moral alienation; with nervous diseases such as hysteria, hystero-epilepsy, epilepsy; or with general paralysis of the insane.[12]

The derangement or degeneration of the will—whether inherited, the product of disease, or the result of injury or trauma—could express itself in one of two ways, in either lack of impulse or in lack of inhibition. Aboulia, the want of impulse or will, was recognized in England and especially in France as a dysfunction of the will common in neurasthenics.[13] In particular, agoraphobia, with its resulting fear of leaving a protected interior space, was thought to be the expression of aboulia. The German physician, Cordes, who suffered from aboulic agoraphobia, studied the condition in himself and concluded that its basic cause was "a paresic exhaustion of the motor nervous system of that part of the brain which presides not only over locomotion, but also over the muscular sense" (*DPM*, 1367). Conversely, the hysteric was thought to be afflicted with a want of restraint and inhibition: "[T]heir prodigious instability, their caprices, which incessantly appear, keep them in a permanent condition of disequilibration and of moral ataxy" (*DPM*, 1368).

In Conrad's fiction, the theme of restraint is firmly rooted in medical issues that are both intimately personal and the subject of broader medical and social discourse. The most obvious illustration of this connection between the personal and public levels of Conrad's fiction occurs in the early texts, when Conrad had recently survived his Congo travels; when he was most actively seeking medical attention for his medical disorders; and when he was struck, with intimate force, by the difficulty of male/female relations.[14] I am wary of using "The Return" as a paradigmatic example, due to Conrad's ambivalence toward the story and due to the understandable critical condemnation it has received. But the issues of male restraint and feminine hysteria are developed with such large brush strokes that it provides a pellucid example with which to begin, and, as Paul Wiley long ago observed, in "content and technique . . . it holds an important place in [Conrad's] development."[15] Since "The Return" is a seldom-read text, I will highlight important aspects of the story's conflict.

The epitome of healthy bourgeois respectability, Alvan Hervey is "stunned" (*TU,* 125) when he reads his wife's letter announcing she has left him, and, before his imagination has fully grasped his predicament, he is "amazed" (139) by her abrupt return. The painful exchange that follows, much like the conversation of cross-purposes between the Verlocs but without any undercurrent of humor, focuses on representative and unbridgeable differences between the sexes.[16] Mr. Hervey reveals his gender biases, exclaiming incredulously at his wife's choice of "an effeminate, fat ass" for a would-be lover, and Mrs. Hervey initially submits to the suffering she must endure from a husband more offended than injured. Her offense is to the body of social, "moral propriety" (121) held in shape by self-restraint: "Do you care for no one's opinion—is there no restraining influence in the world for you—woman?" (148). Universalized into "woman," her lack of restraint will be medically diagnosed by her husband, and one suspects that Mrs. Hervey, residing near the "circle train . . . West-End" (118) station, represents the Harley Street reduction of the female sex:

> "Is this letter the worst of it?"
> She had a nervous movement of her hands.
> "I must have a plain answer," he said, hotly.
> "Then, no! The worst is my coming back." . . .
> He said authoritatively—
> "You don't know what you are saying. Your mind is unhinged. You are beside yourself, or you would not say such things. You can't control yourself. Even in your remorse . . ." He paused a moment, then said with a *doctoral* air: "Self-restraint is everything in life, you know. It's happiness, it's dignity . . . it's everything." (155, emphasis added)

The description of Hervey's "doctoral air" suggests how closely Conrad was attuned to the moral tone of medico-psychological discourse. Compare, for instance, Dr. Charles Mercier's discussion of restraint in Sir Clifford Allbutt's *A System of Medicine*. Writing for the volume on mental disease, Mercier warned, "self restraint is a quality so valuable, so essential to the constitution and integrity of a community, that any conspicuous exhibition of self-indulgence is abhorrent to the witness of it, quite apart from any consideration of resulting ill-effects."[17] The social consequences of such lost restraint would be devastating to Hervey: "'You see where the want of self-restraint leads to. Pain—humiliation—loss of respect—of friends, of everything that ennobles life, that . . . All kinds of *horrors*,' he concluded, abruptly" (*TU,* 155, emphasis added). In the context of *Tales of Unrest,* "The Return" is an inverted "Outpost of Progress"—a kind of "Suburb of the Quotidian"—whose irony is less comic than its companion story. But in the larger context of Conrad's career, it is also a companion piece to *Heart of Darkness,* focusing on themes of the brutal metropolis of empire, the loss of civilized restraint, and the ascendancy of horror and madness.[18]

Of course, Mr. Hervey's "dull severity" lacks the eloquence of Kurtz or the probing inconclusiveness of Marlow. When he overextends his lecture on "restraint, duty, fidelity" and "adherence to what is right," Mrs. Hervey interrupts, simply but provocatively, asking, "What is right?" He responds with another medical accusation: "'Your mind is diseased!' he cried, upright and austere" (*TU,* 156–57). But this restrained male superiority thinly disguises his own nervous degeneration: "He foamed at the mouth while she stared at him, appalled by this sudden fury" (163). Their dialogue, pulsating with extremes of hysteria and enervation, ends with Mrs. Hervey's sobbing laughter, a "shrill peal followed by a deep sob and succeeded by another shriek of mirth" (166). Concerned that the neighbors might hear, Hervey disappears and returns—socially predictable in word and deed—

> striding at her, and with a tumbler of water in his hand. He stammered: "Hysterics—Stop—They will hear—Drink this." She laughed at the ceiling. "Stop this!" he cried. "Ah!"
>
> He flung the water in her face, putting into the action all the secret brutality of his spite, yet still felt that it would have been perfectly excusable—in any one—to send the tumbler after the water. He restrained himself, but at the same time was ... convinced nothing could stop the horror of those mad shrieks. ... Her face was streaming with water and tears; there was a wisp of hair on her forehead, another stuck to her cheek; her hat was on one side, undecorously tilted; her soaked veil resembled a sordid rag festooning her forehead. (167)

The story's complexity and significance lie not in its narrative art but in the tension between the ironic presentation of English male restraint and the genuine pain of lost self-possession and the ascendancy of madness. On the one hand, Hervey is the contemptible "man of purpose" Conrad describes in *An Outcast of the Islands* (*OI,* 197), the man who, convinced of his own superiority, never looks deeply into things on his way to the grave; as such, Hervey's unthinking advocacy of restraint represents the willful "denial of feeling in upper middle-class life," a system of manners Conrad called "the gospel of the beastly bourgeois" (*CL,* 1:393).[19] On the other hand, Hervey is one of a series of Conrad's male protagonists struggling with women who verge on madness. But while "The Return" engages this pattern of Conrad's mature career and a number of related motifs, the story (as literature) lacks the complexity of other explorations of the entangling of male restraint and feminine emotions. In Conrad's later dialogic fiction, either sex can attain to either gender trait, for the theme of restraint comprehends but extends beyond the monolithic gender roles of the English character to encompass a wider constellation of related ideas pertaining to civilization, restraint, and madness.

Civilization, Restraint, and Madness

Since Chinua Achebe's attack on Conrad in the late 1970s, the body of criticism on Conrad's fiction has grown and diversified and has reflected the comprehensive range of approaches to modernist literary study, as wide a range as any author-centered body of criticism (one perhaps thinks of Joyce studies here). Many of those significant studies have variously meditated upon Conrad's complex treatment of "civilization."[20] The present study also requires a discussion of Conrad's idea of civilization, though not in a comprehensive manner that offers a philosophic inquiry on civilization or in an obviously useful way that can improve the world. Rather, I wish to focus somewhat narrowly—and, to the extent possible, without engaging ideological argument—on the connection Conrad makes between the restraints of civilization and the threat of madness. I wish to avoid engaging such ideologies not from a desire to avoid polemical discussion but to show that the issues critics have debated in the last twenty-five years are deeply rooted in Conrad's personal preoccupation with the theme of restraint as response to the threatened loss of sanity. We can witness the interplay between civilized restraint and the threat of insanity in such tropes as savagery, anarchism, and failure of duty.

The Trope of Savagery

Conrad's early fictions are generally about sane men who leave their civilizations to help expand empire and who encounter "Other" civilizations that are unfamiliar, incomprehensible, and inscrutable. And frequently, these male characters lose their will, abandon restraint, and endanger their sanity when they leave the familiar, the comprehensible, behind and encounter the unknown —what Conrad often calls "savagery."[21] At first glance, savagery seems a fairly monolithic or univalent concept associated in the earliest fiction with dark-skinned people, especially women. But even in these early works, simple gendered representations of civilization and savagery are complicated and subverted.[22] Robert Hampson and Andrew Michael Roberts have each recently argued that Conrad's early Malay fiction initially engages the reader with received ideas that reinforce the civilization/savagery hierarchy but quickly moves to destabilize essentialized, binary relations between European/Asian or male/female. Hampson shows how Conrad's "covert plots" and Roberts shows how "irony and ambiguous narrative technique" both function like a Conradian reader trap to engage the expectations of the reader only to complicate, destabilize, and make problematic essentialized ideas about race, gender, and civilization.[23] In *Almayer's Folly,* for instance, savagery is the "natural" state of Lingard's captured and then adopted daughter who, to counteract her natural state, is educated by the nuns of the Samarang Convent: "She bore it all; the restraint and the teaching and the new faith, with calm submission, concealing her hate and contempt for all that new life" (*AF,* 19). At Lingard's "abrupt demand," (18) Almayer marries her and they have a child, Nina, but his wife "soon commenced to treat him with a savage contempt expressed by sulky silence only occasionally varied by a flood of savage invective." Mrs. Almayer, a product of her bicultural experience, is nervous like a European (evident in the extremes of silent enervation and hysterical invective) and "savage" like a Malay. Jealous of the closeness of father and daughter, Mrs. Almayer rebels, "burning the furniture and tearing down the

pretty curtains in her unreasoning hate of those signs of civilization," and Almayer is "cowed by these outbursts of savage nature" (21). The simplicity of Conrad's formulas of racism and
civilization, which would have had immediate recognition by
and appeal to his readership, is borne out in Nina's divided allegiance between white and Malay blood. After Almayer sends her
away from Sambir to be "civilized" by Mrs. Vinck, Nina returns to
her family, to her "savage mother," to "a life devoid of all the
decencies of civilization." But through Nina Almayer, Conrad
quickly undermines such unexamined premises of the differences in "civilized" versus "savage" cultures. Nina's intimacy
with both cultures renders her incapable of falsely discriminating
between the very similar human natures and activities evident in
the two cultures:

> It seemed to Nina that there was no change and no difference.
> Whether they traded in brick godowns or on the muddy river
> bank; whether they reached after much or little; whether they
> made love under the shadows of the great trees or in the shadow
> of the Cathedral on the Singapore promenade; whether they
> plotted for their own ends under the protection of laws and ac-
> cording to the rules of Christian conduct, or whether they sought
> the gratification of their desires with the savage cunning and the
> unrestrained fierceness of natures as innocent of culture as their
> own immense and gloomy forests, Nina saw only the same mani-
> festations of love, and hate, and of sordid greed chasing the un-
> certain dollar in all its multifarious and vanishing shapes. To her
> resolute nature, however, after all these years, the savage and un-
> compromising sincerity of purpose shown by her Malay kinsmen
> seemed at last preferable. (34–5)

Otherness here dissolves into sameness, and Nina casually re-
verts to native preferences that now compete on an equal basis
with more newly constructed European values.[24] Recognizing
she is the product of a marriage arranged for the convenience of
Almayer's career, Nina consequently, and "naturally," falls in
love with Dain, "a man totally untrammelled by any influence of
civilized self-discipline" (50), with whom she will depart from
her father.

The "farewell" exchanged between Almayer and Nina becomes for Almayer a sentence of mental alienation that will finally lead to dementia. The issues of civilization and savagery
are thus closely allied to mental disease: "Leaping up madly in
the sudden fear of his dream" that borders on incestuous desire,
Almayer shouts, "'I will never forgive you Nina!'" to which she

responds devastatingly, "and you will never forget me" (144–5). Almayer's decline is marked by symptoms of general paralysis of the insane—anticipated and confirmed by his hystero-epileptic fit in *An Outcast of the Islands*—as he ironically abandons the final restraints of civilization in the obsessive adoration of his half-Malay daughter. Near his end, Almayer is discovered by his fellow trader, Ford, in the attitude of an unchained lunatic, "sitting on the floor of the verandah, his back against the wall, his legs stretched stiffly out, his arms hanging by his side. His expressionless face, his eyes open wide with immobile pupils, and the rigidity of his pose, made him look like an immense man-doll broken and flung there out of the way" (152–3).[25] Almayer's final loss of restraint, descent into madness, and death occur when he burns the house built for Nina, dubbed "Almayer's Folly" by his Dutch compatriots (the word *folie* in French means madness). In its place he inhabits the "House of Heavenly Delight" (154), Jim-Eng's opium house, where he can forget his daughter with an overdose of what was euphemistically known in the medical community as "chemical restraint."[26]

The connection between loss of civilized restraint, feminine savagery, and insanity is again evident in *An Outcast of the Islands,* which complicates this matrix of issues with the added Conradian theme of cannibalism. Conrad's treatment of Aïssa, whose parents are Arab and Malay, is based more on the dictates of romance conventions than on contemporary conventionalized standards of beauty in the sexualized Other. Those standards typically placed the African "Hottentot" at the lowest extreme and the European white woman at the highest level of beauty.[27] For his purposes, Conrad minimizes the sexuality of the "primitive" female but in no way diminishes her beauty. Like the magnificent savage woman of *Heart of Darkness,* Aïssa is quite literally arresting in her physical beauty: "Willems also stood still for a minute. ... He took in every detail of the tall and graceful figure. ... She stood straight, slim, expectant. ... yellow rays descended upon her head, streamed in glints down her black tresses, shone with the changing glow of liquid metal on her face, and lost itself in vanishing sparks in the sombre depths of her eyes that, wide open now, with enlarged pupils, looked steadily at the man in her path. And Willems stared at her, charmed with a charm that carries with it a sense of irreparable loss" (*OI,* 68–9). The nervous description of light and dark, charm and loss, is the Conradian evocation of Yeatsian "beauty like a tightened bow," beauty that (inverting power relationships) arrests the gazer, fascinates, and threatens to destroy. And, as in *Heart of Darkness,* the woman of color is associated with the destructive allure of the wilderness and the nervous abandonment of restraint:

> He had been baffled, repelled, almost frightened by the intensity of that tropical life which wants the sunshine but works in gloom; which seems to be all grace of colour and form, all brilliance, all smiles, but is only the blossoming of the dead; whose mystery holds the promise of joy and beauty, yet contains nothing but poison and decay. He had been frightened by the vague perception of danger before, but now, as he looked at that life again, his eyes seemed able to pierce the fantastic veil of creepers and leaves, to look past the solid trunks, to see through the forbidding gloom—and the mystery was disclosed—enchanting, subduing, beautiful. He looked at the woman. Through the checkered light between them she appeared to him with the impalpable distinctness of a dream. The very spirit of that land of mysterious forests, standing before him like an apparition behind a transparent veil—a veil woven of sunbeams and shadows. (70)

Willems resolves never to return to the place where he met Aïssa, but of course he does with the "giving way of his will" (78). Otherwise retaining a sense of blamelessness and self-worth, he feels, with each tryst, "disappointed with himself. He seemed to be surrendering to a wild creature the unstained purity of his life, of his race, of his civilization" (80). Aïssa thus becomes the scapegoat and objectification of his moral corruption that accompanies the betrayal of European "civilization."[28] In his final stages of mental decline, Willems laments her taking over his civilized being: "I did not know there was something in me she could get hold of. She, a savage. I, a civilized European, and clever! She that knew no more than a wild animal! Well, she found out that something in me. She found it out, and I was lost" (269).

Similarly, in *Heart of Darkness,* the woman/wilderness "getting hold of something" in the man who is then "lost" to civilization represents the feminine act of cannibalism and the failure of masculine restraint to maintain itself. Kurtz has been incorporated by the wilderness, which "had taken him, loved him, embraced him, got into his veins, consumed his flesh" (*HD,* 115); in this state of degeneration, he "lacked restraint in the gratification of his various lusts" (131) and commits "unspeakable rites," which commentators have often assumed implies cannibalism.[29] By implication, Kurtz performs the rite that initiates his atavism. He becomes feminine and savage. But if Marlow is horrified by

Kurtz's loss of civilized restraints, he is likewise mystified by the male cannibals aboard the steamer, who despite their extreme hunger and superior numbers have restrained themselves from dispatching and consuming the white crew, an act that would (with a certain simplicity of presumption) be both natural and satisfying to them. Marlow recognizes "something restraining, one of those human secrets that baffle probability, had come into play there. . . . Restraint! What possible restraint? Was it superstition, disgust, patience, fear—or some kind of primitive honor?" (104–5). Marlow's fascination with the nightmare of Kurtz losing restraint and his wonderment at the restraint of the famished cannibals is in fact a spectrum of response reflected in contemporary periodical literature on cannibalism. At the time Conrad traveled to the Congo, *Blackwood's* published an article on cannibalism that begins by alluding to "A Modest Proposal" and observing that Swift's irony depends upon an audience "who regarded cannibalism with such horror and loathing as do the European nations. The horror must of course be instinctive, because we find it existing in the lowest grades of society; but the instinct is confined to civilized man. The word cannibal is associated in our minds with scenes of the most debased savagery that the imagination can picture." As *Heart of Darkness* was being serialized in *Blackwood's,* a much less visceral article appeared in *Current Literature,* which portrays "Congo cannibalism" from the African point of view as anything but an "unspeakable rite"; rather, it is "an ancient and, to them, perfectly natural rite." The latter essay, from 1900, is more anthropological, and like an 1897 article published in the *Contemporary Review* with the catchy title "Eaten with Honour," it articulates a view of "cultural cannibalism" as opposed to "survival cannibalism": "It is sheer mental prejudice against strangeness, which puts even the innocent and affectionate cannibal below the moral offender. . . . Institution varies from land to land and age to age . . . [and] each people are only responsible for acting up to the code of their own time."[30] Marlow's issues are thus consonant with English opinion, which would read both Kurtz's and the cannibals' actions in relative terms. Kurtz's moral insanity and the horror of his actions derive from his failure to act in accordance with European codes of civilized masculinity.

Instances of literal cannibalism are likewise at the heart of "Falk: A Reminiscence," which explores the relation of "civilization," savagery, and restraint. For the less resilient members of the crew, European associations between cannibalism and madness portend. The Marlovian narrator of "Falk" anticipates the outcome of Falk's history, since his crew members are ill, weak, and (like Kurtz and Marlow) "ready to catch any tropical disease going. Horror, ruin and everlasting remorse. ... I had fallen amongst a lot of unfriendly lunatics!" (*T*, 189). Falk's steamship, the *Borgmester Dahl,* experiences a mechanical break-down and the crew runs low on rations; the "bonds of discipline" and the "organized life of the ship" (228, 231) likewise break down and degenerate into "madness, suffering and despair" (232), culminating in cannibalism. Falk—unambiguously masculine, mentally sane, conventionally heroic, and not nearly as interesting as Kurtz—survives it all. Falk's restraint underpins the firmness of mind he engages as he overcomes his culturally conditioned horror of cannibalism and consumes his remaining crew members. Falk's stoicism, his singular duty to the instinct of self-preservation and preservation of order on ship, ensure his survival, but not without the loss of delicacy and sensitivity of imagination. (One cannot imagine Marlow, for instance, ever resorting to cannibalism or even being so remiss as to refrain from commenting on such abominable acts.) Indeed, here the European's cannibalism is synonymous with a simplistic firmness of mind reminiscent of MacWhirr, and Falk (who admittedly will become a vegetarian) restrains his cultural restraints in order to survive. Variations on the literal theme of cannibalism are developed more figuratively in later fiction, most notably in *The Nigger of the "Narcissus"* and *The Secret Agent.*

In *The Nigger of the "Narcissus,"* the consumption of human tissue occurs quite literally as infectious disease in the form of Jimmy Wait's pulmonary consumption, tuberculosis, which in oblique fashion is related to the cluster of themes under discussion. It is a critical commonplace that the *Narcissus* represents a microcosm of society and that Jimmy—a black "savage" amidst the white crew—represents at first reckoning a threat to the civilized order of the ship. But Conrad quickly complicates the obvious allegory. The paragraph introducing Jimmy begins by describing him as "calm, cool, towering, superb" and ends with the evocation of "a face pathetic and brutal: the tragic, the mysterious, the repulsive mask of a nigger's soul" (*NN*, 18). And during the course of the *Narcissus's* home voyage, this "savage"—clearly evoked by the image of the Africanist "repulsive mask"—paradoxically becomes an insidiously humanizing influence among the European crew, fostering their degeneration through the subversion of masculine restraint. While at first the crew suspects Wait of shamming his illness and shirking his duty, they later recognize his physical disease when "his cheekbones rose, ... the face was all hollows, ... a disinterred black skull, fitted with two restless globes of silver in the sockets of eyes. He was demoralizing."[31] The crew refrains from mentioning his illness because they were "becoming highly humanised, tender, complex, excessively decadent ... as though [they] had been over-civilised, and rotten" (139). The restraint shown here, to placate Wait's fear and perpetuate the illusion that he is not about to die, is a false restraint because it is based on a feminine delicacy of feeling. The "over-civilised" crew is typified, in exaggerated form, by Belfast, who is the least able to admit the truth about Jimmy and, by morbid fascination, is drawn to the very thing he fears most. As a compensatory behavior, his restraint in the presence of Jimmy is counterbalanced by lack of restraint with the crew. He thus in fact represents the disintegration of order aboard ship that occurs with the degeneracy of masculine restraint: "It was at that time that Belfast's devotion—and also his pugnacity—secured universal respect. He spent every moment of his spare time in Jimmy's cabin. He tended him, talked to him; was as gentle as a woman, as tenderly gay as an old philanthropist, as sentimentally careful of his nigger as a model slave-owner. But outside he was irritable, explosive as gunpowder, sombre, suspicious, and never more brutal than when most sorrowful" (140). The feminizing of the crew, the inversions of masculine restraint into demonstrations of feminine expressivity, and the threatened disintegration of collective mental health come to a crisis at the macabre burial service for Wait, who, even in death, clings to the life of the ship and the plank inclined to effect his departure:

> "He won't go," stammered one of the men, shakily. ... Mr. Baker waited, burying his face in the book, and shuffling his feet nervously. All the men looked profoundly disturbed. ... "Jimmy!" cried Belfast in a wailing tone, and there was a second of shuddering dismay.
> "Jimmy, be a man!" he shrieked, passionately. Every mouth was wide open, not an eyelid winked. He stared wildly, twitching all over; he bent his body forward like a man peering at an horror. "Go!" he shouted. ... His fingers touched the head of the body, and the grey package started reluctantly to whizz off the lifted planks all at once, with the suddenness of a flash of lightning. The crowd stepped forward like one man; a deep Ah—h—h! came out vibrating from the broad chests. ... Belfast, supported by Archie, gasped hysterically. (160)

Jimmy's burial at sea reestablishes the crew's collective masculinity, as they step forward "like one man" to witness the disappearance of the body and acknowledge the death with a collective and deep male vocalization. Only Belfast—whom Jimmy calls a "little Irish lunatic" (38)—retains his nervous, feminized self, shrieking and gasping hysterically during the ceremony.

The emotional proximity of these themes to Conrad's mental state is suggested by the fact that he began *The Nigger of the "Narcissus"* immediately after completing "The Idiots," the story that revealed the "fragments of [his] innermost being," and while he was thinking, as he wrote to Garnett, about "the treachery of disease" (*CL,* 1:293, 300). After all, James Wait dies of tuberculosis, the disease that claimed the lives of Apollo and Ewa Korzeniowski, that was thought to be hereditary, that in certain forms was thought to begin with an onset of dyspeptic and anemic symptoms, and that sometimes culminated in "Phthisical Insanity," the symptoms of which James Wait exhibits (*DPM,* 943).[32] Notwithstanding the differences in race, Jimmy Wait represents Joseph Conrad's self-consuming tandem fears of insanity and death that troubled him in his early married life, a time when he apparently believed he had but a few years to live.

The Trope of Anarchism

If Conrad explores a range of ideas on civilization and savagery through the competing exercise of restraint and cannibalism in his Eastern and African fictions, he explores a like range of ideas on civilization and revolutionary anarchism in his European political fictions, where restraint and figurative cannibalism define characters and serve as an index to their mental states. This use of the restraint and figurative cannibalism theme is especially evident in *The Secret Agent,* in which many of the so-called revolutionists and anarchists exist in the borderland of insanity; they challenge the customary restraints of civilization, evince some degree of physical degeneration and mental disorder, and practice some kind of social cannibalism.

The chapter that introduces Verloc's colleagues begins with the words of Michaelis, who has violated the restraints of civilization by his "complicity in a rather mad attempt to free some prisoners from a police van" (*SA,* 84), a caper that ended in the death of a police escort, a family man and enforcer of society's restraint who thus represents the "bedrock" of civilization.[33] During his fifteen years of confinement, Michaelis (by the admission of his own revolutionist colleagues) loses the power of consecutive thought (63) and (by "indictment" of the Assistant Commissioner) becomes a "humanitarian sentimentalist, a little mad" (87). His eyes are "a little crazy in [their] fixity" (39), and when he orates, he talks to himself. A member of his audience, Yundt exhibits a "worn out passion, resembling in its impotent fierceness the excitement of a senile sensualist" (38) and an incipient dementia revealed by his tendency, when ambulatory, to "stop as if to think, and ... not offer to move again till impelled forward" (44). Yundt's barely intelligible revolutionary vision calls for "a band of men absolute in their resolve to discard all scruples in the choice of means, strong enough to give themselves frankly the name of destroyers, and free from the taint of that resigned pessimism which rots the world" (38). Though he advocates the subversion of civilized restraints as a means to revolution, he had never in his life "raised personally as much as his little finger against the social edifice" (42). The last revolutionist, Ossipon, seems sane at the beginning of the tale and restrained by virtue of self-interest, but Conrad suggests predispositions of mind that point to Ossipon's decline toward insanity at the novel's end. "Free from the trammels of conventional morality" (222), Ossipon is nonetheless prone to mental fixation and susceptible to demagoguery. A failed medical student, he is a devotee of Lombroso, whose anthropological reductionism appeals to and supports an array of bigotries. Ossipon "scientifically" classifies Stevie (the moral center of the novel) a classic degenerate type, yet Ossipon is not objective enough to recognize that his "Negro-type" features and "almond-shaped eyes" (39) would likewise categorize him as a criminal degenerate in the scheme of Lombroso and his phrenological followers.[34] In an ironic reversal, Lombroso seems in force here, for Ossipon is morally insane early in the novel and is "scientifically afraid of insanity" as the novel concludes.

Thus, despite Conrad's misgivings about Lombroso, he uses physical descriptions and the health of the revolutionists as an index to their mental state, but this is not surprising given the conventions of the novel and given Conrad's first-hand knowledge of the close relationship between somatic and psychological ills. In fact, leading medical psychologists who would have been highly skeptical of Lombroso's phrenological theories were themselves comfortable with the assumption that certain mental disorders were reflected in bodily attitude and facial expression (see Fig. 10). And this sort of medical assumption is consistent

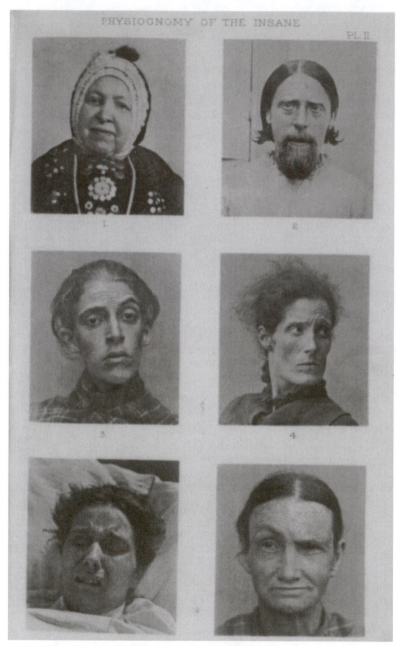

Fig.10. Physiognomy of the insane, D. Hack Tuke's *A Dictionary of Psychological Medicine*, 948. (Memorial Library, University of Wisconsin, Madison. Photo by Dan Schlies and Mark Summers)

with Conrad's emphasis on the physical degeneration of the anarchists. Michaelis, after his fifteen-year incarceration on a diet of fatty foods, emerges "like a tub, with an enormous stomach and distended cheeks of pale semi-transparent complexion" (37). For his health problems, he is sent by his patroness, three seasons running, to Marienbad for a cure but was excluded from the "healing waters" by police when his presence competed with the celebrity of a royal patron. Yundt is toothless, bald, with "extinguished eyes. . . . [and] a skinny groping hand deformed by gouty swellings" (38). The physical descriptions and mental degeneration of Michaelis, Yundt, and Ossipon likewise reflect their cannibalistic (if decidedly unvoracious) sexuality and inverted gender roles. Michaelis, who exists as a social eunuch for a group of progressive socialites, is sponsored by a wealthy patroness, and thus, despite his condemnation of the rich, he feeds off the very class he condemns. Yundt's sensuality is "senile" and the emblem of his sexuality, his goatee, hangs "limply from [the] chin" of his toothless jaw (38). The old terrorist, like Michaelis, is protected by women, but in Yundt's case, he is "nursed by a blear eyed old woman, a woman he had years ago enticed away from a friend, and afterwards had tried more than once to shake off into the gutter" (45). Ossipon likewise is a man who lives at the expense of his women friends and takes the advice of the Professor when he suggests that Ossipon "fasten [him]self upon [Winnie] for all she's worth" (64). All of the revolutionists in this way are sexually/economically "cannibalistic," the very quality Yundt has ironically criticized English society for exhibiting (44).

No character in *The Secret Agent* acts upon his private principles with so much austerity and so little conventional restraint as the Professor, who summarizes with supreme self-confidence his ideas on civilization and restraint when he compares himself to the police: "Their character is built upon conventional morality. It leans on the social order. Mine stands free from everything artificial. They are bound in all sorts of conventions. They depend on life, which, in this connection, is a historical fact surrounded by all sorts of restraints and considerations, a complex organised fact open to attack at every point; whereas I depend on death, which knows no restraint and cannot be attacked" (57). Though the Professor portrays himself as superior, stronger than life itself, and able to conduct his business without the aid of civilized restraints—he is literally a "wired" individual absolutely constrained by his private codes of conduct. Physically weak, with a skull "which looked frail enough for Ossipon to crush between thumb and forefinger," he is a "dingy little man in spectacles"; the Professor has the physical being of a chronically malnourished, undersexed neurasthenic, his "flat cheeks, of a greasy, unhealthy complexion, were merely smudged by the miserable poverty of a thin dark whisker" (52). But his mental degeneration has progressed beyond the constitutional weakness associated with neurasthenia. The Professor's clear intellect but social alienation clearly point to moral insanity. He is, in Chief Inspector Heat's words, a "Lunatic" (78).

The theme of political anarchism in *The Secret Agent* has, as its correlative, the theme of domestic anarchism; for, as the Assistant Commissioner observes to the Home Secretary, we are "in the presence of a domestic drama" (168). And, like the theme of political anarchy, domestic anarchy—the degeneration of the home—is connected to madness. As the simple tale begins, each member of the Verloc family performs certain ritualized, restraining roles that maintain the household as an operating social unit but one poised on the brink of dysfunction. Verloc, "a seller of shady wares, exercised his vocation of a protector of society, and cultivated his domestic virtues" (11) that are based on "a philosophical unbelief in the effectiveness of every human effort" (16); thus he treats his wife as his "chief possession" (137) and his brother-in-law like a "household dog" (142). Winnie attends to the shop "with an air of unfathomable indifference" (10), maintains a "quasi-maternal affection" and a "material vigilance" for her brother Stevie, offers the "usual remedies" (48) for Mr. Verloc's giddiness, and generally "does not look too deeply into things." "Easily excitable" (156) by his nature, Stevie mopes at the foot of the clock (142) or, "very good and quiet" at the deal table, draws innumerable concentric circles "rendering cosmic chaos, the symbolism of a mad art attempting the inconceivable" (40). The Verloc family, like a "perfect detonator," is a tightly restrained and delicate domestic mechanism that is easily disturbed by Mr. Vladimir's insistence that Verloc earn his pay as an agent provocateur. The act of terrorism Vladimir requires must be "purely destructive" (30) and apparently mad, for in Vladimir's view "madness alone is truly terrifying" to civilization. Asserting he is a "civilised man" (31), Vladimir orders an anarchist outrage against the "learning" of civilization symbolized by the Greenwich Observatory. Verloc is thus a double agent against civilization. To protect members of civilized English society depicted taking the morning air on Rotten Row, Verloc stages a purely destructive act of madness when he lazily slaughters his innocent brother-in-law at the behest of a civilized diplomat of a foreign power. The Assistant Commissioner speaks the truth when he suggests to Sir Ethelred that a double agent's "occupation is free from all restraint" (109).

When Verloc returns to Brett Street, "shaken morally to pieces" (174) by the events of the day, we take the irony of understatement as the primacy of meaning, for Stevie has suffered a far worse literal and physical fate. But without diminishing that primary meaning, the phrase also suggests that Verloc's moral being has fully disintegrated. His loathing of "unhygienic labor" and his simple, amoral expedient of getting Stevie to do his work—knowing that "as errand boy [Stevie] did not turn out a great success" (13)—indicates not only that "the mind of Mr Verloc lacked profundity" (177) but also that he is, in Victorian terms, morally insane. Verloc's "affective insanity" (another name for "moral insanity") is registered in the domestic virtues he displays in chapter 11, the brilliant depiction of domestic degeneration Conrad extensively revised during the bleak days of 1907 at Montpellier and Champel, when the Conrad family all but disintegrated due to disease and ill health.

Of all the members of the Verloc household, Stevie most obviously departs from normal human intellectual capacity. The narrator specifically notes that while Stevie is not "mad," he is "not wise enough to restrain his passions" (129–30) and thus might be judged borderline insane by English society; but if he thinks and speaks with difficulty—with a rhetoric of enervation—he feels, at times hysterically so, with "great[] completeness and some profundity" (131–2). Stevie's overflow of passion is in direct contrast to Verloc's affective insanity. Verloc's poverty of feeling is evident in his contemplation of a scenario in which Stevie, like his real mother, might be institutionalized. Speaking to the Chief Inspector, Verloc both defends and condemns himself: "The lad was half-witted, irresponsible. Any court would have seen that at once. Only fit for the asylum. And that was the worst that would've happened to him if—" (160). Verloc here seems familiar with the prevailing judicial practices, specifically with the Lunacy Act of 1890, passed four years before the fictional action of the novel, which forbids the commitment of an individual to an asylum except by judicial authority.[35] Ironically, by this stage of the drama, *all* the surviving Verlocs are clinically "disturbed": Verloc himself by virtue of his moral insanity, where the intellect remains clear but the moral being is corrupt, and Winnie by her sympathetic degeneration into a controlled, but insanely murderous, fury.

The Verlocs' familial degeneration accelerates with the departure of the family matriarch, who demonstrates a "sudden mania for locomotion" (118). In the "Cab of Death" chapter, Winnie grows increasingly nervous. Stevie enjoins Winnie not to worry about flagging down a bus back to Soho after depositing the mother in her new, institutional home. "Don't be nervous, Winnie. Mustn't be nervous! 'Bus all right" (131). Winnie is also noted as growing nervous due to Mr. Verloc's taciturnity (136) and Stevie's moping about the house when he is not out walking (in fact, rehearsing) with Verloc (141). Such references to nervousness increase as the novel moves toward a conclusion and spread contagiously to Verloc and finally to his replacement, Ossipon.[36] Winnie's increasing nervousness is transformed into a Kurtzean moral insanity when she realizes that with Stevie dead, she is now, like Kurtz, "released from all earthly ties. ... She was a free woman" (189).

Conrad's portrayal of Winnie in the moments leading to Verloc's murder illustrate stunningly how clearly Conrad understood the clinical concept of moral insanity. While Verloc is depicted cannibalistically, partaking in "funereal baked meats for Stevie's obsequies, ... ravenously, without restraint and decency" (190), Winnie exercises the newly found awareness of her freedom with increased control of her physical person. Moral anarchy and willful restraint operate simultaneously. With Verloc wallowing on the sofa,

> [h]er face was no longer stony. Anybody could have noted the subtle change on her features, in the stare of her eyes, giving her a new and startling expression; an expression seldom observed by competent persons under the conditions of leisure and security demanded for thorough analysis, but whose meaning could not be mistaken at a glance. ... Her wits, no longer disconnected, were working under the control of her will. ...
>
> Mrs Verloc was [a] free woman. She commanded her wits now, her vocal organs; she felt herself to be in an almost preternaturally perfect control of every fibre of her body. It was all her own, because the bargain was at an end. She was clear sighted. She had become cunning. ... She did not wish that man to change his position on the sofa. ... (196)

Winnie is acting with great intellectual and bodily restraint, but has abandoned all conventional, moral restraint, because the social contract of marriage has been violated by Verloc's cannibalization of Stevie. Verloc's rational apprehension of what is happening to him is perfectly clear but is characteristically indolent, "leisurely." Recumbent, with a full stomach and hoping for sexual gratification, he takes with disappointment the "full meaning " that "his wife had gone raving mad—murdering mad" and that he must struggle with an "armed lunatic." But the penetrating force of Winnie's savage passions, guided by the strength of insanity, is unstoppable: "Into that plunging blow ... Mrs Verloc had put all the inheritance of her immemorial and obscure descent, the simple ferocity of the age of caverns, and the unbalanced nervous fury of the age of barrooms" (197). With hysterical passions restrained by an amoral intellect, Winnie releases the inherited savagery of primitive man and couples it with the nervous, urban degeneration of modern London to exact her revenge for the loss of her brother and for the seven years of her life she bartered away.

The Trope of the Betrayal of Duty

In "A Familiar Preface" to *A Personal Record,* Conrad observes that he "would not unduly praise the virtue of restraint," then admits that "it may be my sea training acting upon a natural disposition to keep good hold on the one thing really mine, but the fact is that I have a positive *horror* of losing even for one moving moment that full possession of myself which is the first condition of good service" (*PR,* xviii–xix; emphasis added).[37] In his fiction, Conrad does not establish a duty/restraint verbal connection as strong as his civilization/restraint connection, but he does create as strong a verbal link between the lack of restraint and savagery/cannibalism as he does between the betrayal of duty and the failure of nerve.[38] But as always, Conrad complicates the pattern, for the most obviously dutiful of Conrad's characters are presented as comical due to their literal-mindedness, their slavish devotion to detail, or their dense talent for leading the unexamined life. Social duty may be said, for instance, to be the prime motivator of a character like Mr. Hervey in "The Return," who is, above all, duty-bound to upholding appearances. The Accountant in *Heart of Darkness* is another quasi-comical character whom Marlow clearly recognizes to be as ludicrous as a "hairdresser's dummy" in his "starched collar [and] white cuffs" but whom Marlow nonetheless respects for keeping up appearances amidst the great "demoralization of the land. ... That's backbone," Marlow observes (*HD,* 68). Even slavish devotion to duty is valuable when the loss of "backbone" (read, the loss of nerve) is the alternative. Captain Whalley, proud of his personal appearance (187) like the Accountant, is obsessively methodical in winding his chronometer but truly devoted to his daughter; the bookish and literal-minded MacWhirr sees his ship though the typhoon; Singleton steers with care; Chief Inspector Heat methodically tracks down his leads; Falk doggedly survives his "breakdown"; and Brierly, despite his ultimate loss of restraint in abandoning his command, leaves all in "applepie order" in his devotion to duty. Like Marlow's view of the Accountant, Conrad's awareness of the limitations of these characters who show neither moral imagination nor wisdom is tempered (with the exception of Brierly) by the outcome of their endeavors.

The betrayal of duty, the failure of nerve, and various forms of mental insanity are linked in a range of Conrad texts. In perhaps his first extended exploration of this nexus, Conrad is centrally concerned in *The Nigger of the "Narcissus"* with whether James Wait is feigning sickness in order to refuse duty, an issue that threatens the restraints of order and discipline aboard ship. But Conrad's underlying themes are psychological, for the most difficult duty aboard the *Narcissus* is confronting human mortality honestly while retaining one's mental health. The passage with Jimmy tests the sanity of the crew and officers both in the storm and when the ship goes over (where all fear immediately for their lives) and in the slow days of Jimmy's confinement (where the threat of immediacy is replaced by the dread of inevitability). The moment when the ship is righted literally articulates the relationship between performance in the extremity of duty, the exercise of nervous force, and borderland of insanity. As the crew begins to wear ship, haul, and then square the main yard, the ship, as if personifying the whole crew, begins to right itself:[39] "The ship trembled, trying to lift her side, lurched back, seemed to give up with a nerveless dip, and suddenly with an unexpected jerk swung violently windward, as though she had torn herself out from a deadly grasp." In response, the crew "all spoke at once in a thin babble; [and] had the aspects of invalids and the gestures of maniacs" (*NN*, 88). Even Captain Allistoun "gesticulated madly" in excitement. The nervous being of the ship is brought to life by the performance of duty under the most extreme conditions. Subsequently, during the relative leisure of a becalming spell, the nerves and sanity of the men will again be tested by their confrontation with death and phthisical madness in the person of Jimmy.

Connections between the failure of duty, the loss of nerve, and the threat of insanity are likewise evident in the central events of *Lord Jim* and "Youth." Although Jim does not articulate his thoughts or motivations at the time of his jump from the *Patna*, the result is apparently loss of nerve and failed duty. The explicit motivation for the leap is absent in the text (though I will later supply a medical explanation) and inspires the same kind of shocking horror that Marlow feels when he wakes to find Kurtz missing from his bunk. "'I had jumped . . . ' He checked himself, averted his gaze. . . . 'It seems'" (*LJ,* 111). The morally shocking act induces a communal mental instability. Afterward, in the lifeboat, the men laugh "hysterically" and call each other variously "idiot," "fool," "lunatic," and "mad" (115–17). Reflecting upon Jim's description of the crew of the *Patna* who had failed in their duty and were now at sea in a lifeboat, Marlow "was struck by the suggestive truth of his words. There is something peculiar in a small boat upon the wide sea. Over the lives borne from under the shadow of death there seems to fall the shadow of madness. When your ship fails you, your whole world seems to fail you; the world that made you, restrained you, taken care of you. It is as if the souls of men floating on an abyss and in touch with immensity had been set free for any excess of heroism, absurdity, or abomination" (120–21). Jim asserts that he did not get "brain fever" (126), but other characters in Conrad's fiction of this time do. In "Youth" Abraham goes insane when his nerves fail during a storm: "[T]here he was, sitting in his bunk, surrounded by foam and wreckage, jabbering cheerfully to himself. He was out of his mind; completely and for ever mad, with this sudden shock coming upon the fag-end of his endurance" (*Y,* 13). Later in the story, Captain Beard (the namesake of the medical purveyor of neurasthenia) goes temporarily insane when he loses the *Judea,* his first command. From a narrow viewpoint, one might argue that most of Conrad's fiction in the first half-dozen years of his publishing career focuses on the restraints of duty, the loss of nerve, and the threat of insanity.

In sum, crisis occurs in Conrad's fiction when the restraints of duty are observed or betrayed, when nerves hold or fail, when sanity or insanity prevails. Thus, it is reasonable to expect this pattern of issues to emerge in the fictions that immediately precede Conrad's breakdown of 1910. In "The Secret Sharer," the young captain feels the restraints of competing duties, one duty to himself as (in a conventional reading of the story) he tests the degree to which he conforms to the ideal conception of himself and the other duty to his crew and ship as he begins his first command. The tension between these obligations nearly drives him insane in a number of crises when the presence of Leggatt is at the point of discovery by the crew. One episode of near-discovery ends after the young captain "dominates [his] nervousness," refrains from betraying his agitation, and rejoins his double after the Steward's departure: "I saw him standing bolt-upright in the narrow recessed part. It would not be true to say I had a shock, but an irresistible doubt of his bodily existence flitted through my mind. Can it be, I asked myself, that he is not visible to other eyes than mine? ... Motionless, with a grave face, he raised his hands slightly at me in a gesture which meant clearly, 'Heavens! what a narrow escape!' Narrow indeed. I think I had come creeping quietly as near insanity as any man who has not actually gone over the border. That gesture restrained me, so to speak" (*TLS,* 130).

Many personal symbols and associations are at work here. While I do not want to psychoanalyze the passage, I do wish to call attention to the personal significance of the "bath-room," an integral part of Conrad's treatment for his loss of nervous health. Likewise, the sense of claustrophobia and paralysis are symptoms associated with the neurasthenic state. Indeed, Leggatt's very presence suggests a personification of neurasthenia; although there is no physical (organic) evidence of his existence, he is the source of mental anxiety that the sufferer hides from his fellow men. The young captain, on the border of insanity, is able to draw back from the edge due to the "restraining," intimate gesture from a hidden part of himself. The betrayal of duty as an abstraction would be complicated were the captain to lose his gamble on Leggatt's behalf and be found out; for the young captain risks an official inquiry into his motivation, where the nature of his attachment to Leggatt would necessarily refocus the moral issues from murder to sexual orientation and promiscuous dereliction of duty.

The same complex themes of doubling and gender identity are evident in *Under Western Eyes,* which Conrad was near finishing when he wrote "The Secret Sharer" and approached his 1910 collapse. During Razumov's exile in Geneva—through chance encounters, ironic misreadings of his political affinities, and the activity of his moral imagination—Razumov works himself into a state of mental anxiety that comes to a head in his interview with the radical Peter Ivanovitch, "The Great Feminist." Remorseful, defensive, and mentally exhausted by his moral and political duplicity, Razumov makes a covert, hysterical confession to Ivanovitch:

> "All these days you have been trying to read me, Peter Ivanovitch. That is natural. I have perceived it and I have been frank. Perhaps you may think I have not been very expansive? But with a man like you it was not needed; it would have looked like an impertinence, perhaps. And besides, we Russians are prone to talk too much as a rule. I have always felt that. And yet, as a nation, we are dumb. I assure you that I am not likely to talk to you so much again—ha! ha!—"
>
> Razumov, still keeping on the lower step, came a little nearer to the great man.
>
> "You have been condescending enough. I quite understand it was to lead me on. You must render me the justice that I have not tried to please. I have been impelled, compelled, or rather sent—let us say sent—towards you for a work that no one but myself can do. You would call it a harmless delusion: a ridiculous delusion at which you don't even smile. It is absurd of me to talk like this, yet some day you will remember these words, I hope. Enough of this. Here I stand before you—confessed! But one thing more I must add to complete it: a mere blind tool I can never consent to be." (*UWE*, 228–29)

Unable to restrain his nervous verbal effusiveness, Razumov prattles until Ivanovitch grasps him physically and becomes a force of psychological restraint that will reestablish Razumov's characteristic silence and his usefulness. To Razumov, the oblique "confession" is inadequate to his moral needs and destabilizes his psychological equilibrium. And at least superficially, his experience is similar to that of the young captain in "The Secret Sharer," who shares the experience with a double figure. "He felt, bizarre as it may seem, as though another self, an independent sharer of his mind, had been able to view his whole person very distinctly indeed. ... 'This is an effect of nervous exhaustion,' he reflected with weary sagacity. 'How am I to go on day after day if I have no more power of resistance—moral resistance?'" (*UWE*, 230). But Razumov's double, Peter Ivanovitch, is a psychological counterpart with whom Razumov shares an uncomfortable affinity, for neither man is what he appears to be. Razumov's mental extremity is based on the ambiguity of his position in a complex constellation of issues, his identity adrift amidst nebulous alliances of nationalism, political and gender ideology, and moral outlook. To reestablish his identity, moral sanity, and psychological stability, Razumov will need to seclude himself from the competing interests and meditate upon his moral situation.

Conrad has carefully prepared for this connection between restraint, nervous exhaustion, and moral duty in the novel's earlier description of Peter Ivanovitch's personal history. Given Conrad's professed hatred of Russia, his critique of revolutionary liberalism, and his ridicule of sentimental mysticism, it would be a mistake to take the satirical history of Peter Ivanovitch too seriously. On the other hand, Conrad takes Razumov seriously as a psychological and moral focal point; so Peter Ivanovitch, a double for Razumov, is a serious character. He, like many Conrad heroes, has become an outcast from his culture, but "civilization" in this case is Russia. He attempts to strike off the restraining chains of an authoritarian Russia—"that simple engine of government"— with a file given to him by a woman whose love has been destroyed by the same repressive government. Unable to entirely remove the chains himself, he skulks about the bogs of Siberia, a living allegory, half-human and half-beast, "his tawny naked figure glimpsed vaguely through the bushes with a cloud of mosquitoes and flies hovering about the shaggy head." Once a fugitive from repression, he discovers there are "two human beings indissolubly joined in that enterprise. The civilized man, the enthusiast of advanced humanitarian ideas thirsting for the triumph of spiritual love and political liberty; and the stealthy, primeval savage, pitilessly cunning in the preservation of his freedom" (*UWE,* 122). In "a form of temporary insanity" (123) he roams the bush until he is liberated by the compassion of a young woman and her proletariat blacksmith husband, who strikes the remaining chains from his legs. Voila! The Great Feminist is born. Though Ivanovitch is the object of Conrad's pointed satirical criticism for being a poseur, a charlatan, and a sycophant, he takes on the rather serious role of being the parodic double of Razumov, what Razumov (and I believe Conrad) would least like to become.

Marlow, Duty, and the Rhetoric of Restraint

Aside from Conrad's comments in *A Personal Record,* the restraint of duty is articulated and illustrated most clearly in *Heart of Darkness.* We have already seen that the understanding of restraint is key to Marlow's exploration of civilization, savagery, and cannibalism; and his thinking about those issues is related to the performance of duty, both in the fictional events of the African action and in the moral significance of the Thames tale-telling.[40] In other words, Marlow's story is literally about the restraints of duty/work/action in Africa, while Conrad's story is anagogically about the restraints of duty/writing/imagination to the artist who must "render the highest kind of justice to the visible universe" (*NN*, xi) and, while recognizing the risks of that process and telling the truth, stay sane.

Marlow says that he "finds himself" in his work or duty not by making money for the Company or himself but by virtue of keeping the old "tin-pot steamboat" off the bottom of the river: "[F]or a seaman, to scrape the bottom of the thing that's supposed to float all the time under his care is the unpardonable sin" (*HD*, 94). Marlow offers this reflection at a critical point in the story, during the first intermission of the tale. Speaking of his duty to attend to surface reality, Marlow fancifully compares tight-rope walkers, sailors, and prostitutes, all of whom perform their various "tricks" for "half a crown a tumble."[41] Marlow's word play on acrobatic "trick," the nautical term "trick" (for one's turn at duty), and the vulgarism for sexual "trick"—compounded with the acrobatic and sexual meanings of "tumble"—offends at least one of his friends. "Try to be civil, Marlow," growls one of the listeners (94). The comparison also suggests the close connection between civility and the moral basis of masculine duty. This moment of narrative rupture in Marlow's tale occurs when his civilized verbal restraint fails and he commits the unpardonable Victorian sin of alluding to prostitution in polite company, so that his "civilized" audience interrupts him (and in effect defuses any similar feelings in his actual readership). The unrestrained intimacy of the ideas has made the men edgy, nervous.

Marlow describes the realities of Africa immediately after the novella's title passage (where the phrase "heart of darkness" occurs in a defining sense) that has been analyzed frequently, most often focusing on moral issues but more recently with a focus on cultural value, racism, and empire.[42] But Marlow's realities and understanding of restraint also have a medico-psychological significance, for the symbolic suggestiveness of the crippled steamer—like an irritable nervous system that is always on the verge of blowing up, losing steam, and suffering a breakdown—would escape neither Marlow, Marlow's lunatic dance partner (a boilermaker), nor Conrad. The realities that necessarily occupy Marlow's waking moments are "the mere incidents of the surface"—patching steam pipes, cutting wood, avoiding snags—while "the reality ... fades. The inner truth is hidden—luckily, luckily" (*HD*, 93). The "inner truth" to which Marlow refers is the "overwhelming realities of this strange world" of Africa, observed by Marlow in "moments when one's past came back to one ... in the shape of an unrestful and noisy dream" (*HD*, 93). Most generally, "one's past" refers to the history of the species, but it may also be more personal. Marlow is here very close to Conrad, whose personal past includes the nightmare of approaching madness, insanity. The inner reality, so difficult to bear, is the simultaneous fear and allure of madness, paradoxically described in objectified terms as the African landscape and its humanity, by which Marlow journeys on his way to Kurtz: "The steamer toiled along slowly on the edge of a black and incomprehensible frenzy. The prehistoric man was cursing us, praying to us, welcoming us—who could tell? We were cut off from the comprehension of our surroundings; we glided past like phantoms, wondering and secretly appalled, as sane men would be before an enthusiastic outbreak in a madhouse" (*HD*, 96). Quite understandably, recent commentators have focused on Conrad's attitude toward the African people and culture that are presented as primitive Other, the savage foil to the European. But the antitheses that Conrad compares are, I think, more personal and confessional than are such cultural readings. Just as James Wait is an objectification of Conrad's fear of his own medical diathesis for phthisical insanity, so the African nation (land and people) on the shore are somehow analogous to the history of Conrad's own mental health.[43] Once on the borderland of insanity, Conrad had been allowed to draw back and conquer his monstrous fear: "'The earth seemed unearthly. We are accustomed to look upon the shackled form of a conquered monster, but there—there you could look at a thing monstrous and free'" (*HD*, 96). "The shackled form of a conquered monster" could, theoretically, refer to the "criminals" of the Company Station. But where has Marlow grown "accustomed" culturally to such an image or representation? Surely not in England, unless the shackled, conquered monster is not literally the African, but, metonymically, insanity, which was connected by some theorists in Conrad's day to race and was medically regarded as an "accursed inheritance." "Ever any madness in your family?" asks the Company doctor in Belgium (*HD*, 58). In Conrad's own life, his monstrous nervousness was clearly "an accursed inheritance" that he "subdued at the cost of profound anguish and excessive toil" (*HD,* 95). In addition to narrating the history of empire, Conrad is here narrating his own medical history.

Marlow suggests that maintaining one's grip on sanity depends upon patching one's leaky pipes, monitoring dangerous pressures, and keeping one's eyes on the current ahead. This exercise of restraint occurs only with profound anguish and excessive toil, for the wild and passionate uproar, while it is ugly, is also appealing: "[I]f you were man enough you would admit to yourself that there was in you just the faintest trace of a response to the terrible frankness of that noise, a dim suspicion of there being a meaning in it which you ... could comprehend. And why not? The mind of man is capable of anything" (*HD,* 96). While Marlow does not join the Africans for a "howl and dance," this exercise of restraint occurs after his earlier howl and dance with the foreman—"a boiler-maker by trade"—a "lank, bony, yellow-faced man" (85) who is similar to Marlow in appearance: "I don't know why we behaved like lunatics," Marlow recalls. "I put my finger to the side of my nose and nodded mysteriously. 'Good for you!' he cried, snapped his fingers above his head, lifting one foot. I tried a jig. We capered on the iron deck. A frightful clatter came out of that hulk, and the virgin forest on the other bank of the creek sent it back in a thundering roll" (86). The capering jig, a moment of ceremonial lunacy, is a ritual parody of madness meant to stave off the real thing: to vaccinate and to develop resistance to the contagious appeal. Marlow argues that one needs more than the superficial principles and trappings of society—"acquisitions, clothes, pretty rags"—to meet the truth. One needs a deeper kind of restraint, an "inborn strength" based on "deliberate belief" to check the allure of abandoning oneself to passion, of turning one's back on the toil of duty, of giving in to the ease promised by the muddy bank where Kurtz is buried. Even the African helmsman, curiously lured by the "fiendish row" (97) and unprotected by either his race or culture, pays the price for losing restraint and drawing back the protective shutter for a glance. "Poor fool!" reflects Marlow. "If he had only left that shutter alone. He had no restraint, no restraint—just like Kurtz—a tree swayed by the wind" (119).

Marlow admits that the abdication of restraint is alluring, and what saves him is the duty to complete his work and to tell others about it: "An appeal to me in this fiendish row—is there? Very well; I hear; I admit, but I have a voice too, and for good or evil mine is the speech that cannot be silenced" (*HD,* 97). Marlow's speech endures because he practices a rhetoric of restraint that modulates between the extreme rhetorics of hysteria and enervation. John McClure identifies the two forms of rhetoric in *Heart of Darkness,* one defined by Kurtz's "eloquent but immoral" speech and one by Marlow's speech that "derives its power of illumination from his habit of self-restraint."[44] As such, Kurtz's speech is closely allied to Michael Finn's notion of the "language of hysteria," which covers over silence and suppresses reflective thought.[45] As Marlow recalls, Kurtz's voice "survived his strength to hide in the magnificent folds of eloquence the barren darkness of his heart" (147). The quality of lavish eloquence hiding or covering over barrenness of thought is evident in his essay, "Suppression of Savage Customs," which typifies a rhetoric of hysteria:

> It was eloquent, vibrating with eloquence, but too *high strung,* I think. Seventeen pages of close writing he had found time for! But this must have been before his—let us say—*nerves,* went wrong, and caused him to preside at certain midnight dances ending with unspeakable rites, which—as far as I reluctantly gathered from what I heard at various times—were offered up to him—do you understand?—to Mr. Kurtz himself. But it was a beautiful piece of writing. . . . He *soared* and took me with him. The peroration was magnificent, though *difficult to remember,* you know. It gave me the notion of an exotic Immensity ruled by an august Benevolence. It made me tingle with enthusiasm. This was the *unbounded power* of eloquence—of words—of burning noble words. There were no practical hints to interrupt the *magic current of phrases.* (*HD,* 117–18; emphases added)

The flowing eloquence of "unbounded power"—which takes the reader soaring but does not define a memorable argument or a constructive reenactment of experience—is clearly a rhetoric of hysteria that Marlow combats in *Heart of Darkness.*[46]

Marlow's rhetoric of restraint is first evident when he intrudes upon the narrator's framing apparatus, which begins the novel with a clichéd, "eloquent" description of "the memories of men and ships" who have used the Thames to pursue "the dreams of men, the seeds of commonwealths, the germs of empires." Marlow's narrative interrupts this rhetoric of hysteria, the flow of words that covers over meaning, with an abrupt interlocution: "'And this also,' said Marlow suddenly, 'has been one of the dark places of the earth'" (*HD,* 47–48). McClure observes that with this interruption, Marlow begins a rhetoric of restraint that will check the flow of received ideas and constantly probe his own presentation of the "inconclusive" story.[47]

The operation of Marlow's rhetoric of restraint is clearly seen in one of the tale's intermissions, one that delineates the relationship between restraint, nervousness, and masculinity. Narrating the final approach to Kurtz, Marlow describes his attention being divided between the surface reality of steering the steamboat around snags and the greater reality of human mortality evident in the dying helmsman, whose blood is saturating Marlow's shoes. For Marlow, the personal impact of the episode centers on his fear that the aggressive reception at the inner station means that Kurtz is dead and that he, Marlow, will never be able to meet the man or hear the voice. In his retelling of the story, Marlow has recaptured the nervous excess of the moment and has assumed the rhetoric of hysteria that flows with emotion: "'Now I will never hear him.' ... The point was in his being a gifted creature, and that of all his gifts the one that stood out preëminently, that carried with it a sense of real presence, was his ability to talk, his words—the gift of expression, the bewildering, the illuminating, the most exalted and the most contemptible, the pulsating stream of light, or the deceitful flow from the heart of an impenetrable darkness. ...'I will never hear that chap speak after all,—and my sorrow had a startling extravagance of emotion, even such as I had noticed in the howling sorrow of these savages in the bush'" (*HD*, 113–14).

Marlow has let his passions run away with him, and, like the savages on shore who appear as an "enthusiastic outbreak in a madhouse," Marlow recounts the brink of nervous exhaustion in a mimetic rhetoric of hysteria: "I couldn't have felt more of lonely desolation somehow, had I been robbed of a belief or had missed my destiny in life. . . . Why do you sigh in this beastly way, somebody? Absurd? Well, absurd. Good Lord! mustn't a man ever—Here, give me some tobacco" (114). Worried that Marlow is being carried away by his own hysterical rhetoric and may step over the bounds of proper masculine restraint, his friends interrupt and provide him with the opportunity to exercise a rhetoric of restraint that is conventionally masculine but that allows an interrogation of that clichéd rhetoric. The sentence that begins "mustn't a man ever—" is surely completed by the word "cry," as we learn from the next paragraph, when Marlow, the hysterical flow of words checked by his male peers, questions the validity of the culturally constructed gender roles: "Absurd! My dear boys, what can you expect from a man who out of sheer nervousness had just flung overboard a pair of new shoes! Now that I think of it, it is amazing I did not shed tears. I am, upon the whole, proud of my fortitude" (*HD,* 114). Marlow, narrating about the verge of nervous collapse in a rhetoric of hysteria, restrains himself, regales his masculinity with some vigorous draws on his pipe, makes a few requisite slights about women, and continues with his tale.

Fairly warned and now self-controlled, Marlow concludes his tale, exercising a probing rhetoric of restraint defined by a pondering speech pattern, constantly revising his own ideas and language as he searches for the words to represent his experience. A typical example of the rhetoric of restraint occurs metalinguistically when Marlow discusses Kurtz's symbolic heads and restraint: "They only showed that Mr. Kurtz lacked restraint in the gratification of his various lusts, that there was something wanting in him—some small matter which, when the pressing need arose, could not be found under his magnificent eloquence. Whether he knew of this deficiency himself I can't say. I think the knowledge came to him at last—only at the very last" (*HD,* 131). Unlike a rhetoric of hysteria that piles up adjectives and stacks received phrases, Marlow's language here probes by qualification, refinement, or resonant phrasing. The shrunken heads, which symbolize the lack of restraint, become "some small [brain] matter" not found under Kurtz's eloquence, and lack of restraint is finally defined as "this deficiency," the opposite of Marlow's saving efficiency. The knowledge of this deficiency comes to Kurtz, Marlow supposes, "at last." Marlow finally settles on "only at the very last."

The deficiency, as Barbara Gates has observed, is moral insanity. Marlow's reflection that "[a]ll Europe contributed to the making of Kurtz" (*HD,* 117) anticipates the (previously noted) pronouncement of Baron Stott-Wartenheim in *The Secret Agent:* "Unhappy Europe! Thou shalt perish by the moral insanity of thy children!" (*SA,* 27). Kurtz, a child of Europe, shows classic symptoms of moral insanity in Marlow's "diagnosis" of his deficiency. Marlow notes in passing and with characteristic understatement that the problem is *not* failed nerves but the moral perversion of nerves, that is, nerves gone wrong (*HD,* 117). Kurtz's nervous collapse leads to more severe mental disease, but not, Marlow argues, to full-blown insanity. Marlow insists that when he was negotiating with Kurtz to extract him from his project, Kurtz was not insane: "I wasn't arguing with a lunatic either. Believe me or not, his intelligence was perfectly clear. ... But his soul was mad" (144–5). As noted earlier, this is the defining characteristic of "moral insanity." In his chapter "Moral Insanity" in *Insanity and*

116

Allied Neuroses, Dr. Savage defines the illness as a "mental disorder in which the intellect is either fairly developed or unaffected by disease, and yet in which great moral disorder or defect is present. . . . There are people who have not the power of controlling their lower instincts; in whom the animal propensities may override the intellectual."[48] This definition of the disorder accounts for Marlow's response to Kurtz's absence from his cabin, which "unnerved" Marlow "by a sheer blank fright." Marlow defines the fright as a "moral shock . . . as if something altogether monstrous, intolerable to thought and odious to the soul, had been thrust upon me" (141). Unable to control his "lower instincts," Kurtz allows his "animal propensities . . . [to] override the intellectual," and he crawls off on all fours toward the "unspeakable rites." Something monstrous, like the frenzied crowd on the shore, has been unshackled. At the very end, Kurtz's pronouncement—"The Horror! The Horror!"—is thus the deathbed recognition of his moral insanity, a victory to Marlow in its "expression of some sort of belief." Marlow's summary of Kurtz's last moments—"it had the appalling face of a glimpsed truth—the strange commingling of desire and hate"—is precisely the feeling Marlow has as he steams by the frenzied "madhouse" crowd on shore. He is appalled but also thrilled by the appeal of their "horrid faces," the "truth—stripped of its cloak of time" that he successfully navigates past, but which Kurtz glimpses and then fatally embraces.

The interesting and vexing question that remains is why Conrad—who had long suffered precarious health and struggled with neurasthenic symptoms, depression, and the fear of insanity—should find any appeal in the passion on the frenzied bank.[49] The answer, I believe, is found in Conrad's choice of Spenser for his own epitaph: "Sleep after toyle, port after stormie seas." Succumbing to the enemy that one continually and fearfully resists is to rest after great toil. Conrad had long struggled with a fear of insanity, "at the cost of profound anguish and excessive toil." Relaxing the grip on himself, easing the constant exercise of self-restraint, giving way to the passions—all must have covertly appealed to Conrad, who labored in a state of constant unrest and self-control, with his hesitating foot always on the "threshold of the invisible."

Chapter 6
Solitude/Seclusion

To be alone and to think, those are my terrors.—Joseph
Conrad and Ford Madox Ford, "The Nature of a Crime"

The conception and naming of The Retreat in York during
the last decade of the eighteenth century set in motion the transformation of the madhouse into the asylum. If the madhouse was
a place where lunatics were locked away and restrained in
chains, The Retreat was so named "to convey by this designation
[the founders'] idea of what such an establishment should be,
namely, a place in which the unhappy might obtain refuge; a
quiet haven in which the shattered bark might find a means of
reparation or of safety" (see Fig. 11).[1] In Tuke's history of The
Retreat, rural seclusion is presented as the condition and place of
The Retreat's conception and the site of patient treatment. This
romantic view is recorded in Tuke's 1892 quotation of a poetic
tribute to the founding of The Retreat, penned circa 1807 by
Wilkinson, a Lake Poet friend of Wordsworth:

On a fair hill, where York in prospect lies,
Her towers and Steeples pointing to the skies,
A goodly structure rears its modest head;
Thither, my walk, the worthy founder led.
Thither with Tuke, my willing footsteps prest,
Who oft the subject pondering in his breast,
Went forth alone and weigh'd the growing plan,
Big with the last help for suffering man.

The Retreat is thus romantically conceived, Tuke founding his
project in the beneficent rural landscape and seeking a cure for

Fig.11. The Retreat, York, 1792, from *Journal of Mental Science* 38 (1892): 339. (Bio-Medical Library, University of Minnesota, Minneapolis. Photo by Dan Schlies and Mark Summers)

the insane through the healing solitude of the same natural world. Wilkinson's verses, apparently published only in Tuke's history of The Retreat, describe how, while approaching the grounds, he "passed with fearful tread, / With apprehensive eye, and heart of lead; / But soon to me a motley band appears," and the fear of the insane gives way to a conflicting impression of happy residents in rural solitude afflicted by the mystifying, periodic reemergence of insanity:

> What female form but brightens into glee
> Whilst bending o'er exhilarating tea?
> What man but feels his own importance rise,
> Whilst from his pipe the curling vapour flies?
> But oft, alas! tea and tobacco fail
> When demons wild the erratic brain assail.
> But why this wreck of intellect? Ah! why
> Does Reason's noble pile in ruins lie?[2]

While The Retreat advocated the moral treatment of the insane and is credited with founding the nonrestraint movement, it is interesting to note how humane treatment is poetically depicted as rigorously linked to gendered, even covertly sexualized, activities. The woman patient is represented in domestic pose, bending over a tea service; and the upright male patient draws manfully on his pipe. Tuke makes it clear that the domestic ideal was not always achieved or practicable. When The Retreat's *"homishness"* failed and a resident disrupted the peace, he or she was calmed either by restraint or seclusion in a "separate room, about 12 feet by 8."[3] Humane solitude, an isolation from family and the cares of the world, thus became central to the treatment of the mentally ill, whether in the Victorian asylum or in the "rest cure" of S. Weir Mitchell; and further seclusion became a discipline for those who violated the quiet solitude of the asylum.

At the time of Conrad's 1910 breakdown, when Conrad feared Jessie and Dr. Hackney were going to commit him to an asylum, "seclusion rooms" or "seclusion chambers" were enthusiastically recommended as an alternative to mechanical restraint. "Anyone who desires to read of the beneficial effects of seclusion," writes George M. Robertson, "in the noblest language ever written on this subject by any physician, may do so in the pages of Connolly [*sic*]."[4] In his *Familiar Views of Lunacy and Lunatic Life,* John Conolly advocated seclusion in preference to restraint, which only serves to irritate, humiliate, and physically injure the excited patient. It was much quieter and less harmful to "adroitly pop" the offender into a "seclusion room," described by Conolly with a confidential voyeurism (a "familiar view") that reveals concrete details on therapeutic procedures and the viewer's evident professional satisfaction:

> But let us now approach and peep quietly through a little aperture in what is called the "inspection-plate," which, without the patient's knowledge, admits of his being overlooked in his new apartment. It is a small chamber, called the "seclusion room," wadded all round, and with a floor composed of some mixture of cork and india rubber. This is to prevent his injuring himself by knocking his head about, and it also deadens the noise which would be created by his attempts to break out. The window is guarded by a strong shutter, which is perforated to admit a modified light only. In the corner is a bedstead, with a mattrass [*sic*] enclosed in extremely strong ticking, which will resist great efforts to destroy it. Upon this, after a few ineffectual attempts to break loose, he will most likely throw himself in a little time, and fall into a sound sleep.[5]

The duration of treatment in the "seclusion room" varied, depending upon the patient, but if the patient were not sufficiently docile to rejoin the others, then he or she would be introduced to an "airing court or gallery" where in solitude the patient could benefit from "strong muscle exercise" that would again induce a beneficial fatigue.[6] By 1910, Robertson suggests that Conolly's "locking" excitable patients in seclusion was probably unnecessary. If the seclusion room were sufficiently pleasant, with especially comfortable furniture, and if a "moral stigma were allowed to be present" for being consigned to the room, then seclusion would also attain the benefit of "self control," that is, restraint; patients could self-assign voluntary seclusion and finally not need it at all.[7] Robertson's emphasis on self-control, staff observation of multiple patients, and the development of moral restraint illustrate Victorian panopticism as a discipline for insanity, a seclusion within a solitude that was controlled and officially observed.

"The Two Solitudes"

Conrad's view of solitude, in his life and fiction, is problematic. Commentators often note that his work values preeminently the virtue of solidarity, a value implicit in Conrad's ethic as a seaman, which recognizes the necessity of order and concerted labor aboard ship. Yet the primacy of solidarity and its enforcement by restraint of duty are constantly destabilized by the romantic allure of solitude.[8] Every soul, Conrad recognizes in the "Preface" to *The Nigger of the "Narcissus,"* must, like the artist, labor in an "uneasy solitude," with those who look on and wonder "what the fellow may be at" (*NN,* xv). Conrad's profession that solitude is one of the painful truths of human existence reveals his intimacy with the work of Maupassant.[9] Yet these ideas are peculiar to neither writer, for they are based on conventional public attitudes toward solitude/seclusion. But not surprisingly, Maupassant's and Conrad's views are more intensely felt or expressed than conventional attitudes and are dominated by a tone of angst, for solitude is associated in their work with the dangerous borderland of insanity. In Conrad's early letters to Marguerite Poradowska—letters in which he is sometimes histrionic but is nurturing a genuine intimacy with his correspondent—Conrad writes that "solitude loses its terrors when one knows it; it is a bitterness which, for the courageous people who have brought the cup to their lips without wincing, is changed to a sweetness whose attraction one would not exchange for anything else in

121

the entire universe" (*CL,* 1:100). The comments on solitude in Conrad's letter reveal two distinct and, again, "contrary stresses" in his views on solitude, one view as a punishing terror and the other as a curative for the soul. The solitude Conrad fears is apparently the existential solitude of mental alienation from one's kind and from ontological meaning.[10] But if the terror of that existential loneliness and the resulting temptation of suicide can be overcome or mitigated by a romantic solitude of individual connection with some higher meaning, then solitude may become a thing of superlative value. Moreover, as Conrad's letter illustrates, such individual connections can be shared with others.

The ideas expressed in Conrad's letter to Marguerite Poradowska are consonant with the contemporary mythography of solitude evident in popular discourse, where romantic solitude obviously treads dangerously close to sentimental solitude. An 1896 article in *The Spectator* entitled "The Two Solitudes" defines the two kinds of solitude: What may be termed romantic solitude is illustrated by "the aloneness" evoked in Wordsworth poems such as "I wandered lonely as a cloud," and what I have termed existential solitude is typified by the urban "loneliness" that may occur even in a crowd.[11] "Here, then," *The Spectator* philosophizes, "are the two most opposite states we can conceive;—the solitude which is the deepest in the world, and yet can be shared, and which is all the deeper and more thrilling for being shared with one or two others,—and the solitude which is mere loneliness, and is all the lonelier because you are not alone, but are hemmed in and spied upon by cold, curious, familiar observers."[12] The solitude of loneliness is thus an urban anxiety of the panoptical society, where insanity was thought to be in steep ascendancy and needed to be watched. This solitude of loneliness differs little from the experience of Conolly's patient in the seclusion room, alone but under "cold" observation. Romantic solitude is retrospective and, in *The Spectator,* tends toward a sentimental antidote to modern mental alienation. "We cannot see truly and happily into our own selves without the consciousness of a mighty atmosphere of mind in the presence of which we are braced and fortified, and so lifted out of ourselves that we can gaze back into ourselves." Indeed, the kind of solitude found in the natural world is akin to a kind of rest cure. "All solitude that is really renovating, all solitude that really rests the mind and heart, opens the man to himself and gives him a greater insight into his own nature and his own powers."[13] In much of Conrad's fiction, we see these two solitudes: a loneliness that terrorizes and isolates one from one's kind and higher meaning, a solitude that objectifies the human; and an aloneness that romanticizes human solitude and facilitates introspection, that invites mystical subjectification and union with a higher wisdom.

Conrad's romantic solitude is more difficult to achieve than the sentimental solitude described in popular discourse, and it is neither abundant in Conrad's fiction nor unqualified. Old Singleton in *The Nigger of the "Narcissus,"* facing his own mortality as he scans the indifferent sea, illustrates how solitude that promulgates terror can move beyond that terror to strengthen mental fortitude and produce what the narrator of the tale calls "completed wisdom": "Old! He moved his arms, shook his head, felt his limbs. Getting old . . . and then? He looked upon the immortal sea with the awakened and groping perception of its heartless might; he saw it unchanged, black and foaming under the eternal scrutiny of the stars; he heard its impatient voice calling for him out of a pitiless vastness full of unrest, of turmoil, and of terror. He looked afar upon it, and he saw an immensity tormented and blind, moaning and furious, that claimed all the days of his tenacious life, and, when life was over, would claim the worn-out body of its slave" (*NN*, 99). The solitude and wisdom of old age are likewise apparent in "The End of the Tether." We are introduced to Captain Whalley at the moment he must adjust to a "radically new view of existence," after he has sold the *Fair Maid:* "In the solitude of his room he smoked thoughtfully, gazing at the two sea-chests which held all that he could call his own in the world." He realizes that his identity is "indissolubly connected with ships" (*Y,* 184–5) and reemerges from a brief retirement, but only to enter a more insidious solitude. His solitude may be thought romantic in several ways. Most obviously, his solitude contrasts the self-interested and petty society of his crew aboard the *Sofala,* including the obsessive and persecuted owner-engineer Massey, who fears he shall go mad (318), and the "raving fool" Jack (312), the solipsistic second engineer, who is an episodic drunkard. Additionally, Whalley inhabits the seclusion of growing blindness, which he endures for the sake of his daughter with a silence and dignity that attains to a kind of stubborn heroism. Finally, his solitude is shared by and masculinizes Mr. Van Wyck, a retired naval officer, in "retreat from his profession and from Europe," who lives as a fastidious, solitary dandy: "His fluffy, fair hair, thin at the top, curled slightly at the sides; a carefully arranged moustache, an ungarnished forehead, the gleam of low patent shoes peeping under the wide bottom of trousers cut straight from the same stuff as the gossamer coat, completed a figure recalling, with its sash, a pirate chief of romance, and at the same time the elegance of a slightly bald dandy indulging, in seclusion, a taste for unorthodox costume" (280–1). From his decadent seclusion, which connotes some form of degeneration, Van Wyck's finer sensibilities and humane intelligence are engaged by the heroic solitude of Whalley, who, sharing his aloneness, draws him into an understanding of himself and the humanity of Whalley's situation: "He sat on the verandah with a closed book on his knee, and, as it were, looked out upon his solitude, as if the fact of Captain Whalley's blindness had opened his eyes to his own. There were many sorts of heartaches and troubles, and there was no place where they could not find a man out. And he felt ashamed, as though he had for six years behaved like a peevish boy" (215). The heroic confrontation with blindness in effect lends a clearer-sighted existence to those who share his solitude. Romantic solitude, in the vein of Singleton and Whalley, reflects a rock-solid mental stability and wisdom but without restless depth.[14] Other characters in Conrad's fiction, such as MacWhirr and possibly Falk, seem to parody this type of romantic isolato.

The solitude constructed by Lord Jim is a romantic solitude that ends much like Whalley's but more tragically, for Jim is a young man and not chronologically "at the end of his tether." "'He is romantic—romantic,' [Stein] repeated. 'And that is very bad—very bad. . . . Very good, too,' he added" (*LJ*, 216). Stein's contradiction is in some sense self-congratulatory, for Stein is likewise a qualified romantic who "lived solitary, but not misanthropic, with his books and his collection, classing and arranging specimens, corresponding with entomologists in Europe, writing up a descriptive catalogue of his treasures" (207). Jim's romantic solitude, his living in seclusion from European culture in Patusan, is like the "butterfly in solitary grandeur," that specimen of beauty in Stein's collection. But Jim, called by his European colleagues at his leave-taking a "reckless kind of lunatic," severs correspondence with that culture, and his romantic solitude expresses an impractical heroism as he enacts his own romantic history of extreme beauty. Stein, on the other hand, while a connoisseur of exquisite beauty, is capable of unflinching pragmatism in the pursuit of his ideals. When Stein collects his magnificent specimen, his practical and ideal worlds intersect in perfect balance. The story he tells Marlow showcases his physical ability to dispatch three armed assassins and remain composed enough to notice the shadow of a butterfly that flickers over the face of one corpse. With a gun in one hand to protect himself from further intrusions from the practical affairs of life, Stein tracks the elusive specimen and eventually captures it with the other hand, "flop" with his hat. Once sure of the perfection of his extraordinary specimen, his legs then go weak with emotion, not for killing three men but for realizing his ideal of beauty. In this exemplum of romanticism triumphant, Stein is what the Marlow of *Heart of Darkness* would like to be, cruising upriver under attack from the bronze bodies in the undergrowth ashore. The practical Marlow must look out for the surface truth of snags in the river, while the romantic Marlow has just glimpsed the higher and hidden reality of an age-old truth about human nature, veiled from him but lurking on shore. Stein balances his solitary romanticism with the practical needs of the world better than either Jim or Marlow, who is attracted to vital primitivism but admits he is happy that the higher reality is hidden.

In *Lord Jim,* Marlow is frustrated and mystified by Jim's solitary romanticism. The "lesson" Marlow exacts from his consultation with Stein is the desirability of mastering existential solitude, for Stein brings Marlow to the realization that human ills (Jim's excessive romanticism, for instance) have no remedy, no cure. The problem is to learn "how to be" (*LJ,* 213). Simply stated, more problematically mastered. This conundrum frames the balance of Marlow's tale of Jim and leads to the climactic interviews of the novel, the first between Marlow and Jewel, the second at the parting of Marlow and Jim. Both sequences in the novel develop complex imagery and symbolism. In the first interview, the imagery of solitude evokes a Conradian nervous description, where opposing forces lead to a sense of enervation or immobility; the second interview culminates with an imagery of solitude where opposing forces lead to a sense of the romantic mystification of human loss.

The interview between Marlow and Jewel is, in effect, an inversion of Marlow's visit with the Intended in *Heart of Darkness,* for in this revision of the male/female interview Marlow does not spare Jewel's "beautiful world" when he speaks the truth about Jim's reputation among Europeans. And Jewel, "with amazing pluck" (*LJ,* 321), bears up under the truth to preserve Jim's masculine dignity as Marlow makes his "escape." The landscape Marlow afterward traverses mirrors his conflicting emotions, which, in turn, reflect the opposing states of the romantic and existential solitude. The hill Marlow climbs as night deepens rears its "double summit coal-black in the clear yellow glow of the rising moon" (322), which, due to Marlow's ascent up the hill, appears to have fallen from the sky and then rests "glittering through the bushes at the bottom of the chasm" (322). As Marlow watches, the moon begins a leisurely ascent into the sky and "in this mournful eclipse-like light the stumps of felled trees uprose very dark" (322). The nervous description of light and dark, rising and falling (felled trees that rise dark in the moonlight), anticipates an intersection of the living and the dead, suggested by the shadow of a cross from a "solitary grave" that is projected by moonlight across the path Marlow walks in an eerie, perfumed atmosphere: "In the darkened moonlight the interlaced blossoms took on shapes foreign to one's memory and colours indefinable to the eye, as though they had been special flowers gathered by no man, grown not in this world, and destined for the use of the dead alone. Their powerful scent hung in the warm air, making it thick and heavy like the fumes of incense" (322). As Marlow pauses before the grave, the "lumps of white coral"—the skeletal remains of marine life—appear to Marlow in the moonlight as "bleached skulls" and in the silence—where all life, marine and terrestrial, unites in death—"all sound and all movement in the world seemed to come to an end" (322):

> It was a great peace, as if the earth had been one grave, and for a time I stood there thinking mostly of the living who, buried in remote places out of the knowledge of mankind, still are fated to share in its tragic or grotesque miseries. In its noble struggles, too—who knows? The human heart is vast enough to contain all the world. It is valiant enough to bear the burden, but where is the courage that would cast it off?
>
> I suppose I must have fallen into a sentimental mood. (323)

Marlow, in a moment of sentimental solitude, reflects on the essential aloneness and unity of all creatures who are united in death—thoughts not unlike those of Gabriel Conroy at the conclusion of Joyce's "The Dead." And, like the conclusion of "The Dead," the moment of sentimental or romantic illumination is complicated by a simultaneous and opposing emotion of existential aloneness.

But Marlow's sentimental ideas, as they verge on the hysterical, are checked by a rhetoric of restraint; as he begins to reflect on the miseries of the human heart that unite all of mankind (a variation of "the human mind is capable of anything"), his mood modulates into a more austere existential solitude: "I stood there long enough for the sense of utter solitude to get hold of me so

126

completely that all I had lately seen, all I had heard, and the very human speech itself, seemed to have passed away out of existence, living only for a while longer in my memory, as though I had been the last of mankind" (*LJ*, 323). The solitude Marlow feels here is "a strange and melancholy illusion," an air of unreality occasioned largely, in the fictional context, by his seclusion from his native civilization: "This was, indeed, one of the lost, forgotten, unknown places of the earth; I had looked under its obscure surface; and I felt that when to-morrow I had left it for ever, it would slip out of existence, to live only in my memory till I myself passed into oblivion" (323). The echoes of *Heart of Darkness* grow quite obviously strong from here to the very end of the passage, where Marlow shifts his time frame from a more sentimental reverie to the fictional present, suggesting to his listeners that he is trying to "hand over to you, as it were," the story's "very existence, its reality—the truth disclosed in a moment of illusion" (323). In *Heart of Darkness,* Marlow suggests that it cannot be done; it is "impossible to convey the life-sensation of any given epoch of one's existence—that which makes its truth, its meaning—its subtle and penetrating essence. It is impossible. We live, as we dream—alone" (*HD*, 82). Both passages suggest the Sartrean mantra, "existence precedes essence." The artist's attempt to distill experience into some kind of truth and to convey it to others is an impossible task, for we live as we dream, in an existential solitude.

In *Lord Jim,* as in *Heart of Darkness,* the dream sensation Marlow describes verges on the dreamworld of the artist. Though a raconteur, Marlow is not Conrad. Yet he enjoys the confidence of Conrad's "hours of solitude" and has trod so dangerously close to the "edge" that his story about the borderland of insanity all but inhabits the landscape it describes.[15] And, like the inner reality on the shore of the Congo—the howl and dance in a madhouse—Marlow's melancholy in Patusan is symbolically framed by lunar imagery that suggests a landscape of hysteria, of irrationality: "I saw part of the moon glittering through the bushes at the bottom of the chasm. For a moment it looked as though the smooth disc, falling from its place in the sky upon the earth, had rolled to the bottom of that precipice: its ascending movement was like a leisurely rebound; it disengaged itself from the tangle of twigs; the bare contorted limb of some tree, growing on the slope, made a black crack right across its face. It threw its level rays afar as if from a cavern" (322). The imagery of "chasm," "precipice," and "cavern" suggest a psychological abyss; the "tangle of twigs," the "contorted limb" that cracks the face of the moon likewise suggest a traditional image of lunacy: the alienation from the earthly world that occurs under the light of the moon. Marlow makes such a comic association in *Heart of Darkness* when he and the boilermaker, dancing their jig on the steamer, behave like lunatics in the moonlit jungle, an "entangled mass of trunks, branches, leaves, boughs, festoons, motionless in the moonlight, was like a rioting invasion of soundless life, a rolling wave of plants, piled up, crested, ready to topple over the creek, to sweep every little man of us out of existence" (*HD*, 54). In both sequences, the jungle and moonlight evoke the borderland of insanity whether it is portrayed in a comic/parodic moment of madcap "lunacy" or a melancholic, existential moment of "utter solitude."

A biographical reason for such contrasting treatments of lunar imagery and the issue of borderland insanity extends from Conrad's medical history. It was in early 1899 that Conrad wrote the madcap, ludic sequence of *Heart of Darkness,* and a year later, on 25 January 1900, he fell seriously ill—an illness Conrad describes as "[m]alaria, bronchitis and gout. In reality a breakdown" (*CL,* 2:248)—and wrote chapter 35 of *Lord Jim* some months after the breakdown and "shattered nerves" (2:251). He probably drafted the chapter, which appeared serially in the September issue of *Blackwood's,* in May or June of 1900.[16] As he labored to finish the novel, Conrad felt a need to go abroad to regain his nervous strength. As he wrote to David Meldrum, his friend and literary advisor for *Blackwood's,* "I fear I must go, and that soon, or I shall become a complete idiot. My nerves are like fiddle strings" (2:272). During the same period, his intimate friend, Stephen Crane, was gravely ill, traveled to the Black Forest in Germany for a last attempt at a cure, and died on 5 June 1900. The secluded night forest and fragmented lunar imagery of Patusan surely correlate to Conrad's own mental state of the late spring and early summer of 1900.

The Conrad tale that most centrally explores various states of solitude is "The Secret Sharer," written by Conrad in the difficult period prior to his nervous breakdown of January 1910.[17] Like the major characters of *Lord Jim,* the young captain and Leggatt, though repeatedly referred to as "doubles," illustrate different personalities responding to solitude and seclusion. Leggatt is imagined by the narrator as more "romantic" in his orientation to solitude. He is an outcast but contemplative, "at home with himself" (as the saying goes), and a more integrated personality than his host: "His expression was concentrated, meditative, under the inspecting light of the lamp I held up to his face; such as a man thinking hard in solitude might wear" (*TLS*, 100). The young captain watches Leggatt a good deal, and when not looking at him he frequently thinks about his sequestered guest. Recent gender studies of the story have suggested the captain's "looking" and Leggatt's enjoyment of the captain's gaze suggest an eroticism secretly shared by the doubles.[18] While I recognize the validity of readings that trace the homoerotic subtext of the tale, the captain also has a more clinical side to his observations that are focused more on a kind of comparative introspection than on Leggatt as an object of desire. The captain is not always "with" Leggatt in the solitude of his cabin, and at times, the captain is in the cabin (with or without other members of the crew) while Leggatt is further secluded behind curtains or doors, not unlike the clinical situation described by Conolly in his *Familiar Views of Lunacy*. Like a neurasthenic "secret self," hidden from public view and privately focused on diet and rest, Leggatt is under observation in a "seclusion room." In keeping with the theme of doubling, one also sees the roles reversed, as when the captain takes breakfast with the crew while Leggatt is in the next room behind curtains in the captain's secluded "bed-place." The voyeurism, the self-reflexive nature of the observation, and the issue of mental health are textually overt: "[A]ll the time the dual working of my mind distracted me almost to the point of insanity. I was constantly watching myself, my secret self, as dependent on my actions as my own personality, sleeping in that bed, behind that door which faced me as I sat at the head of the table. It was very much like being mad, only it was worse because one was aware of it" (*TLS*, 113–14). Who is the observed, who the observer? The young captain is exploring varieties of solitude, one romantic and the other moral and existential; in other words, the captain is both measuring his actions against an "ideal conception" of instinctive, spontaneous action, and, at the same time, testing the parameters of his existence by exploring the borderland of insanity: "I think I had come creeping quietly as near insanity as any man who has not actually gone over the border" (130). The captain, in this respect, is very much like a young Marlow, torn between competing responses to solitude.

There are many more Conradian characters who are romantic or existential "isolatoes," (or parodies and lampoons thereof) whose mental health is problematic. In his full-length study entitled *The Eternal Solitary*, Adam Gillon charts the fate of Conrad's characters and in doing so visually demonstrates the rarity with which Conrad's protagonists "emerge from their isolation." The vast majority either commit suicide, die of disease, experience emotional crises, or turn insane.[19] Gillon's chart is a telling visual paradox, for it groups together bunches of isolatoes and demonstrates the similarity of outcasts. This spatial contradiction reproduces one of the paradoxes of solitude and mental disease seen in the destructive and curative properties of seclusion: the opposing fears of confined or open spaces.

Neurasthenia, Agoraphobia, and Claustrophobia

With the increased incidence of diagnosed nervous disorders in the late nineteenth century, the identification and classification of various kinds of phobia increased, not only in England but in Europe and America as well.[20] George M. Beard and others recognized various phobias as symptomatic of neurasthenia and various hysterical disorders, and chief among these were agoraphobia and claustrophobia.[21] Beard was careful to distinguish between normal fears, which are a natural and necessary function of human life, and so-called "morbid fears," which result from various malfunctions, specifically a "lack of force in the disordered nervous system. The debility of the brain—the nerve impoverishment—renders it impossible to meet responsibility" occasioned by anxiety. "Morbid fear," he concludes, is a "psychical paralysis."[22] Given that neurasthenia was thought to be an urban nervous disorder, it is fitting that the morbid fears most commonly associated with neurasthenia were both connected with environment and space, since modern men and women often found themselves in uncongenial surroundings, whether it was the confining home or crowded marketplace. Beard cites the work of Karl Westphal, who in 1871 published his paper on "agoraphobie"; the phobia's name is based on the Greek *agora,* meaning "an open square" or "marketplace," and suggests, in Beard's view, that it is really a form of *topophobia.* For the agoraphobic individual, closed spaces thus offer a place of refuge from the terrors of the marketplace or open spaces. Beard likewise cites the work of Dr. Meschede, which introduced cases of patients who feared the opposite, *"close, narrow* places," and of Dr. Ball, for naming the reverse condition "claustrophobia," a condition evident in those who fear confinement

130

and enclosure and who cannot stay indoors.[23] Even Max Nordau sensed the close connection between the two phobias and neurasthenia, citing these morbid fears as indicative of degeneration.[24] In Conrad's fiction, both phobias are connected with the terrors or attractions of solitude and figure prominently as indices of the mental health of particular characters.

Agoraphobia and especially claustrophobia are morbid fears that preclude any romantic embrace of solitude, and the Conradian characters that experience either phobia associate solitude with the terror of mental alienation. Commentators on *The Secret Agent* have long recognized that the nervousness or mental instability of many of the novel's characters is registered in either the agoraphobic fear of the slimy, dirty streets of London or the contrasting feeling of claustrophobia created by prisons, narrow byways, and cramped Soho shops and flats. Michael Haltresht catalogs the novel's characters who have some sort of mental disorder—the Professor's paranoia, Michaelis's schizophrenia, Stevie's mental retardation, Verloc's hallucinatory states, Winnie's temporary murderous insanity, Ossipon's alcoholic depression, and Vladimir's observation that "madness alone is truly terrifying"—and concludes that "madness was very much on Conrad's mind" when he produced *The Secret Agent* and that this preoccupation is represented in the contrasting fear of confinement and the dread of space.[25] Whether or not Conrad was himself agoraphobic, as Haltresht maintains, or was consciously depicting the disorder with which his friend Ford had been diagnosed, variations of agoraphobia are used in Conrad's fiction to suggest extreme mental states.[26] Kurtz, whose "nerves went wrong" and whose "soul had gone mad," is described in the face-to-face, midnight confrontation with Marlow in psychospatial terms:

> This alone [the spell of the wilderness], I was convinced, had driven him out to the edge of the forest, to the bush, towards the gleam of fires, the throb of drums, the drone of weird incantations; this alone had beguiled his unlawful soul beyond the bounds of permitted aspirations. And, don't you see, the terror of the position was not being knocked on the head ... but in this, that I had to deal with a being to whom I could not appeal in the name of anything high or low. ... There was nothing either above or below him, and I knew it. He had kicked himself loose of the earth. Confound the man! he had kicked the very earth to pieces. He was alone, and I before him did not know whether I stood on the ground or floated in the air. (*HD*, 144)

The loss of restraint and the soul's madness are suggested by spatial alienation, by an ambience of solitary disconnection and the hallucinatory nightmare of drifting in space. Similar allusions to Cain's estrangement from earth occur in "The Secret Sharer," where Leggatt remarks he is "off the face of the earth" (*TLS*, 132), and in "Amy Forster," where Yanko is "like a man transplanted into another planet, ... separated by an immense space from his past" (*T*, 132). Perhaps the most extended treatment of agoraphobia and madness is evident in the Placid Gulf sequences of *Nostromo*, which culminate with Decoud's extreme existential solitude, madness, and resulting suicide.

When Decoud and Nostromo depart from the Sulaco wharf with their cargo of silver and Señor Hirsch, their entry into the darkness of the Placid Gulf has the effect of "being launched into space" making "no more noise than if she [the lighter] had been suspended in the air" (*N*, 261). The sense of "solitude could almost be felt" (262–3), a synesthesia suggesting a dysfunction of the nervous system. Indeed, the stressful sensation of sailing in the utter darkness is conveyed in part through medical metaphors. Nostromo remarks twice that "this thing"—the desperate affair of protecting the silver in the Placid Gulf—"has been given to me like a deadly disease" (264) that if discovered, will kill him. And the "enormous stillness" of the gulf "affect[s] Decoud's senses like a powerful drug" that induces a sense of suspension in space: "In this foretaste of eternal peace they floated vivid and light, like unearthly clear dreams" (262). While this release from tension is momentarily appealing, the solitude and situation make both men nervous in characteristically different ways. The high risk of failed action makes Nostromo "nervously resentful" (263); later he feels "nervous impatience" (274), and as the Sotillo's steamer probes the darkness of the gulf for the Isabels, he utters "nervous murmurs" (281) to Decoud. Through all of this, Nostromo, a man of action, restrains his nerves. Decoud, a man of skeptical thought, feels his physical and mental strength degenerate as he overextends himself rowing into the gulf, and he barely retains his grip on himself: "'I am on the verge of delirium,' he thought. He mastered the trembling of all his limbs, of his breast, the inward trembling of all his body exhausted of its nervous force" (266). For the desperate present, Decoud restrains himself, "nerved himself for the effort of rowing" (269). As the steamer approaches in the darkness, "Decoud stood as if paralysed; only his thoughts were wildly active" (271). "The very madness of fear" protects Hirsch as he crouches, whimpering in the lighter. "*Nostromo,*" Conrad begins his author's note, "is the most anxiously meditated" of the longer novels following his volume *Typhoon* (*N,* vi). The Placid Gulf is a study of nervous action, nervous meditation, and nervous fear as a response to the anxiety of palpable solitude.

The conclusion of the novel records the responses to solitude by the romantic hero of audacious action and the existential victim of skeptical thought. The death of Nostromo is a function of his moral corruption—the silver a disease that will kill him—which undermines the heroism of his solitary, romantic endeavors. The undermining of his heroism is underscored by his "romantic courting/betrayal" of the Viola girls in the seclusion of the Great Isabel, now the site of his growing moral insanity. Decoud, on the other hand, is cut off from all forms of life and explicitly dies from his island solitude. As if to underscore the intensity of Decoud's experience on the Great Isabel, Conrad reiterates the word "solitude" six times in the two pages of text that lead up to Decoud's suicide: "He died from solitude, the enemy known but to few on this earth, and whom only the simplest of us are fit to withstand. The brilliant Costaguanero of the boulevards had died from solitude and want of faith in himself and others" (*N,* 496). In *Nostromo,* as in *Heart of Darkness,* Conrad speaks of our dependence on the high organization of crowds. Few of us, he argues, experience actual aloneness, though many deal with the loneliness endemic in the urban crowd. Only the "simplest of us," the narrator argues, can withstand the rigors of solitude. What Conrad means by "simple" is evident in a character like Singleton.[27] Decoud's ironic and skeptical refinement fails to sustain him in existential aloneness: "Solitude from mere outward condition of existence becomes very swiftly a state of soul. ... After three days of waiting for the sight of some human face, Decoud caught himself entertaining a doubt of his own individuality. It had merged into the world of cloud and water, of natural forces and forms of nature. In our activity alone do we find the sustaining illusion of an independent existence as against the whole scheme of things of which we form a helpless part" (497). In his paradoxical solitude of spatial plenitude and island confinement, Decoud becomes absorbed in melancholy based on his cultivated skepticism and lapses into a mild dementia, which, in turn, degenerates into a state of existential angst and nervous exhaustion. Ultimately, he "beheld the universe as a succession of incomprehensible images" (498). Unable to transform his "outward condition" of solitude into some romantic formulation of higher meaning, "the solitude appeared like a great void, and the silence of the gulf like a tense, thin cord" (498) that would release him only with his suicide.

Medical opinion classifying agoraphobia and claustrophobia in the professional and popular media of Conrad's day reveals that both conditions were assumed to be closely related to vertigo, vertigo with anxiety, or a number of other possible exciting causes.[28] One prominent contemporary opinion on the origin of the phobias advanced an eclectic mixture of the theories of Darwin, degenerationists, and Freud. Dr. Charles Mercier, a well-published asylum superintendent and lecturer in neurology and insanity at Westminster Hospital, London, suggested that both phobias, so closely associated with modern nervousness, involve the revival of instincts of our primitive arboreal ancestors. Agoraphobia, Mercier argued, is based on the fear of open spaces once felt by primates that ventured too far from the cover and the protection of trees where they were safe from terrestrial predators. Claustrophobia, Mercier reasoned, developed later in our "racial history," in response to the closed shelters (caves, hollows in trees, and so forth) our nearer kin sought during inclement weather. The desire for more open space is here conversely a relic of sleeping in trees under the open skies. "Like the sufferer from agoraphobia," Mercier wrote, "he who suffers from claustrophobia experiences the revival of an ancestral instinct that has been obsolete for untold generations, but that has been lost more recently than that revived in agoraphobia."[29] Mercier apparently offered his theory quite seriously, though not without tongue in cheek. The mild humor he enlists also reveals a telling set of associations between the theories of Darwinian degeneration, the feminine, modern neuroses, and the abandonment of restraint: "The habit of taking shelter in more or less closed spaces was a habit of slow and gradual acquirement; and we may be sure that it was not acquired without many a relapse and many a backsliding. We can almost hear the jeers and scoffs of the stout old Tory anthropoids at the effeminacy of their degenerate juniors, who should seek a shelter that their forefathers would have scorned. The habit has not yet been fully acquired by all our race, for we see, even at this late day, many persons of human status to whom the shelter of a roof is abhorrent, and who prefer, in the worst of weather, to lie about under a hedgeside rather than submit to the restraint of roof and walls."[30] Such a complex of ideas seems both odd and humorous until we reflect that a similar complex of ideas appears in *The Secret Agent,* that novel of tensions between men and women, restraint and freedom, political state and domestic affairs, and between the agoraphobic and the claustrophobic. Consider, in particular, the moment after Winnie kills Verloc: "Into that plunging blow . . . Mrs. Verloc had put all the inheritance of her immemorial and obscure descent, the simple ferocity of the age of caverns, and the unbalanced nervous fury of the age of bar-rooms" (*SA,* 197). Winnie Verloc, "a little swimmy in her head" (200), makes a dash for the door, now a free woman. The fact that Mercier republished his peculiar theories in the 23 March 1907 number of *Scientific American* (subsequent to their original publication in *The Lancet* [London]), just as Conrad was revising *The Secret Agent* for publication as a book, suggests the medical currency of Conrad's claustrophobic "landscape of hysteria."

Without venturing too much into the Freudian analysis that Mercier was apparently beginning to explore, we can see the same constellation of issues in *The Nigger of the "Narcissus,"* which likewise links claustrophobia with degeneration, primitive fear, and femininity as James Wait devolves into phthisical insanity. Jimmy's claustrophobia is occasioned by his entombment in his cabin during the storm and later by his medical confinement—both "feminine" conditions anticipating the utter solitude of death. When the crew realizes that Jimmy is trapped in his cabin during the storm, he is detected by his "screaming and knocking" beneath the boatswain, Archie, Belfast, and Wamibo "with the hurry of a man prematurely shut up in a coffin" (*NN,* 66). During the minutes they struggle to reach Jimmy, "he screamed piercingly, without drawing breath, like a tortured woman" (67). When the men finally break though to Wait, Conrad's narrator describes the scene in what is clearly a birthing sequence, though Jimmy emerges as the embodiment of a primitive, even bestial terror of death. Belfast "clamoured": "'For the love of God, Jimmy, where are ye? . . . Knock! Jimmy darlint! . . . Knock! You bloody black beast! Knock!' He was as quiet as a dead man inside a grave; and, like men standing above a grave, we were on the verge of tears—but with vexation, the strain, the fatigue; with the great longing to be done with it, to get away, and lie down to rest somewhere where we could see our danger and breathe" (69). In the dark, confined space and suffocating atmosphere, the men finally break through with a crowbar, and

Jimmy "rushed at the hole, put his lips to it, and whispered 'Help' in an almost extinct voice; he pressed his head to it, trying madly to get out through that opening one inch wide and three inches long. In our disturbed state we were absolutely paralysed by his incredible action" (69). The association of claustrophobia with the primitive, female, bestial, and nearly "extinct" suggests the constellation of ideas are metonyms for madness.[31] This comparison is further reinforced by the men who are "maddened with excitement"; by Jimmy, who "madly" tries to escape his narrow confinement; and by the disturbed paralysis of the men who witness his mental extremity. If Jimmy's liberation is a birth, it is a rebirth occasioned by the narrow escape from madness, not unlike Marlow in *Heart of Darkness* when he is permitted, on the brink of the soul's madness and death experienced by Kurtz, to draw back his hesitating foot.

Jimmy's confinement caused by the storm is followed by confinement imposed on him by Captain Allistoun, when the master realizes with certainty that Jimmy is mortally ill. That assurance occurs when he witnesses Jimmy "utterly alone in the impenetrable solitude of his fear" (*NN*, 119). The confinement of Jimmy is not a strict medical quarantine, even though seclusion of the phthisical insane was a common procedure at the time *The Nigger of the "Narcissus"* was published, for the crew are allowed to visit Wait in his cabin.[32] Rather, the seclusion of Wait is effected to confine a feminine and humanizing force on board ship; it is a restraint of the insane and diseased Wait, who, under the watchful gaze of Allistoun, is seen in his true light—no longer a functioning member of the crew, already isolated in his "impenetrable solitude" (119).

If the seclusion of Wait in the *The Nigger of the "Narcissus"* is due to a complex of moral/medical/ideological reasons, the same holds true for Leggatt. Leggatt is the embodiment of the neurasthenic predicament, a functional disorder that has no organic etiology and whose presence is inexplicable to the observer. A number of other circumstances in the text suggest that Conrad is narrating his own medical history of neurasthenia. The nature of Leggatt's crime, an unrestrained act during an "anxious sort of job," implies a medical allegory underlying the storm and fit of rage. Leggatt's description of the ship and sea—"the maddening howling of that endless gale"—suggests that the officers and crew were all in precarious mental health when he commits murder. The victim is "half crazed with funk," and when Leggatt strangles him, Leggatt blacks out, for he does not remember anyone prying his hands from the throat of the dead man. He does, however, remember the men "screaming 'Murder!' like a lot of lunatics" and that the skipper, whose "nerve went to pieces" during the gale, was "raving" just like the crew (*TLS,* 102–7). Presumably, the skipper's failure of nerve necessitated Leggatt's heroic but insane act that saves the ship and crew but kills one man. A variety of other details suggest a medical subtext that alludes to neurasthenia and the fear of nervous breakdown. When Leggatt appears, expressing the worry that he might have died from "exhaustion," he is twice described as being in a mysterious glow of "phosphorescence" (review Fig.4); he will likewise disappear in phosphorescence (97–99, 142). Moreover, Leggatt is described in paralytic terms, he appears to the captain "as though he had been ill" (due to being confined to his room for nearly seven weeks), and his face looks "sunken in daylight" (98, 103–5, 114). During their confinement, the captain and Leggatt are by necessity preoccupied with food, as victims of eating disorders might be during a Weir Mitchell rest cure: the captain eats nothing while Leggatt feasts on a variety of delicacies that would generally be forbidden to the dyspeptic or anemic patient: "stewed chicken, paté de foie gras, asparagus, cooked oysters, sardines" (113, 227). In their seclusion, especially during Archbold's visit, the captain presents himself as suffering from "disease." Leggatt's introduction to the new ship is thus "a nerve-trying situation" (116, 123) that brings on an outbreak of mental instability.

The seclusion of Leggatt should be read not as the moral protection of an "ideal conception of self" as is often supposed by commentators, but quite the reverse: as the prudent isolation or moral restraint of an inherited, perhaps even contagious instability.[33] This seclusion is necessary both to command and to gradually heal the self. The claustrophobic atmosphere of the tale thus suggests the difficulty and the necessity of quarantining such emotional force in a confined space: "I went slowly into my dark room, shut the door, lighted the lamp, and for a time dared not turn round. When at last I did I saw him standing bolt-upright in the narrow recessed part. It would not be true to say I had a shock, but an irresistible doubt of his bodily existence flitted through my mind. Can it be, I asked myself, that he is not visible to other eyes than mine? It was like being haunted. Motionless, with a grave face, he raised his hands slightly at me in a gesture which meant clearly, 'Heavens! what a narrow escape!' Narrow indeed" (*TLS,* 130). The narrowness, the "recessed part," the motionlessness, the "grave" face, and the doubting of bodily "existence" all suggest that the claustrophobia of seclusion is associated in the mind of the speaker with a fear of death, a fear closely associated with the horror of insanity. In short, Leggatt is a later version of James Wait. The passage quoted above has been taken by recent gender critics to be part of the evidence suggesting that the captain and Leggatt secretly share a homoerotic relationship, and in this way, too, he is a source (like Wait) not only of potential disease but, as was thought in Conrad's day, moral "degeneration."[34] In addition to Leggatt being "bolt-upright" in the captain's innermost chamber, gender critics cite other scenes of physical proximity; intimate gestures, touching, and conversation; his emergence naked from the sea; and his pleasure in having the captain look at him.[35] A queer reading of the tale complements the present reading as an allegory of impending nervous collapse, for homosexuality was thought in Conrad's day to contribute to or to be symptomatic of neurasthenia.

The Rhetoric of Seclusion

When the narrator of "The Secret Sharer" introduces the reader to the motif of doubling, he shares with the reader a self-conscious admission that he and Leggatt are really not that much alike, but if viewed in seclusion, from a particular perspective, they might well appear as intimate doubles: "His face was thin and the sunburn faded, as though he had been ill. And no wonder. He had been, I heard presently, kept under arrest in his cabin for nearly seven weeks. But there was nothing sickly in his eyes or in his expression. He was not a bit like me, really; yet, as we stood leaning over my bed-place, whispering side by side, with our dark heads together and our backs to the door, anybody bold enough to open it stealthily would have been treated to the uncanny sight of a double captain busy talking in whispers with his other self" (*TLS*, 105). The rhetoric of seclusion is illustrated by this passage, both in the use of distance and involubility, that is, the approach to silence. Conrad critics have long examined the issues of distance and silence in Conrad's fiction.[36] Jakob Lothe defines narratorial *distance* as "a modal category that denotes, essentially, the relation between the narrator and the characters and events he describes. Additionally, distance may also refer to the relationship between the narrator and the author, or more precisely between the understanding, views, and sensations of the narrator and the thematics the author presents." Various kinds of distance may be created by narration, either temporal or spatial, and they indicate "a difference between narrator and character in matters of information, insight, and attitude."[37] The passage from "The Secret Sharer" quoted above illustrates just this difference.

The first thing the reader may notice about the passage is the surprising revelation that Leggatt and the young captain are "not a bit" alike, "really," even though the balance of the story insists upon an apparently misleading "doubling" of the two. Our doubting the young captain's word is in part an effect of the distance between the narrator and his younger self, a distance suggested temporally by the "distance of years" (*TLS*, 116) that separates the events from the narration of them. (Additionally, since we must now question the narrator's reliability, a gap opens between the narrator's understanding and the understanding the reader takes from Conrad's text.) The temporal distance is further complicated. The passage begins with a sense of events in the simple past ("his face was thin ... "), but a sense of present immediacy is created by "as I presently heard" and the lexical juxtaposition of past and present ("as we stood leaning [and] whispering"). Such multiple distancing is even further complicated spatially by the introduction of "anybody who might be bold enough" to open the door and witness their collusion.

The voyeurism implicit in this situation—of looking at or looking on the solitary couple in their seclusion room—is similar to that described by Conolly in his *Familiar Views of Lunacy and Lunatic Life*. The effect of this narrative move is threefold. First, it momentarily positions the narratee at the point of narrative voyeurism as we initially enlist as "anybody bold enough" to gaze on the secret sharers. But almost immediately we see the potential threat of intrusion by the crew as "anybody bold enough," and we physically distance ourselves from the door-frame and defer to the second, imagined intruder as furthering the suspense of the story. This accomplished, we become the narrative audience, willing witnesses to the fictional action that occurs at a distance below us; in so doing, we (Conrad and his readers) create another level of distance in the text's thematic treatment of solitude.

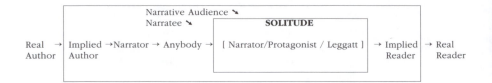

The narrator, it must be remembered, is telling the story from a "distance of years" and thus compounds the distance of time upon the multiple distances of space. And though it is possible to diagram the narrator in relation to the various audiences of the text, the physical setting from which the narrator's voice emanates, is specified—is contextualized—nowhere. In "The Secret Sharer" there is no Marlow narrating aboard the *Nellie* to a circle of friends. The secret sharer is a psychologically motivated vocalization emanating from some secret place, from an utter solitude. And the narrator's story is thus a tale about the operation of the human mind in and on solitude.

Conrad also deploys a complex rhetoric of seclusion in *Lord Jim,* using spatial and temporal distancing to portray the solitude of Jim and, at the same time, portraying Jim himself as a hysterical, nervous voice that is only partially successful in its attempts to recount the psychological trauma of the *Patna* episode and the subsequent sense of isolation that extends from the episode. Jakob Lothe, perhaps the most deft and meticulous analyst of Conrad's narrative structures, has confessed it is impossible to "do justice" to the complexity of the narrative discourse in *Lord Jim.*[38] My diagram below thus comes with an admission that it grossly simplifies the narrative situation of *Lord Jim,* but it does so to make a simple thematic point about Conrad's treatment of solitude:

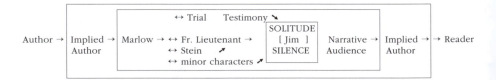

If the process of interpreting Jim's story is central to *Lord Jim,* then the silence at the center of the novel becomes, ironically, a telling silence, for Jim's inability to explain himself must itself be explained by a narrator, known elsewhere for telling his own "inconclusive experiences" (*HD*, 51). Jim often tries to tell his story but is unable to do so due to his chronic hysteria, which manifests itself not only with Marlow's sympathetic fascination but in a variety of more concrete ways.

To the casual reader, an inconspicuous way in which Jim manifests hysteria occurs at the very beginning of the novel, in chapter 2, when Jim is felled by a blow from a loose spar and subsequently falls victim to a debilitating illness. The incident in the novel is based on Conrad's own experience in 1887 when he was chief mate on the *Highland Forest*. Conrad narrates the events in *The Mirror of the Sea:* "A piece of one of the minor spars that did carry away flew against the chief mate's [Conrad's] back, and sent him sliding on his face for quite a considerable distance along the main deck. Thereupon followed various and unpleasant consequences of a physical order—'queer symptoms,' as the captain, who treated them, used to say; inexplicable periods of powerlessness, sudden accesses of mysterious pain. ... The Dutch doctor who took the case up in Samarang offered no scientific explanation. All he said was: 'Ah, friend, you are young yet; it may be very serious for your whole life. You must leave your ship; you must quite silent be for three months—quite silent'" (*MS*, 54–55). Conrad and Jim both undergo a rest cure, Conrad in Singapore and Jim in an "Eastern Port." The text of *Lord Jim* suggests that the mishap in stormy weather is a portentous event that will have devastating consequences on Jim's entire life. "The elemental furies" of the sea come at him "with a purpose of malice ... to smash, to destroy, to annihilate all he has seen, known, loved, enjoyed, or hated ... by the simple and appalling act of taking his life" (*LJ*, 10–11). Clearly there must be a connection between the traumatic event of the spar and the more obvious central event of the novel, his jump from the *Patna*.

Conrad and Jim were both prescribed a rest cure, for in such cases of traumatic injury to the spinal cord, head, or other part of the nervous system, the victim was in grave danger of "hysterotraumatic paralysis," a form of hysteria that would account for the strange "powerlessness" experience by Conrad. The injury to the back and Jim's experience in the solitude of his cabin (before his rest cure)—"many days stretched on his back, dazed, battered, hopeless, and tormented as if at the bottom of an abyss of unrest" (*LJ*, 11)—are similar to that described by Tuke: "The names of *psychical paralysis*, . . . *paralysis by imagination* are well applied. . . . It seems probable that hystero-traumatic paralysis is, among others, formed by the following process: A man predisposed to hysteria has received a blow on the shoulder. This slight traumatism or local shock has sufficed to produce in this nervous individual a sense of numbness extending over the whole of the limb and a slight indication of paralysis; in consequence of this sensation the idea arises in the patient's mind that he might become paralyzed; in one word, through autosuggestion, the rudimentary paralysis becomes real" (*DPM*, 633). The so-called *"paralysis by imagination"* is precisely what Conrad describes in the passage immediately following upon the above description of Jim's "abyss of unrest." "The danger, when not seen, has the imperfect vagueness of human thought. The fear grows shadowy; and Imagination, the enemy of men, the father of all terrors, unstimulated, sinks to rest in the dulness of exhausted emotion" (*LJ*, 11). But when suddenly traumatized, the imagination of Jim will reassert the paralysis. Jim's jump from the *Patna* is thus a neurotic reenactment of paralytic trauma consistent with his hysteria and explains why, prior to his jump, he repeatedly feels a sense of paralysis: "It seemed to take all life out of [his] limbs" (86); "he was tempted to grip and shake the shoulder of the nearest lascar, but he didn't. Something held his arms down along his sides" (87–88); "[h]e stood on the starboard side of the bridge ... arrested, held by an invisible hand on the brink of annihilation" (97); "his feet were glued to that remote spot" (104). As Jim, in the witness box, reenacts his jump, he rises to an attitude of paralysis: "Up, slowly—to his full height, and when his knees had locked stiff ... he swayed a little on his feet. There was a suggestion of awful stillness in his face, in his movements, in his very voice" (110). Jim's jump is thus due directly to his hystero-traumatic paralysis, a hysterical medical condition that will quite literally destroy his life, which will end as he stands "stiffened" (415) to receive the fatal shot from Doramin. More generally in Conrad's fiction, this sense of motionlessness is a chronic reenactment of hysterical paralyses experienced by a range of characters.

The more obvious ways that hysteria manifests itself, at least more conspicuous to an audience reading the text a century after it was written, are Jim's emotional actions. The dinner discussions with Marlow that describe the jump are themselves fraught with emotion and end with Jim bungling his departure: "[A]t the moment of taking leave he treated me to a ghastly muddle of dubious stammers and movement, to an awful display of hesitations" (*LJ,* 155). He ends by literally running away. Similarly, when he refuses to dine with Marlow again, his emotionalism is impulsive (181), and when he quits the employ of Egström, he is so overwhelmed by emotion as he leaves that Egström reflects to Marlow, "I don't know what came over him; he didn't seem able to find the door" (196).

In many of these instances, Jim's hysteria is manifest in his stammering, hesitant vocalizations. An early and notable instance of the language of hysteria and its relation to Jim's solitude occurs during the inquiry, when Jim is alone in the witness box, offering testimony about the *Patna* incident. The tense atmosphere and Jim's anxiety are suggested by "vivid, *nervous* descriptions" that open chapter 4, handled here with greater finesse than those "opposing stresses" described in *An Outcast of the Islands.* The images are hot and cold (winds that make Jim shiver, shame that makes him burn), light and dark (the light from a window makes the inquiry panel "fiercely distinct in the half-light of the court-room" [*LJ,* 28–9] where the audience seems like staring shadows). The opposing stresses of hysterical thought and restrained speech result in Jim's stuttering, hesitant performance:

> He spoke slowly; he remembered swiftly and with extreme vividness. ... he had come round to the view that only a meticulous precision of statement would bring out the true horror behind the appalling face of things. The facts those men were so eager to know had been visible, tangible, open to the senses, occupying their place in space and time, requiring for their existence a fourteen-hundred-ton steamer and twenty-seven minutes by the watch; they made a whole that had features, shades of expression, a complicated aspect that could be remembered by the eye, and something else besides, something invisible, a directing spirit of perdition that dwelt within, like a malevolent soul in a detestable body. He was anxious to make this clear. (30–1)

In the anxiety of the moment, Jim restrains the vivid rush of sensations and details he recalls. The narrative description of those facts consists of a hysterical stacking of adjectives ("visible, tangible," and so forth) that has the opposite effect of the "meticulous precision" for which Jim strives: "He wanted to go on talking for truth's sake, perhaps for his own sake also; and while his utterance was deliberate, his mind positively flew round and round the serried circle of facts that had surged up all about him to cut him off from the rest of his kind: it was like a creature that, finding itself imprisoned within an enclosure of high stakes, dashes round and round, distracted in the night, trying to find a weak spot, a crevice, a place to scale, some opening through which it may squeeze itself and escape. This awful activity of mind made him hesitate at times in his speech" (31). The imagery used to portray his hysterical state of mind is vertiginous ("his mind ... flew round and round"), claustrophobic ("imprisoned within an enclosure"), and suggests his solitude/seclusion ("cut off from the rest of his kind"). The image of the trapped, desperate animal "dashing round and round" is itself a hysterical flow of words seeking an outlet, "a weak spot, a crevice." The hysterical piling up of noun phrases blocks his effective speech and causes Jim to hesitate in the counterdirection of vocal enervation.

Such moments of silence, of failed speech, happen often to Jim, and evidence in the text suggests that Conrad consciously ascribes to Jim symptoms of clinical hysteria, not unlike when Almayer, in *An Outcast,* suffers a hysterical fit. In *Lord Jim,* Jim is precluded from speech by the "globus hystericus" or "the choking sensation as of a lump in the throat, felt by hysterical persons. . . . It is frequently observed as one of the immediate warnings or auræ of a hysterical fit" (*DPM,* 547–8). After Jewel saves Jim from assassination, "'Jim turned to the girl, who had been a silent and attentive observer. His heart seemed suddenly to grow too big for his breast and choke him in the hollow of his throat. This probably made him speechless for so long. ... He did not tell me what it was he said when at last he recovered his voice. I don't suppose he could be very eloquent'" (*LJ,* 303–4). This hysterical moment experienced by Jim, and other characters in the novel (see Egström's speech: *LJ,* 196), occurs at moments when characters, male or female, experience extraordinary sensitivity: "[T]here are moments when our souls," Marlow reflects, "as if freed from their dark envelope, glow with an exquisite sensibility that makes certain silences more lucid than speeches" (304). The silence induced by the *globus hystericus*—that "lump in the throat" experienced in moments of intense anxiety or emotion—occurs when Jim's nervous force peaks, is checked, and deflates.

Conrad and Ford's epigraph to this chapter—"To be alone and to think, those are my terrors"—implies several things about solitude. First, to be alone in a thoughtless state or to be alone in a mental state that somehow transcends thought is not terrifying. Indeed, this sort of solitude as experienced by Singleton—a character, Conrad wrote, who "does not think"—is a balance of romantic and existential solitude that is rarely experienced by characters in Conrad's fiction.[39] Most Conradian protagonists face the terror of thought in a state of solitude or seclusion, where they confront their separation: their state of social, cultural, and mental alienation. In this sense, the Conradian solitary hero is like the writer. Within a fortnight of Conrad's reflections on Singleton, Conrad wrote to A. T. Quiller-Couch, "Writing in a solitude almost as great as that of the ship at sea the great living crowd outside is somehow forgotten; just as on a long, long passage the existence of continents peopled by men seems to pass out of the domain of facts. . . . As he writes he thinks only of a small knot of men—three or four perhaps—the only ones who matter." For the writer who confronts the terrible solitude of his existence, that terror is mitigated by the presence of a few intimate readers who connect with the author. "It is like seeing unexpectedly a friend's face in the crowd at the dock head after a two years' voyage ending with four months at sea" (*CL,* 1:430). For Conrad, water, solitary meditation, and writing were inextricably linked.

Chapter 7
Water

The sea is strong medicine.—Joseph Conrad,
A Personal Record

"Remember," Conrad wrote to his friend Ted Sanderson, "dysentery (like salmon) lurks in water: in the babbling brook and the smooth-flowing river" (*CL,* 1:239). The remark, made by Conrad in response to Sanderson's news that he had had a "tussle with [Conrad's] old enemy," dysentery, is typical of the Manichean vision of water evident throughout Conrad's fiction. If water is host to beauty and animal vitality, the sea is also a disintegrating and indifferent force of nature. Almost five years earlier, in a more genteel and literarily romantic comment to Marguerite Poradowska, Conrad reflected, "I believe that I feel homesick for the sea, the desire to look again on the level expanse of salt water which has so often lulled me, which has smiled at me so frequently under the sparkling sunshine of a lovely day, which many times too has hurled the threat of death in my face with a swirl of white foam whipped by the wind under the dark December sky" (*CL,* 1:62). The same dualism, expressing the magnificent but indifferent physical universe of late-nineteenth-century naturalism, becomes a spectrum of oppositions that characterize the world view of Babalatchi in *An Outcast of the Islands*. Turning with relief from the claustrophobic jungle to the open spaces of the Pantai River, Babalatchi senses the "unconcerned" and "selfish discourse of the river": "The brown water was there, ready to carry friends or enemies, to nurse love or hate on its submissive and heartless bosom, to help or to hinder, to save life or give death; the great and rapid river: a deliverance, a prison, a refuge or a grave" (*OI,* 214). Babalatchi's river seems the transparent expression of Conrad's "moral being" as described in the author's note to *An Outcast,* the embodiment of "contrary stresses which produced a state of immobility" (*OI,* ix).

Writing a mere chapter on the subject of water in Conrad's fiction is, of course, a daunting task, for water is everywhere in Conrad. It is the elemental force and geographical setting in the genre of his sea novels, a conspicuous presence in the epistemological clouds and fog of Conrad's jungle fiction, and in the dampness and slime of the London streets.[1] Water is the allegorical/mythical threshold of Marlow's psychological journey, the archetypal medium of Nostromo's night voyage and rebirth, and the conventional grave of the fallen woman and the sailor buried at sea.[2] Jacques Berthoud suggests that in *The Nigger of the "Narcissus"* the "sea is *itself* an historical concept. . . . An independent character in the narrative" and, as such, resists symbolization. This historical conception is a dynamic, constantly changing force that compels the men on the *Narcissus* to "register [their] existential predicament." The sea, Berthoud argues, is at once a "curse and a cure" that offers the men the paths represented by Wait and Singleton: "diseased introspection and unreflecting action."[3] If the sea is itself a historical concept that mirrors the alternative ontological paths of the men aboard the *Narcissus,* it was also a mirror for Conrad that allowed him to narrate his own medical history and his alternative activities of introspection and action. Conrad's observation that "the sea is strong medicine" (*PR,* 100) suggests the palliative effects of the ocean solitudes but also the bitterness and power of a storm at sea. Thus, in addition to serving as traditional settings, symbols, and allegorical functions, water has an idiosyncratic meaning in Conrad that grows out of his treatment at Champel and his personal view of the association between water and mental health. It is to those specific and special considerations that this chapter will attend.

The hydrotherapy at Champel would have reinforced Conrad's sense of the simultaneously beneficent and malevolent forces of water. Given that Conrad was treated for both anemia and neurasthenia, the water baths prescribed for him would have been alternately invigorating and relaxing.[4] We know from Conrad's Champel letters that he was subject to "active fire hose (twice a day)" (*CL,* 1:212), medically called the "douche" bath (in France, sometimes a *douche à la Charcot)* and described by Tuke as a "stream of water directed on some part of [the patient's body] through a hose or pipe" (*DPM*, 119). In nervous or mental patients, the flow was often directed at either the head or spine; Conrad may have also been treated on his abdomen to palliate his digestive problems. Care had to be taken not to hose the patients too forcefully or the resulting shock could produce faintness, vomiting, shivering, and, afterward, depression (*DPM*, 120). Given the potentially adverse side effects, by 1892 Tuke recommended such treatment only in the case of raving mania. Dr. Glatz at Champel apparently retained what he called the *"jet brisé"* in his arsenal of baths for those anemic-neurasthenic patients who needed both stimulating and calming baths.[5] The calming baths, in the form of a shower bath, were a "modification of the douche, being the douche delivered though a rose, so as to form a shower of water" (*DPM*, 120). The shower bath pictured in the Champel brochure could produce a temperate or warm shower, a hot, cold, or alternating hot/cold shower; what appear to be hot and cold pipes with separate valves are joined at the "rose" or shower head (see Fig. 8). Other calming baths at Champel included the temperate swimming pool and various vapor baths. Clearly, the range of nearly thirty kinds of showers and baths available would have reinforced Conrad's sense of water as something to both endure and enjoy.[6] Indeed, the various therapeutic regimens at Champel mirrored the entire spectrum of his life and his medical experience, which, as Conrad suggests in his letters and writing, is also true of maritime experience: "Everything can be found at sea, according to the spirit of your quest—strife, peace, romance, naturalism of the most pronounced kind, ideals, boredom, disgust, inspiration—and every conceivable opportunity, including the opportunity to make a fool of yourself—exactly as in the pursuit of literature" (*PR*, 109). The sea is thus a meta-experiential and metafictional mirror in which all human experience is reflected and in which the writer finds the inspiration for his or her narrative that both reflects human experience and offers a cure from any ills that may arise from it.

Destructive and Curative Elements

Potency and palliative conjoined, the sea was thus a kind of psychological medicine for Conrad, providing a cure that was fraught with danger. This paradox is most clearly articulated in the oft-examined interview between Marlow and Stein, a good place to begin this discussion because it shows so clearly the metonymic relationship in Conrad's mind between water and issues pertaining to mental health. Stein explicitly articulates this paradox in the famous passage from *Lord Jim,* where he intones to Marlow, "A man that is born falls into a dream like a man who falls into the sea. If he tries to climb out into the air as inexperienced people endeavour to do, he drowns. ... The way is to the destructive element submit yourself, and with the exertions of your hands and feet in the water make the deep, deep sea keep you up" (*LJ,* 214). Water is here both the destructive element and the medium that sustains the swimmer threatened with annihilation, keeping him up. The medical (and perhaps sexual) implications are conspicuous, for Marlow remarks that Stein's pronouncements on Jim's romanticism are like a doctor's clinical observations:

> 'I understand very well. He is romantic.'
> He had diagnosed the case for me. ... Indeed our conference resembled so much a medical consultation—Stein, of learned aspect, sitting in a arm-chair before his desk; I, anxious, in another, facing him. . . .
> 'What's good for it?' ...
> 'There is only one remedy! One thing alone can us from being ourselves cure!' (212)

The cure, of course, is to learn how to live, "how to be." And that process of learning centrally involves confession and narration, on the part of Jim, Marlow, and Conrad. The dangerous process of confronting the horror, of telling about the confrontation, is itself curative.

In his preface to *Lord Jim,* Conrad defended the narrative method of the novel against unfriendly reviewers, who complained that the novel becomes incredible due to the sheer length of Marlow's narratives: "They argued that no man could have been expected to talk all that time, and other men to listen so long" (*LJ,* vii). Conrad in his preface underestimates Marlow's individual narrations at something less than three hours, and then offers an apparently facetious defense—"that there must have been refreshments on that night, a glass of mineral water of some sort to help the narrator on" (vii)—a defense that brings to mind the narrator/Marlow in "Youth" who repeatedly asks his companions to pass the bottle of claret. But Conrad's apparently facetious remark about mineral water masks, I think, his serious intent if we consider what Conrad says elsewhere about Marlow and Conrad's relationship to his familiar narrator. In the preface to "Youth" he speaks about his relationship to his narrator: "The man Marlow and I came together in the casual manner of those health-resort acquaintances which sometimes ripen into friendships. This one has ripened. ... He haunts my hours of solitude, when, in silence, we lay our heads together in great comfort and harmony" (*Y,* x). Mineral water, indeed. The laying together of heads is quite literally a posture of intimacy assumed by men in a communal bath, tête-à-tête, or perhaps side-by-side in two chaise longues on the spa terrace, sharing a tale in solitude as part of their health-resort cure. In point of fact, the typical daily schedule at Champel-les-Bains included, between 6:00 and 8:30 in the evening, a two-hour rest in the open air on a chaise longue.[7] Conrad the health-resort patient may well have heard or delivered such lengthy post-prandial narratives. This imagined meeting between the author and Marlow, the relationship they develop, and the activities they engage in constitute what might be called the spa situation. In a number of Conrad tales, the narrative begins with men who share some social activity accompanied by a tale that is meant to serve as a maritime exemplum of "how to be," that is, how to survive the destructive element of water and stay sane.

The most extended trial of nerves immersed in the destructive element occurs in "Typhoon." Though MacWhirr's nerves are rock-solid—so much so that he fails to recognize in himself the "fatigue of mental stress" (*T,* 86)—other men aboard the *Nan-Shan* approach varying degrees of mental collapse with the "seething mad scurry of each wave" (53). The full fury of the storm "penetrated" Jukes, who is "absorbed by it" (53), but he does not suffer as much as his subordinates. One of the sailors complains the darkness "was making him crazy" (54); the seasoned boatswain feels "a nervous anxiety to get out of that bunker" (57); the helmsman, who "was anxious not to get muddled and lose control of [the ship's] head . . . suffered from mental stress" (64). The second mate shows clinical signs of mental collapse: "He had fixed himself in a corner with his knees up, his fist pressed against each temple; and this attitude suggested rage, sorrow, resignation, surrender, with a sort of concentrated unforgiveness" (64). MacWhirr relieves him of duty and later remarks to Jukes, "'The second mate's lost. . . .' ... 'Lost his nerve. ... Gone Crazy'" (67–8). Less obviously, the "Chinamen" in the hold, thrown about by the storm and fighting over the storm-tossed dollars, are described in terms that suggest an insane asylum: "Jukes convulsively opened the door. ... Rancorous, guttural cries burst out loudly on their ears, and a strange panting sound, the working of all these straining breasts. A hard blow hit the side of the ship: water fell above with a stunning shock" (62). The images of animalistic cries and panting, of writhing bodies, and tumult in a closed and claustrophobic space all suggest an image of the asylum. And water, falling from above with a stunning shock, is a feeling Conrad would have known not only at sea but at Champel. Even the imperturbable MacWhirr has to admit with verbal outrage, "Damme, if this ship isn't worse than Bedlam!'" (100). "Typhoon" is a psychodrama of the threat of insanity.

The seascape and storm of *The Nigger of the "Narcissus"* are described in the destructive terms of mental insanity. The *Narcissus* is "tossed about, shaken furiously, like a toy in the hand of a lunatic" (*NN,* 53); later "a big, foaming sea came out of the mist; it made for the ship, roaring wildly, and in its rush it looked as mischievous and discomposing as a madman with an axe" (57). As in "Typhoon," which describes the "disintegrating power of a great wind" (*T,* 40), the storm in *The Nigger of the "Narcissus"* is "discomposing" because it breaks the order and routine of the ship, it threatens death and decomposition, and it mirrors James Wait, the decomposing and phthisically insane crewman locked in his cabin. Finally, the storm threatens to discompose the solidarity of the crew. At the height of the disorienting wind, with Belfast dangling half overboard in his attempt to rescue Jimmy, the crew break down and laugh in the face of death. "In our extremity nothing could be terrible. ... Some one began to laugh, and, as if hysterically infected with screaming merriment, all those haggard men went off laughing, wild-eyed, like a lot of maniacs tied up on a wall" (*NN,* 64). The metaphor of infection is important here; it suggests the popularly held but mistaken notion that the "rise of lunacy" in England was due to the mechanism of contagious disease, and it also suggests the connection between Wait's tuberculosis, his growing insanity, and his impending death. All are metonymically inseparable from the destructive element of the sea, which, like the disease consuming the lungs and the sanity of Wait, is ravaging the ship and men. Indeed, the crew of the *Narcissus,* even more than those aboard the *Nan-Shan,* are pictured in attitudes of the insane:

[The crew] seemed to have become much thinner during our absence, as if all these men had been starving for a long time in their abandoned attitudes. ... Here and there a man stirred a little, but most of them remained apathetic, in cramped positions, muttering between shivers. ... The faces were earthy, and the dark patches under the eyes extended to the ears, smudged into the hollows of sunken cheeks. (*NN*, 74)

The two smooth-faced Norwegians resembled decrepit children, staring stupidly. ... A seaman, lashed by the middle, tapped the deck with his open hand with unceasing quick flaps. In the gathering greyness of twilight a bulky form was seen rising aft, and began marching on all fours with the movements of some big cautious beast. (74–5)

Others, alarmed at not feeling any pain in their fingers, beat the deck feebly with their hands—obstinate and exhausted. Wamibo stared vacant and dreamy. The Scandinavians kept on a meaningless mutter through chattering teeth. ... A man yawned and swore in turns. Another breathed with a rattle in his throat. ... A sudden voice cried into the cold night, "O Lord!" (77)

Now and then, by an abrupt and startling exclamation, they answered the weird hail of some illusion. ... In the dark and on all fours he resembled some carnivorous animal prowling amongst corpses. ... A man near him began to make a blabbing noise with his lips, all at once and very loud, as though the cold had broken brutally through him. (78)

This is madness, the asylum Joseph Conrad feared. The commonplace observation that the multinational ship represents a microcosm of mankind obscures Conrad's more poignant interest in narrating his own medical history: in portraying the vulnerability of the human psyche, exposed to and threatened by insanity in the "destructive element," but also in portraying the endurance of the human mind, able to restrain itself at the point of utter discomposition.

In *Heart of Darkness,* Marlow's remark that the human mind is capable of anything accounts for those who can embrace simultaneously "the civilized" and "the savage," those who can immerse themselves in the destructive element, remain calm, and survive. One might reasonably argue that in *Heart of Darkness* the jungle is the destructive element since it is a cannibalistic force that gets into the veins of men and consumes from within. But water is also a destructive element in *Heart of Darkness,* for it is the element that conveys Marlow to the "culminating point of his experience," his flirtation with madness. Commentators have often observed Marlow's admission that the river is a snake that fascinated him early in life and charms him (*HD,* 53) and lures him up the river toward Kurtz, that "enchanted princess. . . in a fabulous castle" (106). Navigating the Congo is a dangerous endeavor, physically, psychologically, and epistemologically. Marlow is prepared for the psychological difficulties by the Belgian doctor, who inquires into the mental history of Marlow's family, takes Marlow's cranial measurements, admits to an interest in alienism, and finally warns Marlow to avoid "[nervous] irritation" (58). The psychological departure of steaming upriver toward Kurtz is a discomposing entry into a melancholic state (introduced by a sentence fragment) that shades into existential angst and finally into epistemological uncertainty: "An empty stream, a great silence, an impenetrable forest. ... The long stretches of the waterway ran on, deserted, into the gloom of the overshadowed distances. ... The broadening waters flowed through a mob of wooded islands; you lost your way on that river as you would in a desert ... bewitched and cut off for ever from everything you had known once" (93). As captain of the steamer, Marlow must keep his command afloat, literally on the surface level of the destructive element that continuously impedes his progress. To lose his command, "to scrape the bottom of the thing that's supposed to float all the time under his care is the unpardonable sin" (94). The river with its maze of islands, sandbars, snags, relentless current, and shoreline intermittently lined with alarmed Africans is a source of fascinating attraction and constant anxiety for Marlow, placing him under continual temptation and psychological pressure. So too is water pressure, or more precisely steam pressure, also a constant source of anxiety for Marlow. The leaky steam pipes power his vessel but are irritable in the extreme; overloading the vertical boiler, letting it run out of water, or risking a safety valve malfunction would take a "terrible vengeance" (98). Water, like nervous force, both supports life and threatens it. Marlow's nervousness, his medical prescription to avoid irritation and exercise calm, and the fact of Kurtz's nervous degeneration all contribute to the textual building of pressure that is released just below the inner station. With the steamer at anchor, a thick fog arises and the destructive element literally engulfs Marlow and the steamer in an eerie loss of atmospheric pressure. The fog, which isolates Marlow and his crew from contact with their surroundings, has an effect similar to Kurtz's moral insanity, which cuts him loose from the earth.

The pressure from the destructive element is reversed when the steamer turns around and is borne down the river: "The brown current ran swiftly out of the heart of darkness, bearing us down towards the sea with twice the speed of our upward progress" (147). The structural pace of the novel is thus analogous to the sequences of a neurasthenic nerve storm, a building and release of pressure traceable in the novel's water imagery.

If water is a dangerous, even destructive element in the course of Marlow's travels in the Congo, it seems a palliative for the framing narrator, the auditors, and Marlow in the opening pages of the narrative apparatus, but the palliative effects wear off during the course of Marlow's unrestful story. While it is tempting, due to Marlow's low key, to focus on him as a functionary of the narrative apparatus, Marlow's "full-life" dimensions are suggested by the difference between water in Africa and the waters of the Thames. As the story unfolds, the waters above Gravesend have a healing quality for Marlow, who was brought in Africa to the brink of his grave and who must, on those luminous, calming waters of the Thames, tell his story of immersion in the destructive element. To the authorial imagination, Marlow mirrors the "health-resort acquaintances" of Conrad's Champel experience and, one suspects, reminds Conrad of himself. A number of commentators, for instance, have noted that in his various tales Marlow narrates his misogyny, his homoerotic attractions, and his fear of heterosexuality, all predispositions that have been attributed to Conrad.[8] What is conspicuous to me, given the focus of this study, is his neurasthenic aspect, apparent in his undernourished countenance, his nervousness, and the defensiveness about his masculinity. Consider the descriptions of Marlow in the opening of *Heart of Darkness:* "He had sunken cheeks, a yellow complexion, a straight back, an ascetic aspect" (*HD,* 46), and later in the novel, in one of the tale's intermissions, his "lean face appeared, worn, hollow, with downward folds and dropped eyelids, with an aspect of concentrated attention" (114). It is during this intermission—after Marlow has broken off his tale with "mustn't a man ever—"—that Marlow confesses, "My dear boys, what can you expect from a man who out of sheer nervousness had just flung overboard a pair of new shoes? Now I think of it, it is amazing I did not shed tears. I am, upon the whole, proud of my fortitude" (114). The emaciation, the admitted nervousness, the competing emotionality and desire to defend his manhood, all point to a neurasthenic personality in a male, of any sexual orientation, who wishes to avoid the social stigma of homosexuality. This explanation arguably accounts for Marlow's masculine bravado and his "typically male" demeaning comments about the female sex while he hints, consciously or unconsciously, that his visit to the Intended may be based on romantic attraction.[9]

At one time neurasthenic (and possibly hysterical) himself, Conrad knew firsthand the palliative effects of a water cure, and the narrative opening of *Heart of Darkness* suggests the calming properties of water despite the foreboding gloom of nightfall: "The day was ending in a serenity of still and exquisite brilliance. The water shone pacifically; the sky, without a speck, was a benign immensity of unstained light; the very mist on the Essex marshes was like a gauzy and radiant fabric, hung from the wooded rises inland, and draping the low shore in diaphanous folds" (*HD*, 46). The narrative situation of *Heart of Darkness* exemplifies the curative, communal "spa situation," a situation of "contrary stresses" where men gather in homosocial confraternity to endure a talk cure. They are brought together in a state of repose to dispel—through the act of unrestful narration—the ethical horrors of life, those choices of nightmare that life dishes out. *Heart of Darkness* begins thus, at dusk, when "the sea and the sky were welded together" in a "luminous space." As the waters of the flood tide wash the *Nellie* in a moment to tidal equipoise, the men "felt meditative and fit for nothing but placid staring. . . . the water shone pacifically" (45–6). To Conrad, who by 1900 had benefited from three water cures at Champel-les-Bains, this is the salutary spa situation, an antidote to the "brooding gloom" that lies over the distant metropolis. And so Marlow begins his therapeutic narrative to the meditative men, all of whom participate, if somewhat reluctantly, and strengthen their bond as they bear witness to Marlow's proto-Freudian talking cure. But if the rehearsal of Marlow's unrestful tale is palliative for him, for the primary narrator it will have an unsettling and sobering effect. His "pretty fictions" about men, ships, and empire with which he begins the narration are transformed into a terse, dark comment at the tale's end. His cure is a somber one.

The Conradian talking cure—in which mental health, water, and narration are linked—is nowhere more obvious than in "The Secret Sharer," a story about a young captain who is "distracted ... almost to the point of insanity" (*TLS*, 114), a story written by an irritable Conrad on the brink of his own nervous breakdown. This confessional tale, told by an elderly and retired sea captain, begins and ends with descriptions of water, which are an index to the mental and moral state of the narrator. The tale begins with a series of inchoate, incomplete images that delineate the transitional space 'twixt land and sea: "there were lines of fishing-stakes, resembling a mysterious system of half-submerged bamboo fences," which the narrator describes as "incomprehensible, ... crazy of aspect as if abandoned, ... suggesting ruins." The prospect of the Gulf of Siam, by contrast, is described as "the flat shore joined to the stable sea, edge to edge, with a perfect and unmarked closeness, in one levelled floor half brown, half blue under the enormous dome of the sky" (91). Water, on the one hand, reflects incomprehensibility where it adjoins land and, on the other hand, mirrors stability: the dichotomy of imagery is thus an introductory, performative trope that describes and illustrates the potential for simultaneous, dual states of mind in both the old narrator and young protagonist/captain.

Leggatt will share with the young captain a "cure" for his formlessness as a commander; he appears much as an intimate, male bather would in dim light, "something elongated and pale floating very close to the ladder. ... A faint flash of phosphorescent light, which seemed to issue suddenly from the naked body of a man, flickered in the sleeping water with the elusive, silent play of summer lightning" (*TLS*, 97). The disorganized body parts of Leggatt are finally arranged into the appearance of a "headless corpse," the phallic implications of which (mirrored by the dropped cigar) have not escaped recent commentators.[10] The re-assembled parts of Leggatt suggest that the cure Conrad speaks of here is closely related to gender identity and to the literal construction of mature masculinity (on the captain's part) and the telling about that process (on the narrator's part). The issue of mental health is further developed by Leggatt having jumped ship from a vessel where another skipper, the victim, and crew (including Leggatt) are respectively described as "out of his mind," "half-crazed," and "lunatics" and by his subsequent confinement with the nervous but otherwise sane young captain. As the young captain judges himself in relation to Leggatt's standard—which involves the competing forces of restraint and insanity in the face of the destructive element—the reader is tempted to confirm Leggatt as an ideal of spontaneous action. To do so is, I think, to fall victim to a Conradian "reader trap," for the young captain's judgment of Leggatt as an idealized double excuses the murderer's moral insanity and the young captain's close shave of Koh-ring, actions that Conrad would not condone.[11] It is guilt for that youthful moral oversight that prompts the older captain/narrator to rehearse the tale in the tradition of Coleridge's Ancient Mariner.

The narrative end game of "The Secret Sharer" is, like the overture to the tale, gauged by water. The images of water, with the young captain's increased psychic equilibrium, become highly conventionalized and aestheticized, a medium for melodramatic action, when Leggatt appears to reestablish the tale's moral equilibrium: "[W]ith no brand of the curse on his sane forehead ... [Leggatt] lowered himself into the water to take his punishment: a free man, a proud swimmer striking out for a new destiny" (*TLS*, 142–43). The aesthetic contrasts between the initial water images of confusion and the closing water imagery of melodramatic simplicity—as the ship turns from the ominous shadow of Koh-ring and Leggatt swims to his problematic freedom—indicates the ritualized, curative process of the taletelling for the guilt-ridden old captain but may also call its genuine efficacy or profundity into question.[12] For it is Leggatt, taking his punishment, who remains sane, and the captain/narrator, who escapes the immediate punishment of grounding, must relive and retell his adventure. Accepting the burden of moral insanity from Leggatt by sheering the cliffs of Koh-ring and risking the lives of his crew, the narrator lives, like the Ancient Mariner, in a state of moral guilt that he secretly shares with his audience. The promise of a simple cure for life's horrors is dangerously alluring.

Composed at the same time as "The Secret Sharer" but distinguished by Conrad as his "most deeply meditated work" (*CL*, 5:695), *Under Western Eyes* provides a more somber resolution to the same set of problems explored in the relatively comedic "The Secret Sharer." Early in the novel Razumov leads a private life in his native Russia, apparently orphaned and aloof from friends. "He was as lonely in the world as a man swimming in the deep sea. The word Razumov was the mere label of a solitary individuality" (*UWE*, 10). By the end of the novel, Razumov has endured a protracted struggle with his moral imagination and has come to the brink of nervous exhaustion that can be avoided only through the process of solitary communion with his conscience. Razumov's meditation is solitary, rationally restrained, and wedded to water. The site of his meditation and written confession is the headwaters of the Rhône River, formed by the voluminous outflow of Lac Leman. In the company of the English-language teacher, Razumov is transfixed by the destructive power of the current: "He hung well over the parapet, as if captivated by the smooth rush of the blue water under the arch. The current there is swift, extremely swift; it makes some people dizzy; I myself can never look at it for any length of time without experiencing a dread of being suddenly snatched away by its destructive force. Some brains cannot resist the suggestion of irresistible power and of headlong motion" (197).

Though it is difficult to trust the dis/ingenuous teacher, the water here is aptly characterized as a destructive element, seductive in its promise of overpowering force. But suicide is not a moral alternative for Razumov. Nor will the water of the Rhône itself serve to cleanse him in a conventionally symbolic way. The third part of the novel, which prepares Razumov for the confession with which the section concludes, begins with the objective narration: "The water under the bridge ran violent and deep. Its slightly undulating rush seemed capable of scouring out a channel for itself through solid granite while you looked. But had it flowed though Razumov's breast, it could not have washed away the accumulated bitterness the wrecking of his life had deposited there" (198). At the headwaters, Razumov confronts his action, "thinking, like a secret dialogue with himself" (198).

Though water cannot simply "wash away" the bitterness in Razumov's soul, it is the destructive element that provides him with the refuge from his fellow men as he begins writing. As Razumov approaches the Île Rousseau, as yet unaware he will seek its seclusion, he wonders at the source of his lassitude, questions his health, worries he may have a "conventional conscience," but concludes he must write by way of confession. Some ironic providence, he surmises, has led him to the "absurd island" where he could secure the "solitude" necessary for his writing. If his earlier confession to Peter Ivanovitch was hysterical, his written confession in the company of the "exiled effigy" of the sentimental J. J. Rousseau is deliberate and rational. He meditates before he begins his "scribbling." Though Razumov realizes the irony of his writing in the presence of Rousseau, the romantic confessor, the reader apprehends a deeper irony, for Razumov's "fine ear" has lulled him into a state of self-forgetfulness. Given his torment, it is surely a welcome relief. Razumov concludes that "the sound of water, the voice of the wind" are the only sounds that are truly curative, for they are "completely foreign to human passions. All the other sounds of this earth brought contamination to the solitude of the soul." Whether the reader concurs with the narrator that "in Mr. Razumov's case the bitterness of solitude from which he suffered was not an altogether morbid phenomenon" (291–2) is of course deliberately problematic. Conrad, I suspect, assigns this judgment to the English-language teacher in order to undermine, problematize, and ironically distance himself from the conclusion toward which he steers the reader. After all, we can only be thankful that Razumov moves toward moral sanity.

Water: The Rhetoric of Rest and Unrest

As Conrad struggled to write "The Sisters," a tale that might have been his third novel, he was apparently deflected from the project by Edward Garnett, who urged Conrad to follow his natural impulse to write a tale of the sea that would call upon his wealth of maritime experience and be "commercially viable."[13] The story Conrad started, "The Rescuer," proved unseaworthy and would not be finished for more than twenty years, though Edward Garnett told Conrad that in these early drafts he had "*never done better than in the part of 'The Rescuer'* which you sent me. At last you have got to the real sea."[14] Garnett reinforced his own praise with that of his sister-in-law ("who loves the sea herself") and suggested to Conrad that he may have found his true voice: "[A]ll is in your best style—& rather a new style for you—so crisp, so admirably firm and concentrated in the handling & presentation. It is really extraordinary how *real* how wonderfully *actual & vivid* your characters are in the midst of your poetry, your exquisite poetry. You have done something in drawing that storm at sea, that stands by itself in its vigour its delicacy its *magic*. I will send you some notes on various passages, notes of *encore* & still *encore*. I think the public will be hit & brought down as well as the critics."[15] Two things are notable in this passage. First, Garnett suggests that Conrad has achieved a more masculine prose style than the vivid nervousness of *An Outcast of the Islands*. The new style is vivid but more "firm" and "concentrated," more "crisp" and "real." Praise for the sparer, more masculine style suggests that Garnett detected Conrad's restraint of the hysterically active voice that covers over silence with thick description. But the conventional masculine qualities are admixed with conventionally feminine epithets of refinement: "exquisite" and "delicate." Second, Garnett's description of the more modern prose style anticipates the aesthetic that Conrad articulates at the completion of, and in the preface to,

The Nigger of the "Narcissus," the early novel that confirmed Conrad in his career as a writer and upon which Conrad was later content to let his artistic reputation stand or fall.[16]

Richard Ambrosini has argued that in writing about the sea, Conrad was able to render the complexity of his vision of the natural world, its relation to the human community, and, in so doing, create his writing voice: "[T]he sea allows Conrad's language to develop its natural cadence and verbal richness" and serves as the "central verbal device for descriptions, ironical juxtapositions, and authorial commentary."[17] The contemplation of the sea and the working crew of the *Narcissus* offered Conrad the opportunity to think about his role as an artist and his professional relation to the reading public, in other words, to define and refine the rhetoric of his fiction and to sell it—what fiction must attain to in order to appeal to a reading audience. There must be a direct appeal by the temperament of the artist to the collective temperaments of the reading audience: "Fiction—if it at all aspires to be art—appeals to temperament. And in truth it must be, like painting, like music, like all art, the appeal of one temperament to all the other innumerable temperaments whose subtle and resistless power endows passing events with their true meaning, and creates the moral, the emotional atmosphere of the place and time" (*NN*, xiii).

Conrad's reader-based rhetoric suggests it is not the author's direct discourse or "persuasion," through the heavy application of descriptors, that creates the moral and emotional power of a work of art; rather, the emotional power of a work of art is created by the artist's *appeal* to the historically situated reading audience.[18] Such a reader-based rhetoric affirms Jacques Berthoud's view "that for Conrad the sea is *itself* an historical concept," presented to the reader not as a static and culturally constructed symbol but as an "independent character," as a "stupendously impersonal reality."[19] For Conrad, the sea is an *archetrope,* an all-encompassing overarching figure that mirrors all the processes of nature, all life and death, and the human intercourse with those processes. The sea is thus (as it is for many of Conrad's characters) the perfect subject of contemplation and, by extension, the perfect object of tangency between the artist and audience. Conrad's ideal artist aspires, through the written word, to make that synaptic connection that Edward Garnett first congratulated Conrad for making in his fictional possession of the sea. "All art," Conrad writes, "must strenuously aspire to the plasticity of sculpture, to the colour of painting, and to the magic suggestiveness of music—which is the art of arts. And it is only through complete, unswerving devotion to the perfect blending of form and substance; it is only through an unremitting never-discouraged care for the shape and ring of sentences that an approach can be made to plasticity, to colour, and that the light of magic suggestiveness may be brought to play for an evanescent instant over the commonplace surface of words: of the old, old words, worn thin, defaced by ages of careless usage" (*NN,* xiii). Like the scientist and thinker, the artist must "speak authoritatively" to "our desire of peace or to our desire of unrest," not through reason and intelligence, but through the supple and colorful nuances of language, the beautiful form and resonance of a sentence that perfectly conveys sensation, which, apprehended by the audience, renders "the highest kind of justice to the visible universe" (*NN,* xi) and attains to meaning.

The urgent sense Conrad conveys in his preface to *The Nigger of the "Narcissus"* reveals his need for reassurance and encouragement; it also explains in part why the sea and water generally might provide Conrad with a verbal talisman throughout his writing career. Conrad's ideal language must approach the plasticity and color of the visual arts and the magic suggestiveness of music, qualities that echo the observations, aesthetics, even the cadence of Garnett's encouraging letter of 17 June 1896. Garnett praises Conrad's "drawing that storm at sea . . . in its vigour its delicacy its *magic*" and promises to send Conrad "notes of *encore* & still *encore*."[20] The development Garnett particularly admired in the drafts of "The Rescuer" is a new "crisp," "firm," and "concentrated" style to replace the thick appliqué of adjective and phrase characteristic of the hysterical voice in his earlier fiction. The nervous and compulsive piling on of description, the excess of nervous force followed by enervation, is replaced by a more restrained "desire of peace" and "desire of unrest." One might argue that the equanimity of Conrad's balanced phrases is a mere semantic difference, but it is also a stylistic refinement that marks a greater verbal control (restraint) and a more distanced apprehension of competing desires that earlier led to alternating verbal irritability or paralysis. The trope of rest/unrest in Conrad's fiction emerges just at a point when he moves beyond the health problems of his early adulthood and early married life, and as he exchanges thoughts of working the sea for writing professionally about it. Water, rest, and unrest thus became inextricably linked in Conrad's imagination and psyche both as an index to his mental and emotional health and as an expression of himself as an emergent writer. We can thus trace the evolution of Conrad's mature style and rhetoric by tracing the rhetoric of rest and unrest in the early fiction and how it is transformed in the later fiction.

Early in Conrad's career, the theme of rest/unrest is associated with the sea. Following the "vivid, *nervous* descriptions" of the first chapter of *An Outcast of the Islands,* the second chapter begins with an extended description of the sea that enlists an all-encompassing catalog of oppositions: "The sea, perhaps because of its saltness, roughens the outside but keeps sweet the kernel of its servants' soul. The old sea; the sea of many years ago, whose servants were devoted slaves and went from youth to age or to a sudden grave without needing to open the book of life, because they could look at eternity reflected on the element that gave the life and dealt the death" (*OI,* 12). Bitter and sweet, youth and age, life and death are all reflected in the sea, which is epitomized by its conventional association with a "beautiful and unscrupulous woman" who capriciously embodies rest and unrest: The sea is alternately smiling and angry, "a thing to love, a thing to fear," charming and cruel, "it lulled gently into boundless faith" and "then with quick and causeless anger it killed." In its continuous mutability, it is the "restless mirror of the infinite" (12). Restlessness is thus characterized by the "contrary stresses" that, paradoxically, end in paralysis, which is distinguished from "rest" or "peace." By the end of the novel, Willems's state of unrest has devolved to a state of psychological paralysis, embodied in the person of Aïssa, who defines the cruelty of his solitary confinement by Lingard. Though Willems is with his one-time lover, he is described as one condemned to "the cruel solitude of one abandoned by men; the reproachful silence which surrounds an outcast ejected by his kind" (327). Willems inhabits the borderland of insanity described as a state of perpetual unrest: "He moved on, and on; ceaseless, unresting, in widening circles, in zigzagging paths that led to no issue; he struggled on wearily with a set, distressed face behind which, in his tired brain, seethed his thoughts: restless, somber, tangled, chilling, horrible and venomous, like a nestful of snakes" (328).[21] Language of hysteria is here fully expressive, engaging the audience in a recursive reading process that mimics the rhythms of the sea through verbal repetition, verbal adornment and qualification, and the compounding of adjectives. Such rhythmic mimesis also suggests mental fatigue and the failure of mental discrimination. The final image of a nestful of snakes conjures the image of

Medusa, the daughter of Neptune, and refocuses the reader's attention on Aïssa as a prison guard for Lingard, whose flattering Malay title "Raja Laut," means "the King of the Sea" (14), that is, Neptune. Mental unrest, described in Conrad's early fiction with the language of hysteria, is thus deeply associated with the mythos and mythology of the sea.

Conrad's stories in *Tales of Unrest* all depict mental extremity, and all but one are set on water (I exclude "The Return," though technically it is set on the Thames), and in most cases water is incorporated into the matrix of ideas that includes neurasthenia, hysteria, and other forms of mental unrest. Karain, for instance, is described in "Karain: A Memory" as "haggard, as though he had not slept for weeks; he had become lean, as though he had not eaten for days. His cheeks were hollow, his eyes sunk, the muscles of his chest and arms twitched slightly as if after an exhausting contest. Of course it had been a long swim off to the schooner; but his face showed another kind of fatigue, the tormented weariness, the anger and the fear of a struggle against a thought, an idea—against something that cannot be grappled, that never rests—a shadow, a nothing, unconquerable and immortal, that preys upon life" (*TU,* 23). While medical opinion varied as to which forms of mental disease were prevalent in non-European peoples, Karain is clearly the picture of the exhausted neurasthenic.[22] He is not unlike the picture drawn by Conrad of the "sallow, sunken face and the deep-set, dark eyes of the young Cambridge man," W. H. Jacques, who read an early portion of *Almayer's Folly,* monosyllabically encouraged Conrad to finish it, and haunted Conrad's memory.[23] "The Idiots" ends in the hysterical suicide of a "lunatic," who refers to her marine grave as "Home!" (83). Kayerts, the "lunatic" of "An Outpost of Progress" set on a river, murders Carlier and, unable to compose his "disturbed nerves" (115), likewise commits suicide. "The Return" ends in a hysterical domestic dissolution characterized by the literal gnashing of teeth. Rain and wetness of London are an evocative backdrop to the dreary tale: from the "misty rain [that] settled like silvery dust on clothes" (119) in the opening pages, to Mrs. Hervy's skirts—"wet and splashed, as though she had been driven back there by a blind fear through a waste of mud" (140)—to the "clap of thunder" referred to during the tale and in the tale's conclusion (138, 186). Water here is the rain of Hemingway, a depressing rain of disaster and despair that presages the characters' "restless fate" (173). Water, too, is a metaphor that slows the pace of the already excruciatingly drawn-out confrontation "like a mist of facts thickening between" the husband and wife. Events are likened to a slow flood tide:

> He saw [the servant girl] come up gradually, as if ascending from a well. At every step the feeble flame of the candle swayed before her tired, young face, and the darkness of the hall seemed to cling to her black skirt, followed her, rising like a silent flood. ... It rose over the steps, it leaped up the walls like an angry wave, it flowed over the blue skies, over the yellow sands, over the sunshine of landscapes, and over the pretty pathos of ragged innocence and of meek starvation. It swallowed up the delicious idyll in a boat. ... It rose higher, in a destructive silence. ...
>
> He watched the rising tide of impenetrable gloom with impatience, as if anxious for the coming of a darkness black enough to conceal a shameful surrender. ... And on her track the flowing tide of a tenebrous sea filled the house, seemed to swirl about his feet, and rising unchecked, closed silently above his head. (*TU,* 181–2)

Although Conrad abhorred the tale, water, prose rhythm, and narrative pace are used here with considerable finesse to convey to the reader simultaneous impatience and maddening lethargy, simultaneous rest and unrest. Conrad would perfect this rhetorical device, which he used with astonishing effect in chapter 11 of *The Secret Agent,* the scene in which Verloc is murdered in slow motion (*SA,* 196–7).

In his later work, Conrad's rhetoric of rest and unrest is evident in water imagery, and the narrative manipulation of rhythm and pace, especially in *The Nigger of the "Narcissus," Heart of Darkness,* and "The Secret Sharer." Each of these works is a story of unrest contextualized by the framing distance of some sort of rest or calm. The contrary stresses of rest and unrest do not resolve with closure that suggests "paralysis," as Conrad notes was the case for *An Outcast of the Islands,* but rather with a problematic "calm" suggestive of restraint and healing that may sadly be superficial. Conrad's preface to *The Nigger of the "Narcissus,"* for instance, calls the novel an "unrestful episode in the obscure lives of a few individuals" (*NN,* xii). This sense of unrest is felt by the reader in Wait's ill health, in the relentless fury of the storm at sea, in the attitudes of insanity of the crew when the ship goes over (as discussed above), and in the disintegration of duty and order aboard ship. These events increase the pace of the story until the death of Jimmy and the becalming, which suggest the unrest of life followed by the rest of death. But the narration does not end with Jimmy's death and burial. Subsequently, in a narrative pattern that mimics the first sequence, the ship is driven briskly to home port. The narrative shift that occurs with this final movement from unrest to rest has long occupied commentators who seek to explain the tale's narrative technique.[24] The shift from a third-person authorial voice to first-person (and more potentially unreliable) narrator allows Conrad to unambiguously distance himself from the tale's conclusion that veers toward a rhetoric of rest, what Roland Barthes calls a "text of pleasure" that tends to adopt received ideas and confirm conventional wisdom.[25] The sentimental closure—the increasing velocity of return, the exclusion of Donkin from the company with a "bad discharge" (*NN,* 169), and the predictable words of good fellowship—all contribute to the closure of rest, calm, and peace from which Conrad apparently wished to separate the implied author and himself.

Heart of Darkness is a tale of unrest framed by a qualified rhetoric of rest. Clearly the story of Marlow's encounter with Kurtz, the European driven by social inadequacy to participate in "unspeakable rites" and the plundering "conquest of the earth," is a tale of unrest focusing on what was then seen as mental and moral degeneration. The framing mechanism that Conrad employs is nominally a "tale within a tale," but the "contrary stresses" of *Heart of Darkness,* which complicate the straightforward frame, create a kind of rhetorical palimpsest. The tale clearly begins with calm placidity due to the external narrator's glib but gorgeous "jabber," his descriptions of the Thames dusk, his received notions on the history of British commerce on the Thames, and so forth. Similarly, Marlow's narration of his lie to the Intended recounts his "real-life" attempt to put the history of Kurtz to rest and to end the tale he tells (to the Intended) in a manner that confirms received ideas about male chivalry and the preservation of female naïveté. To do this, in Marlow's view, is to end the history of Kurtz in the most humane, "civilized" way, that is, with a lie to spare the beautiful beliefs of the Intended. To distance himself from Marlow and his "tale of pleasure"—to modify Barthes's phrase—Conrad uses the external narrator to dislocate the restful ending proposed by Marlow to the Intended. Virtually simultaneous to Marlow's putting Kurtz to rest (lies have the flavor of mortality), the frame narrator's contextualizing ends the story with an abrupt rhetorical flourish of unrest: the "tranquil waterway ... flowed sombre under an overcast sky—seemed to lead into the heart of an immense darkness" (*HD*, 162). The layering of a conventional "lie of pleasure"—to modify even further Barthes's phrase—with a painful truth that disrupts the frame narrator's naïve, masculine historical sense, creates a rhetorical palimpsest upon which the author transcribes multiple voices.[26]

As suggested by my earlier analysis of "The Secret Sharer," the opening pages of which describe water as a destructive and curative element, the story begins with a narrative palimpsest of a simultaneous rhetoric of rest and unrest. If the "right-hand" view of abandoned bamboo fish traps suggest a "crazy ... aspect" of the "incomprehensible" and the left-hand view of islets suggests further "barren[ness]" and "ruins," then the sea provides a contrasting stability that, conjoined with a distant flat shore, provides little upon which the eye can "rest" in the "monotonous sweep of the horizon" (*TLS*, 91–92). These visual phenomena are mirrored in the various narrative distances in the tale: between the fictional action and the narrated event; between the protagonist captain and the narrator captain; and, most importantly, between the narrator and Conrad. The rhetorical effect is a *discordia concors* that sets up the theme of psychological doubling that the story explores. The conclusion of the tale moves toward a "resolution of pleasure," both sentimental and melodramatic. But the text of pleasure—which narrates the restful, conventional wisdom that one must take chances in order to gain something—is undermined by the restlessness implied by the narrator's compulsion to tell his tale of penance.

Rest and unrest are, in sum, suggestive, ambiguous words and themes in Conrad's life and fiction. Conrad sought rest cures or water cures that were conceived to isolate patients in solitude, away from life's troubles, and to restore them to emotional equanimity. So conceived, rest has positive associations through the calming and curative qualities of water as counterdistinguished from the restlessness and agitation of modern, nervous life. Of course, in its extremity as an opposition to life, rest is conventionally a euphemism for death (as in "final resting place") that makes death a welcome conclusion to the turbulence of life. Conrad's choice of epitaph from Spenser suggests the appeal of this conventional idea: "Sleep after toyle, port after stormie seas / Ease after warre, death after life, does greatly please."[27] But the concept of unrest also suggests the irrepressible vitality of life or the relentless agitation of approaching death that serves to reaffirm life, not the attraction of death, as suggested by the speaker of Spenser's quote, Despayre.

Chapter 8
Medical Allegory in the Later Novels

> I hardly thought of my other self, now gone from the
> ship, to be hidden forever from all friendly faces, to be a fu-
> gitive and a vagabond on the earth, with no brand of the
> curse on his sane forehead to stay a slaying hand . . . too
> proud to explain.—Joseph Conrad, "The Secret Sharer"

During Conrad's years at the Pent Farm when he traveled
overland by trap to Canterbury, he would turn uphill onto the
old Roman road called Stone Street, pass under the canopy of
trees, and ascend to a high plateau where the road straightens, as
Roman roads are wont to do. A few miles from Canterbury, on a
road now called Iffin Lane, he would have looked across farm-
land into Cartham Down and the valley of the Stour, where the
Canterbury Cathedral could be seen. Whether or not Conrad
could also see the Kent County Asylum, founded in Cartham near
Canterbury in 1875 and housing eleven hundred beds for lunatics, he was surely aware of its presence; it was situated only
about one and a half miles from Stone Street.[1] The nearest "lunatic asylum" in Kent, it is probably the particular asylum he
feared following his 1910 breakdown in Aldington. The suspicion that his wife and family physician might commit him extends not so much from unwarranted mistrust as from the power
this asylum, and the very words and concept of "The Asylum"
generally, had on his imagination.[2] The product of exaggeration
and hypochondriacal tendencies, Conrad's fears were reasonably based on his family medical history (of gout, tuberculosis,
and suspected epilepsy); sociomedical discourse on perceived
fin-de-siècle epidemiological trends of degeneration; and the

material publishing of his "innermost self" that, in effect, realized the meta-narrative of his medical history.

Conrad's medical history and fear of insanity—narrated in tropes of restraint, solitude, and water—were intimately associated with his sexuality and evolving attitudes toward gender identity. When Conrad returned from the Congo in 1890, he had been suffering from and continued to endure the symptoms of malaria and dysentery. These medical problems were complicated by a series of nervous and digestive disorders that culminated in depression; in his day, this pattern of symptoms would have been diagnosed as neurasthenia, which, complicated by continuing bouts of malaria, was known as malarial neurasthenia. This illness seriously imperiled his maritime career. During the early and mid-1890s, Conrad struggled with the knowledge that his very masculine profession was threatened by a medical disorder that was recognized (when it was recognized by English physicians) as a typically feminine disease. As a result, Conrad sought medical help from European physicians, who recognized neurasthenia as a legitimate medical complaint, accepted male neurasthenia, and treated it as such. He confessed these innermost worries to Marguerite Poradowska, a French woman writer nominally related to him, who was remarkably similar in temperament. At this time, Conrad struggled to accept his "feminine" side—his nervousness, his sensitivity, and his penetrating insightfulness—and sought the friendship of men and women (Poradowska, the Garnetts, the Sandersons) who understood and accepted his sensibilities. In mid-career, he sought the companionship and collaboration of Ford Madox Ford, himself a diagnosed neurasthenic, and Conrad thus shared the same medical problems, physician, and artistic projects with a like-minded individual. As Conrad struggled with his health, writing, and self-acceptance, he produced some of his most "nervous" fiction, which vibrates with a host of "contrary stresses." During the twentieth century, ethical critics, formalists, psychoanalytical critics, post-structuralists, and more recently critics of empire, gender, and culture have all been fascinated with these tensions that typify the transition from the Victorian to the modern. For Conrad, it was simply pain, work, and the restraint of his fears.

Conrad's breakdown in the winter of 1910 was a watershed. To Sir Hugh Clifford Conrad would write in the spring of 1910, "[I]t seems I have been very ill. . . . The horrible nervous tension of the last two years (of which even my wife knows nothing) had to end in something of the sort." Conrad's refusal to refer explicitly to his nervous breakdown by name and his supposedly withholding the truth from his wife reveals his embarrassed masculinity. His confession to Clifford that "I am ashamed to show my face to you even from a distance—in writing" confirms this Marlovian posture of male pride in the exercise of restraint and fortitude. It also anticipates Conrad's need, in his writing, to distance himself, to hide his face, to bring his fiction to a level of opaqueness via allegory. But to his old friend, Sir Clifford, Conrad also reflects interrogatively, "Perhaps it was the only way of relief?" (*CL,* 4:330). In other letters to his old friends during this period of April and May of 1910—to John Galsworthy, Edward Garnett, Arthur Symons, William Rothenstein—Conrad confesses obliquely the truth of his mental collapse. The letters testify to his need for sympathetic affirmation that he was still worthy of his friends' attentions. And they reveal a man who suspects he has narrowly escaped "general paralysis of the insane." To John Galsworthy, Conrad half joked in May of 1910 that his growing sense of confidence might be due to "incipient softening of the brain!" (*CL,* 4:329), a form of degeneration that was one of the salient pathological indications of "GPI," according to W. Julius Mickle, England's leading expert on the condition and Dr. Clifford Hackney's instructor in "Mental Disease" at University College Medical School.[3]

Whether the 1910 breakdown, as suggested by Thomas Moser, was the fulcrum of Conrad's "achievement and decline" is really a question of literary taste (or perhaps gendered literary taste). The form of the present work, focusing primarily on the fiction leading up to the breakdown and saving four post-breakdown novels for these last two chapters, suggests complicity in a masculinist reading of Conrad's life and work. But the scholarship of recent critics presents compelling arguments that Conrad's post-breakdown fiction was not a decline but rather a shift in his thematic, technical, and career interests.[4] I hope that the present work, emphasizing the nervous fiction leading up to the breakdown, is consonant with these arguments about the later fiction. In my view, the fiction of Conrad after 1910 relaxes even as it retains its complexity, reducing the mutual pressures exerted by "contrary stresses." This reduction of stress happens most clearly, I think, in the work that immediately followed upon his collapse. And, when an increasing sense of tension and conflict returns to his work in novels like *Victory* and *The Shadow-Line,* it assumes not a deeply brooding psychological form but a more aestheticized, allegorical one.[5] And, not surprisingly, the allegories recount Conrad's medical history.

The first fiction Conrad wrote after his breakdown and after revising *Under Western Eyes* was "A Smile of Fortune," a comic story that parodies the romance conventions of frustrated love before it turns to the higher satisfactions of the potato trade. Falling upon the heels of Conrad's darkest, "most deeply meditated novel" (*CL,* 5:695), the opening lines of "A Smile of Fortune" literally break like a ray of sunshine: "Ever since the sun rose I had been looking ahead. The ship glided gently in smooth water. After a sixty days' passage I was anxious to make my landfall, a fertile and beautiful island of the tropics. The more enthusiastic of its inhabitants delight in describing it as the 'Pearl of the Ocean.' ... A pearl distilling much sweetness upon the world" (*TLS,* 3). Though Conrad's nerves were still "just on the balance" (*CL,* 4:330) and though he was unable to write for more than ten minutes at a stretch (*CL,* 4:329), the story explores a ludic view of human activity that rigorously turns away from tragedy. The taciturn indifference of the "masculine" (*TLS,* 63, 65) but strangely alluring Miss Alice Jacobus derives from the deadening habit of familial restraint that represses her emotions and sensuality. These are rather typical pre-breakdown themes that would earlier have been treated quite seriously. But Miss Jacobus is a parodic rendition of Natalie Haldin from *Under Western Eyes,* a comparison that renders the narrator of "A Smile of Fortune" a comedic version of the "teacher of languages" who narrates the former novel. When Alice Jacobus's father presumably witnesses the narrator's sexual advances toward his daughter, he exacts reparation for the captain's inappropriate behavior, not by insistence on a code of moral conduct but by forcing a business deal. The obverse of *Under Western Eyes*'s extended meditation on human remorse, the novella briskly concludes with a material transaction and unexpected profits for all parties. This remarkable shift in Conrad's fictional mode is due to his insistence on a subject and tone that would keep his nerves steady, but the enforced simplicity of the tale could not be sustained in the novels Conrad would write in the coming years.

Composite Temperaments

C*hance* has been recognized as a problematic text by both its detractors and its admirers. Whether it is regarded as evidence of Conrad's declining powers or as a shift in Conrad's fictional and career interests, the novel is difficult to read (I include the sense of "painful" to read) due to the complexity of narration and to Conrad's resurrection of Charley Marlow, narrator of *Heart of Darkness, Lord Jim,* and *Youth*.[6] The Marlow of *Chance* is unlike the younger Marlow, who, in Conrad's own words, was "a most discreet, understanding man," who, "for all his assertiveness in matters of opinion ... is not an intrusive person" (*HD,* x). In *Chance,* Marlow is often indiscreet, overbearing, intrusive, even voyeuristic.[7] He is older, less affable, less restrained and reflective—in fact, at first reacquaintance, completely unlikable. Cedric Watts has shown that a "transtextual" reading of Marlow's biography helps explain the problem of reading the character, for Marlow has been shaped by his previous "human" endeavors, by the fact that he has never become engaged to a woman, and by his missed chance for love (as we know from the end of *Heart of Darkness*).[8] A transtextual reading of Marlow's health can also shed light on his attitudes and narratorial function in *Chance*. We know from *Heart of Darkness* that Marlow is nervous, has a neurasthenic aspect, and is concerned about both his mental health and his masculinity; we know from *Lord Jim* that Marlow is capable of rather intense homosocial desire; and we know from the preface to *Youth* that Marlow is "intimate" with Conrad and likened to a health-spa acquaintance. The Marlow of *Chance* is also described by the frame-narrator in terms of his physical health: "lanky, loose, quietly composed in varied shades of brown, robbed of every vestige of gloss, [he] had a narrow, veiled glance, the neutral bearing and the secret irritability which go together with a predisposition to congestion of the liver" (*C,* 32). Although this medical aside is glibly humorous, Marlow's irritability has a specific medical antecedent and explains, if not excuses, his irascible volatility. It is also in keeping with Marlow's earlier character that he should be interested in the nervous—indeed, at times, the borderland insane—Flora de Barral, who represents the quintessence of nervous "femininity." Vulnerable, passive, and dependent on the limited roles created for her by her culture, Flora fascinates Marlow, who is voyeuristically attracted to her. His inquisitive fascination

171

leads him to assume various narratorial poses and to explore his own attitudes toward gender and sexuality. It is no wonder that the end product, which can be read as a rather conventional romantic history, sold well.

As Marlow recounts Flora's history, from the lip of the quarry cliff to her happy union with Powell, he offers an astonishing array of generalities on the female sex, on gender, and on his own gender profile. Many of his comments are wildly disparate, even self-contradictory, because he seems to try out ideas, as Verloc takes his meat, "without restraint and decency" (*SA,* 190). Indeed, only half tongue-in-cheek, one might assert that he lacks restraint in the gratification of certain narratorial lusts. Chief among these is the curious juxtaposition of his ugly invective against women—he admits that "it's towards women that I feel vindictive mostly" (*C,* 150)—and an insistence of his own femininity.[9] Although Marlow is distanced from Conrad by his disagreeable opinions and by the frame-narrator who remarks that he has "seldom seen Marlow so vehement, so pessimistic, so earnestly cynical before" (*C,* 212), the Marlow of *Chance* is in certain ways as close to Conrad at this time as the more attractive Marlow was to Conrad in the earlier texts. In particular, Marlow's comments about his feminine side resonate with statements Conrad and his friends made about Conrad dating back more than a decade. Like Edward Garnett, who in 1896 reflected that Conrad was "masculinely keen yet femininely sensitive," the Marlow of *Chance* recognizes the two tendencies in himself and calls the combination a "composite temperament" (*C,* 146). The "composite temperament" to which Marlow refers is not a balanced androgynous figure that ideally combines gender traits in a unified being. Marlow is a kind of narratorial loose cannon in *Chance* who has, I believe, Conrad's amused blessing for his misogynism, his anti-feminist sentiments, and his apparently contradictory claim to a masculinity tempered by the feminine. Marlow's irascible masculinity seems a calculated defense mechanism analogous to the manful draws on his pipe in *Heart of Darkness.* But if in the earlier fiction Marlow was unable to finish the sentence "mustn't a man ever—" (*HD,* 114), Marlow in *Chance,* like the new woman of his own day, is liberated from the confines of his earlier gender roles: the mind of the later Marlow is more unrestrained, capable of anything, and quite vocal during the process of trying out ideas. He provides Conrad with an ironic commentator on the allegory of damsel and knight, unaligned with traditional gender roles: modulating from

172

a conservative, masculinist anti-feminist to a progressive, feminine anti-masculinist.

The "contrary stresses" of anti-feminism and anti-masculinism illustrate the deliberate range of Marlow's commentary. Marlow's reaction to Mrs. Fyne's feminist following begins either with a disingenuousness or a bewildered, emergent anti-feminist view: "The girl-friend problem exercised me greatly. How and where the Fynes got all these pretty creatures to come and stay with them I can't imagine. I had at first the wild suspicion that they were obtained to amuse Fyne. But I soon discovered that he could hardly tell one from the other, though obviously their presence met with his solemn approval. These girls in fact came for Mrs. Fyne. They treated her with admiring deference. She answered to some need of theirs. They sat at her feet. They were like disciples. It was very curious. Of Fyne they took but scanty notice. As to myself, I was made to feel that I did not exist" (*C*, 42). Marlow's critique of Mrs. Fyne's feminism—he later argues that "Mrs. Fyne did not want women to be women. Her theory was that they should turn themselves into unscrupulous sexless nuisances" (*C*, 189–90)—suggests Marlow's conservative understanding of the social construction of gender roles. And yet, he is no less critical about Fyne's and his own masculinity. Although the following passage may be read ironically, given Marlow's sometimes surly maleness, I would argue it should be taken straight, though behind a defensive or compensatory feint of irony. Marlow recognizes in himself "that small portion of 'femininity,' that drop of superior essence of which I am myself aware; which, I gratefully acknowledge, has saved me from one or two misadventures in my life either ridiculous or lamentable. ... Observe that I say 'femininity,' a privilege—not 'feminism,' an attitude. I am not a feminist. It was Fyne who on certain solemn grounds had adopted that mental attitude; but it was enough to glance at him sitting on one side, to see that he was purely masculine to his finger tips, masculine solidly, densely, amusingly, —hopelessly" (*C*, 146).

In Marlow's discussion of Fyne's dense masculinity, Conrad anticipates the discourse on social constructionism and essentialism that has occupied recent gender critics. Marlow adheres to an essentialist view that women are naturally women and men, men. But he also recognizes that the restraining gender roles constructed by Victorian culture circumscribe both men and women. Marlow continues, "And if by the obscure promptings of my composite temperament I beheld him with malicious amusement, yet being in fact, by definition and especially from profound conviction, a man, I could not help sympathizing with him largely. Seeing him thus disarmed, so completely captive by the very nature of things, I was moved to speak to him kindly" (*C,* 146). Marlow observes the monolithically masculine Fyne with amusement, but seeing Fyne rendered inept by his obtuse masculinity and rendered "captive by the [essential] nature of things," Marlow (as a male) sympathizes with the disarmed Fyne and speaks to him with feminine kindness. At different points in his narrative, Marlow thus inhabits opposite ends of the spectrum of attitudes toward masculinity and feminism, and through much of *Chance* he hovers at various locations above no-man's-land in the battle between the sexes.

This paradoxical regendering of Marlow is, I would argue, Conrad's exploratory attempt to come to terms with his nervous breakdown (typically a feminine problem), with issues of gender and sexuality, and with the women's movement. Having resisted for two decades coming to terms with his neurasthenia and having feared a feminizing nervous breakdown as a threat to his masculinity, Conrad finally reconciles himself to the loss of masculine restraint and works toward a compromise position in which that loss becomes a refining gain. *Chance* thus becomes a tale of male liberation that retains an essentialist position on matters pertaining to sexuality but that rejects the culturally constructed gender roles. Such roles, Conrad suggests, unduly restrain men by inhibiting the development of feminine sensibilities and imprison women by limiting their options in life. The Marlow of *Chance* thus recants the Nordaudian sentiments uttered by the narrator of *The Nigger of the "Narcissus,"* who warned against the dangers of "becoming highly humanized, tender, complex, excessively decadent, ... over-civilised" (*NN,* 139). The Marlow that Conrad creates after his breakdown has moved beyond these socially constructed masculinist views. So, too, has he moved beyond the rhetoric of restraint evident in, say, *Heart of Darkness.* There is neither a hysterical rhetoric that covers over silence with adjectival impasto nor a rhetoric of enervation that stutters into silence. Thus, the Marlow of *Chance,* conceived after the breakdown of 1910, has no need to exercise rhetorical restraint, and Conrad has moved beyond the need for a Victorian silencing of his composite personality.

Scuttling Mr. Jones

If the Marlow of *Chance* is an intimate of Conrad, particularly in his exploration of gender identity, the gallery of characters in *Victory* may be viewed as allegorical figures in a fictional diorama that depicts Conrad's medical history. Heyst and Lena, not unlike the earlier couple of Willems and Aïssa, form a "composite temperament" that represents "contrary stresses" in Conrad's own being: notably Heyst's romanticism, his aristocratic lineage, his desire for detachment and solitude; Lena's practical fidelity, her natural nobility of character, her eros and capacity for love. Heyst also exhibits rather subtle indications of various medico-psychological conditions that had long preoccupied Conrad. Davidson—who represents a banal normalcy in the novel— thinks of Heyst as a "lunatic" (*V*, 45) for whisking Lena away to Samburan and, echoing the general public sentiment, pronounces him a "queer chap" at the end of the novel (408). While these are not medical observations, Davidson's comments point to Heyst's psychological disorders, for Heyst comes close to the medical profile of "affective insanity" due to his upbringing. Although his rational faculties are perfectly normal, even acute, he is raised in a home devoid of affection and love: "The young man learned to reflect, which is a destructive process, a reckoning of the cost. It is not the clear-sighted who lead the world. Great achievements are accomplished in a blessed, warm mental fog, which the pitiless cold blasts of the father's analysis had blown away from the son" (91–2). The last day of Heyst's fictional life, Davidson surmises that Heyst's upbringing by his nihilist father "upset his head when he was young," and Heyst confides to Davidson, "[W]oe to the man whose heart has not learned while young to hope, to love—and to put his trust in life!" (409–10). He becomes "a masterpiece of aloofness" and follows his father's dying, advisory words: "Look on—make no sound" (175). His lofty superiority, his tendency toward seclusion, both become agoraphobia alternating with claustrophobia, and his passive disengagement develops into aboulia.

Although agoraphobia, claustrophobia, and aboulia are indications of neurasthenia, Heyst is clearly not a nervous personality. He is physically healthy (even a bit robust), temperamentally calm, and taciturn. With the failure of the Tropical Belt Coal Company, the world of commerce recedes, and he is left like a hermit to inhabit his island mountaintop. By remaining in

175

Samburan, he happily insulates himself from the nervousness of the modern world that is run by coal, which is, as the narrator reflects in the opening of the novel, "the supreme commodity of the age in which we are camped like bewildered travellers in a garish, unrestful hotel" (*V*, 3). Retired from his fifteen years of drifting, disengaged from the rootless, bewildering travel and the unrestfulness of the modern world, Heyst becomes "a captive of the islands" (66). Withdrawing from the world of commerce he becomes, as it were, globally agoraphobic, existing within two concentric closed spaces, one small and the other large: his small island, and, when claustrophobia sets in, a larger but still circumscribed range: "[A] circle with a radius of eight hundred miles drawn round a point in North Borneo was in Heyst's case a magic circle. It just touched Manila, and he had been seen there. It just touched Saigon, and he was likewise seen there once. Perhaps these were his attempts to break out. If so, they were failures. The enchantment must have been an unbreakable one" (7). Heyst's agoraphobia is validated by the encroachment of Jones, Ricardo, and Pedro, whom Heyst calls "the envoys of the outer world" (329). In a sense, Jones and crew have a function analogous to that of Lena, since both require some response from a man who has "refined everything away" (329, 350), whether it be the impulse to love or to shed blood.

Heyst has just enough engagement with the world of romantic impulse to "rescue ... a distressed human being" (51), Alma (which means soul). But he is neither impulsive nor willful enough to defend himself and his soulmate against the violent intruders from the world, who represent the opposite end of the nervous spectrum. Indeed, Heyst and his nemeses both appear to have some clinical disorders of the will, conditions associated with neurasthenia. Medical psychologists of the late nineteenth and early twentieth centuries, as indicated in chapter 5, recognized two dysfunctions of the will: want of impulse (aboulia) and want of inhibition (impulsiveness). The will was regarded as the faculty that has "the power to govern ourselves and to co-ordinate our actions with one purpose in view." Clearly, Heyst's will fails in his contest with Jones, and he exhibits many of the symptoms of aboulia outlined in the following textbook case: "The patients have the latent will, but they are unable to bring it into action. One of the earliest observations of this kind is due to Esquirol; it is that of a distinguished and eloquent magistrate who was perfectly well aware of his sad position. 'If they spoke to me about travelling or about looking after his business, he would answer: "I know that I ought to do it, but also that I cannot do it; your advice is very good, and I wish I could follow it, but give me will, give me that will which decides and executes. It is quite certain that I have a will only in order not to will"'" (*DPM,* 1366). The medical case history is like Heyst, who is conscious of what he should do to protect himself and Lena from the intruders but is literally powerless to will any action. His rescue of Lena from Zangiacomo's orchestra is an essentialist act of masculine attraction but an act of will that he is unprepared to sustain. His hermit-like sexlessness and passivity have allowed him to live a life in which the opposing functions of the will—restraint and impulse—have atrophied, and when he allows himself to be tempted into "action— ... the barbed hook" (*V,* 174), he finds himself unequal to demands placed upon him.

Conrad skillfully prepares a close connection between the novel's symbolic geography, its "romance" action, and its moral and medical allegories. Heyst's nervelessness and aboulia are suggested in the opening paragraphs of the novel. "There is," the narrator of the novel reflects, "a deplorable lack of concentration in coal" (*V,* 3). The very means by which Heyst has sustained his livelihood involves the mining of a soft and fissile substance counterdistinguished from the hardness of diamonds. Moveover, the business concern itself is liquidated: "The Tropical Belt Coal Company went into liquidation. The world of finance is a mysterious world in which ... evaporation precedes liquidization. First the capital evaporates, and then the company goes into liquidation. These are very unnatural physics, but they account for the persistent inertia of Heyst" (3). The dissolution of the coal company is objectively correlated in the degenerated compound and landscape surveyed by Heyst under the "flood of cold light" of a full moon: it has "the aspect of an abandoned settlement," the buildings have "vague roofs" surrounded by "broken shadows of bamboo fences" near an "an overgrown bit of road." Even the nearby volcano—a source of potentially deadly, destructive pressure—is characterized by a benign lassitude that mirrors that of Heyst: "His nearest neighbor—I am speaking now of things showing some sort of animation—was an indolent volcano which smoked faintly all day ... and at night levelled at him, from amongst the clear stars, a dull red glow, expanding and collapsing spasmodically like the end of a gigantic cigar puffed at intermittently in the dark. Axel Heyst was also a smoker" (4). The landscape—a domain of silence, inertia, and placidness— lacks natural vitality. Conrad consciously develops this entropic landscape when the romance plot and the allegorical levels co-alesce at a structural crossroads later in the novel.

Lena is adversely affected by this symbolic landscape just prior to the time when Heyst speaks of the "mystery of [his] existence" (*V,* 195) and subsequently "seduces" her. The couple moves through the claustrophobic jungle and heads toward an opening that allows a vista over the expanse of sea, a view that induces in Lena a kind of vertiginous dizziness often associated with agoraphobia:

> Heyst and Lena entered the shade of the forest path which crossed the island, and which, near its highest point, had been blocked by felled trees. ... They left it at a point where the forest was bare of undergrowth, and the trees, festooned with creepers, stood clear of one another in the gloom of their own making. Here and there great splashes of light lay on the ground. They moved, silent in the great stillness, breathing the calmness, the infinite isolation, the repose of a slumber without dreams. They emerged at the upper limit of vegetation, among some rocks; and in the depression of the sharp slope, like a small platform, they turned about and looked from on high over the sea, lonely, its colour effaced by sunshine, its horizon a heat mist, a mere unsubstantial shimmer in the pale and blinding infinity overhung by a darker blaze of the sky.
>
> "It makes my head swim," the girl murmured, shutting her eyes and putting her hand on his shoulder.
>
> Heyst, gazing fixedly to the southward, exclaimed: "Sail ho!" (189–90)

The romance story of Lena and Heyst will soon climax in one of Conrad's most frankly sexual encounters, graphically implied by a rolling cork helmet. The allegorical love story, at this juncture, converges with the moral and medical allegories when Heyst sights the sail of the boat that will bring Jones and his men to Samburan.

The allegorical dimensions of plain Mr. Jones, Ricardo, and Pedro are inescapable. Heyst's reading of the intruders as a moral allegory—Jones an "evil intelligence," Ricardo an "instinctive savagery," and Pedro a "brute force" (*V,* 269)—prompts an allegorical reading that focuses on the moral level of the tale that is satisfying because of its clarity, elegance, and consistency. But a less obvious medical allegory is also at work in the text, related to and hosted by the moral allegory: If Heyst represents the medico-psychological disorder of aboulia (lack of will), then Pedro, Ricardo, and Jones are a study in the medico-psychological problem of impulsiveness (lack of restraint). The trio are described to the reader as "nerveless[]," "irrational," and "exhausted[]" (227–28) and are introduced by Ricardo bludgeoning Pedro as he greedily attempts to drink from the brass water tap that Heyst opens for them. Ricardo reflects, "He has no restraint, no restraint at all. ... That's what will happen to him in the end, if he doesn't learn to restrain himself" (233–34). Ricardo feels that his role as a subordinate of Jones creates a kind of "restraint" (219) that operates until he can no longer resist the temptation presented by Lena. Until that point, "the necessity of prudence had exasperated his self-restraint," and, unused to such a "prolonged effort of self control," he finally succumbs to his predatory sexual impulses: "The self-restraint was at an end: his psychology must have its way. The instinct for the feral spring could no longer be denied. Ravish or kill—it was all one to him" (284–8). Known to Ricardo as the "governor" (284), Jones is a master of restraint who looks upon his "follower's perplexities with amusement concealed in a death-like composure" (274). But Jones is unwilling to submit to the restraints of civilization, and, though apparently born a gentleman like Heyst, he forfeits his social station rather than conform to the expectations of his social class. To Lena, Heyst relates Jones's history as a social outcast, "having been ejected, he said, from his proper social sphere because he had refused to conform to certain usual conventions" (317). Those conventions, the reader gathers, are sexual and psychological, and Jones has been forced or chooses to operate on the margins of the globe, a willed version of Kurtz who has entirely "kicked himself loose of the earth" (*HD*, 144). The contrary stresses of governing restraint and unrestrained impulse, of mounting nervous pressure and deflating inertia, are the hallmarks of the neurasthenic personality. Conrad's comments about plain Mr. Jones are perhaps the most intriguing reflections in his author's note to *Victory*: "I will say nothing as to the origins of his mentality because I don't intend to make any damaging admissions" (*V*, xii). Though the physical being of Mr. Jones is presumably based biographically on an indolent and emaciated gambler Conrad met in the West Indies in 1875 (xii), the origin of Jones's mentality is apparently Conrad himself, otherwise the "damaging admission" of his origin would presumably be a "damaging accusation" against some other person. Though Conrad claims no affinity to Jones's sexuality or gender identity, it is hard to wholly separate "mentality" from sexual orientation or gender ideology. But if Mr. Jones's mentality originates with Conrad, Conrad also snuffs out the character at the novel's end.

Like the Marlow of *Chance,* Jones is clearly antagonistic to women, but unlike the Marlow of *Chance* whose misogynism is ideological, the misogynism of Jones is personally visceral and sexual: "They give me the horrors," Mr. Jones declares about women. "They are a perfect curse!" (*V,* 102). Because Jones reviles women who compete for the attentions of his secretary, Ricardo, the reader is meant to understand that Jones is homosexual, with "his long, feminine eyelashes" (102) and "his delicate and beautifully pencilled eyebrows" (111); significantly, Jones loses his restraint in a "dance of rage" and insane laughter when he realizes Ricardo is "on the scent" of a woman (388–9). But if Jones is the most stereotypically homosexual of Conrad's characters, he is also the most obviously neurasthenic, though this malady has escaped critical attention. Jones is introduced to the reader as possessing a "handsome but emaciated face. ... His body was long and loose-jointed; his slender fingers, intertwined, clasped the leg resting on his knee, as he lolled back in a careless yet tense attitude" (98–9). In a later scene he is described closing his "sunken eyes, as if exhausted. ... In this pose, his long, feminine eyelashes were very noticeable, and his regular features, sharp line of the jaw, and well-cut chin were brought into prominence, giving him a used-up, weary, depraved distinction" (102). Ricardo comments on Jones's episodes of neurasthenic exhaustion, telling Schomberg, "the governor is subject to fits— ... Regular fits of laziness, I call them. Now and then he lays down on me like this, and there's no moving him" (149). If *Victory* can be read as Conrad again narrating his medical history, then the ending of the novel is a ritualistic attempt to put the specter of misogyny and neurasthenia to rest and, at the same time, to resurrect his faith in love. The pessimism of the ending thus seems less aimed at human nature than at the world and indifferent universe in which those humans must operate.

Cheating Contagion, Denying Heredity

Conrad's victory over the specter of neurasthenia was sadly temporary. After the publication of *Chance* and the completion of *Victory,* Conrad experienced the return of despondency and enervation occasioned by creative sterility, the onset of war, and uncertainty about his son Borys's future. But with the war, Borys's coming of age, and the writing of *The Shadow-Line,* the convergence of personal and public history would move Conrad to issues he would again allegorize in his fiction. *The Shadow-Line* is about taking command and specifically about a new generation of command, but just as surely, the novel is about illness, enervation, paralysis, and the will to avoid contagion. While in the author's note, in the dedication, and in the opening pages of the narration Conrad implies that this tale of the narrator's first command was written as an allegory for the war effort of a new generation of soldiers, the history of the story's composition belies this implication, for the story was sixteen years in its generation.[10] It was conceived within a week of Conrad's finishing *Heart of Darkness* (the story about empire and Marlow's first command) when Borys Conrad, to whom *The Shadow-Line* is dedicated, was just one year old. When I suggest that the novel marks a convergence of personal and public history, I mean that *The Shadow-Line* is about war but that it is also about the communication or transmission of infectious disease and, to Conrad, about the generational transmission of disease. It is also a novel in which Conrad reflects most consciously on the problem of becoming modern.

Like *The Nigger of the "Narcissus," The Shadow-Line* is about infectious disease and maintaining sanity in the face of mortality. Indeed, the novella's narrated events unfold from an irrational, "mad" action: "[F]or no reason on which a sensible person could put his finger I threw up my job" (*SL,* 4). When the narrator recounts his act of youthful folly, he notes that Captain Kent stared at him, wondering "what ailed" him (5). The second engineer, a "fierce misogynist," speculates that the instinct to marry must be the basis of his freakish action, and the chief engineer, a "confirmed dyspeptic" with a "deranged liver," offers the narrator a "certain patent medicine in which his own belief was absolute" (6–7).[11] Neither the woman-hater nor the irritable dyspeptic can offer an explanation for what ails the narrator, and well into the narration Captain Giles reflects that "everybody in the world is a little mad." To the narrator's response—"You make no exceptions?"—Captain Giles pointedly asserts, "Why! Kent says that even of you" (42). Thus, it is fitting that the narrator should take his place in the line of command next to his predecessor, whose "brain," according to the first mate, "began to go a year or more before he died" (124). Indeed, the story offers a medical allegory of the challenge of modernity from Conrad's perspective: of resisting nervous dysfunction and continually bringing oneself back from the brink of collapse.[12]

When the narrator, at the recommendation of Captain Giles, approaches the "deputy-Neptune" to apply for his first command, he is understandably nervous and edgy. "When I had come within range," the narrator admits, "he saluted me by a nerve-shattering: 'Where have you been all this time?'" And, as Captain Ellis signs the appointment agreement, the narrator's "head swam a little" and his brain feels like a "seething cauldron" (*SL*, 32, 34). Moreover, he is transported by an impatient steamer captain, who embodies "the spirit of modern hurry," to his new command, a traditional sailing ship, the sight of which fills him with a feeling of contentment: "[T]hat feeling of life-emptiness ... lost its bitter plausibility, its evil influence, dissolved in a flow of joyous emotion" (49). The ship thus becomes a testing ground for the narrator's capacity and a cure for the modern sense of futility epitomized by steamships: "She was a high-class vessel, a harmonious creature in the lines of her fine body, in the proportioned tallness of her spars. Whatever her age and her history, she had preserved the stamp of her origin. She was one of those craft that in virtue of their design and complete finish will never look old. Amongst her companions moored to the bank, and all bigger than herself, she looked like a creature of high breed—an Arab steed in a string of cart-horses" (49). But like an Arab steed she is high-strung. He notices the "fine nerves of her rigging," and the legation doctor's examination of the crew reveals ominous symptoms that correlate their health with that of the ship itself: "He looked after the ship's health, which generally was poor, and trembling, as it were, on the verge of a break-up" (66). Members of the crew, one by one, fall victim to the miasma of the climate, "an invisible monster [that] ambushed in the air, in the water, in the mud of the river bank" (67). In his use of the climate and military metaphors, Conrad suggests that all moderns—whether the men and women on the street in unwholesome, urban London, the merchant seaman steaming under the pressure of time schedules, or the soldier in the trenches who lives in fear of ambush—all function in the borderland of nervous collapse.

Initially, the new captain hopes to escape the contagion of anchorage and, longing for departure, reflects that "the sea was now the only remedy for all my troubles" (*SL*, 71). But once at sea his troubles only multiply, and the balance of *The Shadow-Line* seems a revision of "The Secret Sharer." Like the narrator of

"The Secret Sharer," the narrator of *The Shadow-Line* feels "as if [he] were going mad" (93). He attributes this feeling to "the intense loneliness of the sea [that] acted like poison on [his] brain" (92) and that creates "the creeping paralysis of a hopeless outlook" (93). These feelings deepen: "[T]here were moments when I felt, not only that I would go mad, but that I had gone mad already; so that I dared not open my lips for fear of betraying myself by some insane shriek. Luckily I had only orders to give, and an order has a steadying influence upon him who has to give it" (100–1). Many details of the text specifically invite a comparison with "The Secret Sharer": during the storm and dual manning of the ship, the captain is wearing "only [a] sleeping suit" (114); the captain and Ransome are "the only two fit men in the ship" (123); Ransome acts strenuously "for some distinct ideal" (126); and, near the end of the story, the captain "hate[s] the idea of parting" with Ransome (129). Many of these comparisons, however, also point to the differences between the two stories.

First, while *The Shadow-Line* is not as morally, psychologically, or sexually suggestive as "The Secret Sharer," it is allegorically more complex in its development of well-known Conradian themes. Conrad introduces his familiar "first command" motif most pointedly when the narrator contemplates himself in his new capacity, as if addressed by the "composite soul" of command: "'You too!' it seemed to say, 'you, too, shall taste of that peace and that unrest in a searching intimacy with your own self—obscure as we were and as supreme in the face of all the winds and all the seas, in an immensity that receives no impress, preserves no memories, and keeps no reckoning of lives'" (*SL,* 53). The nature of command represented by a "composite soul" at once suggests anonymity and confraternity, but it also suggests a divided if not fragmented being. The commanding soul will know both peace and unrest, those "contrary stresses" that embody the life at sea, but the sum of those human experiences will leave no lasting impression in the natural arena of their action. The narrator realizes, like Keats, that he is one "whose name is writ in water" and, like Marlow, that the most you can hope for is some knowledge of yourself (*HD,* 150).[13] That is what the narrator of *The Shadow-Line* searches for in his mirrored image:

> Deep within the tarnished ormolu frame, in the hot half-light sifted through the awning, I saw my own face propped between my hands. And I stared back at myself with the perfect detachment of distance, rather with curiosity than with any other feeling,

except of some sympathy for this latest representative of what for all intents and purposes was a dynasty; continuous not in blood, indeed, but in its experience, in its training, in its conception of duty, and in the blessed simplicity of its traditional point of view on life.

It struck me that this quietly staring man whom I was watching, both as if he were myself and somebody else, was not exactly a lonely figure. He had his place in a line of men. (*SL*, 53)

The mood of this passage is quite different from the general tone of "The Secret Sharer." There is no pervading sense of guilt, ago-nized relief in catastrophe averted, or melodramatic heroism at the tale's conclusion. *The Shadow-Line* allows a sense of fra-ternal belonging and a quiet but inevitable sense of futility that marks its increasingly amoral modernity. Indeed, the narrator of *The Shadow-Line* does not dwell on his youthful error in judg-ment (bringing Burns along as first mate) that endangers his first command.[14] Rather, there is a morally neutral self-assurance in the rhetoric of restraint employed by the narrator as he stares back at himself with "the perfect detachment of distance" and yet with curiosity—which implies that he does not yet quite know himself—as if "he were somebody else." And so, like the narrator of the earlier tale, he will need to measure himself against those comparable others but will do so in an allegory that avoids heavy moralizing.

The two others that serve as potential defining doubles in *The Shadow-Line* are Ransome and Burns. Ransome is rather obvi-ously the more appealing alternative: "Even at a distance his well-proportioned figure, something thoroughly sailor-like in his poise, made him noticeable. On nearer view the intelligent, quiet eyes, a well-bred face, the disciplined independence of his manner made up an attractive personality" (*SL*, 67–8). Although Ransome is held hostage by some disorder of the heart, which could result in imminent death, he is able to function effectively by exercising a calm "restraint he put on the natural sailor-like agility of his movements" (73). Indeed, Ransome's restraint is like the *"calme"* advised by the Belgian doctor who examines Marlow and councils him to avoid irritation in the tropics (*HD*, 58). Ransome "was the only one the climate had not touched—perhaps because, carrying a deadly enemy in his breast, he had schooled himself into a systematic control of feelings and move-ments" (*SL*, 68). His restraint affords him a degree of resistance to various contagious threats in the tropics; thus, allegorically, he opposes the figure of Burns (an appropriate name for someone

184

consumed by malarial fever), who "gave up and went to bed in a raging fever without saying a word to anybody." The narrator specifically reflects that Burns's illness is due as much to a failure of the will (that is, lack of restraint) as it is to exposure to infection: "I believe he had partly fretted himself into illness; the climate did the rest with the swiftness of an invisible monster ambushed in the air, in the water, in the mud of the river bank. Mr. Burns was a predestined victim" (*SL*, 67). The potential doubling between the narrator and either of his two companions, Burns or Ransome, is an allegory that must have expressed for Conrad the personal conundrum of how one faces disease and mortality. If at first the answer seems obvious, Conrad undermines that easy moral with the novella's ending: Ransome retreats, "in a blue funk about [his] heart" (133), on his way to the hospital; Burns— though he is last seen "like a frightful and elaborate scarecrow set up on the poop of a death-stricken ship, to keep the seabirds from the corpses" (130)—convalesces. Perhaps Conrad's messenger is Captain Giles, who observes, "Precious little rest in life for anybody. Better not think of it" (132).

Like the novella's dedication, which is both personal and public, the medical history narrated in *The Shadow-Line* mirrors the Conrad family personally but also reflects the more public history of disease and World War I. In *The Shadow-Line,* once malaria became established, it swept through the crew, who become faceless victims, and, like the casualties of war, their lives leave no impress and their deaths are untold: "That disease played with us capriciously very much as the winds did. It would go from one man to another with a lighter or heavier touch, which always left its mark behind, staggering some, knocking others over for a time, leaving this one, returning to another, so that all of them had an invalidish aspect and a hunted, apprehensive look in their eyes; while Ransome and I, the only two completely untouched, went amongst them assiduously distributing quinine. ... But all spring was out of their limbs, and as I looked at them from the poop I could not keep from my mind the dreadful impression that they were moving in poisoned air" (*SL*, 85–6). The dosing with quinine clearly indicates that the men are being treated for malarial fever, and the ravaged look in the eyes of the men and their evident emaciation—Burns, for instance, is described as having "wasted fore-arms" and "fleshless claws" (69) for hands—suggest that the crew also develops a collective neurasthenic aspect. The fact that the men are described as moving about exhausted, in poisoned air, clearly associates disease with the gas of World War I. This convergence of medical allegories is almost surely conscious on Conrad's part, when one considers that the sheer number of men suffering from neurasthenia and shell shock and the fact that the "exciting causes" of neurasthenia among soldiers included a substantial number of cases of malaria and other tropical diseases.[15] These medical issues would become directly personal to Conrad, who had suffered from malarial neurasthenia and, as he began writing *The Shadow-Line,* surely worried about his nervous son at the front lines.

If Conrad worried about his health due to the Korzeniowski and Bobrowski medical histories, he was also keenly aware that the medical history he inherited might likewise be passed on to his own progeny. Borys's months-long episode of poor health in 1906–7—culminating in his whooping cough, measles, and rheumatism in Montpellier and Geneva—must have reminded Conrad of his own ill health as a child. Indeed, when Conrad described the boy's illness, he would sometimes shift from a discussion of Borys's illness to his own health, from one sentence to the next, without transition: "He's under treatment now here [Montpellier]. Morning frictions, salt baths, medicines, special diet. It's rather horrible. He's anemic and very nervous. Pulse constantly near 100, but he looks much more like himself. I am well now. I felt extremely seedy for 10 days or so" (*CL,* 3:432). The decision for both Borys and his father to take a water cure at Champel in 1907 further underscores their medical similarity, which would lead Conrad to express concern in 1924 about the possible return of "neurasthenic symptoms" in Borys.[16] It is possible that Conrad here refers to the nervousness of 1907, but it is more likely that he refers to Borys's nervous problems that developed as a result of shell shock in October of 1918.

As early as the winter of 1915, just as Conrad started writing *The Shadow-Line,* doctors of the Royal Army Military Corps (RAMC) serving in France began seeing a high number of cases of mental breakdown among the victims of the war, in some locales as high as forty percent of the casualties. The symptoms noted were similar to those cases of neurasthenia and hysteria where traumatic events (such as railway accidents) were the exciting cause. The wartime disorder received the name "shell shock" in a February 1915 article in *The Lancet.* During the course of the calendar year, disused lunatic asylums, spas, and other institutions were transformed into hospitals for shell-shocked soldiers, whose numbers swelled to eighty thousand by the end of the war.[17] Borys Conrad was one of those casualties. He describes the experience and treatment in his memoir:

> I became partially buried, with several others, by a salvo of high explosive shells among which the enemy had included several gas shells. The effects of the gas and my temporary interment put an abrupt end to my participation in the War and remained with me for several years. In fact, in a minor degree, they remain with me to this day [1970]. . . .
>
> After three or four weeks in the Rouen Hospital I seemed to be fully recovered physically, but my nervous system was in a very bad state and I was transferred to a "shell-shock" hospital—officially called a Neurological Hospital—in South London which did me no good at all.[18]

In Borys's day, physicians may have told him that mere rest would not cure him due to his family predisposition to neurasthenia. In *Psychoses of the War: Including Neurasthenia and Shell Shock,* Dr. H. C. Marr (also a lieutenant colonel in the RAMC), found that while only two percent of soldiers engaged in battle become neurasthenic, he found that eighty percent of those cases have "a family history of nervous or mental disease" or a previous history of nervous breakdown.[19] Conrad's nervousness had been passed on to his son.

The Shadow-Line—conceived in the week following the completion of *Heart of Darkness,* maturing in Conrad's imagination as Borys Conrad grew, and written in the war years when tens of thousands of casualties suffered from traumatic psychological disorders—is itself a kind of psychodrama. As the dedication suggests, *The Shadow-Line* is offered by Conrad to a whole generation of young men who would know from their military experience the stress, enervation, and sense of paralysis with which Conrad was afflicted all of his adult life. It is also a father's hope that his son—who bore the double burden of a weak, nervous constitution in a combat situation that would try the nerves of all but the most imperturbable—could escape paralysis, gain command of the situation, and remain free of the suffering that his father endured. The layers of allegory do not end there, for the novella is also about the modern historical moment: about moving from the era of the sailing ship into the modern age of the steam ship.[20] And, while the novel laments the passing of the age of sailing ships, it is also a confrontation of the realities of modernism, with its high-pressure pace, its threat to the nerves, and its resolve not to look back. In some ways, Ransome's departure is a sad recognition that "the heart" has gone out of sailing the seas, and unlike Leggatt's departure in "The Secret Sharer" Ransome's departure holds out little hope of a healing cure. What is available to us in the modern world, Conrad seems to be saying, is unrestful labor repaid by a tenuous grip on sanity and the certainty that few will remember our endeavors.

Conclusion
The Heart in Its Perplexity

The modern malady of love is nerves.—Arthur Symons, "Nerves," from *London Nights*

During the winter of 1921, Conrad visited the island of Corsica to absorb its ambience for his "Mediterranean novel," *Suspense,* and to provide a comfortable climate for his wife Jessie's convalescence from yet another knee surgery. On Corsica, the Conrads visited the birthplace of Napoleon Bonaparte and survived encounters with the bandit Romanetti, and Conrad contemptuously declined to read Freud. While staying in Ajaccio, Conrad struck up an acquaintance with Henri-René Lenormand, a young French playwright who admired not only Conrad but Dostoievski and Freud as well. Before Lenormand left Corsica for Paris, Conrad returned the two volumes of Freud that Lenormand had lent him, commenting about the unread books with "scornful irony."[1] The reasons for Conrad's continued hostility to Freud are surely complex and, in this particular instance, may have been exacerbated by Lenormand's coupling his admiration for Conrad with an enthusiasm for Freud and the Russian author. But whatever Conrad's reasons, his disdain for Freud in the 1920s seems surprisingly Victorian. In fact, the relevance of psychoanalysis to various facets of Conrad's family life had increased during the war years, and Conrad's exploration of psychosexual themes in his fiction had become increasingly overt late in his career and, one suspects, self-conscious.

Given the high incidence of war neuroses among British casualties and then the gassing and shell shock of his son Borys near the end of the war, it would be surprising if Conrad were not aware of, and personally interested in, the evolution of treatment for such casualties. As the war dragged on in 1916–7, British medical personnel increasingly believed that the Weir Mitchell rest cure, which was the standard treatment for neurasthenia in women, was ineffective and inappropriate for the male officers suffering from neurasthenia or for an enlisted man exhibiting shell shock.[2] The alternative treatment developed by doctors was aversion therapy, where soldiers were placed into a "treatment" environment to which they were individually hostile, the idea being that such aversion would accelerate the healing process. (One suspects that this approach was really a punishment for those soldiers who failed to keep their nerves steady.) Dr. W. H. R. Rivers devised a more humane alternative to this therapeutic model. An early Freudian, Rivers developed a talking cure that involved discussion rather than repression of traumatic war experience in order to further what he called "autognosis," or the self-knowledge that would enable a patient to understand his fears and more quickly recover.[3] Dr. Rivers's most famous patient, Siegfried Sassoon, had been diagnosed neurasthenic as a pretext to cover for his "Soldier's Declaration": Sassoon's letter of protest sent to his commanding officer, a letter that, without such a medical diversion, might have resulted in his court-martial. A year after Sassoon entered treatment with Rivers in the Craiglockhart Military Hospital near Edinburgh, Borys Conrad was gassed in France and hospitalized for shell shock in Rouen; shortly thereafter, in November of 1918, Conrad had plans to meet with Sassoon. While there is no reason to assume that Conrad agreed to meet with Sassoon to better understand how shell shock might manifest itself and how to medically manage the condition, if Conrad and Sassoon did meet, wartime experiences and their effect on the nervous system would have been a subject of mutual interest.[4]

Given these events in his family life, I suspect (for reasons I will explain) that Conrad was already moving toward a general awareness of the need for psychotherapy to treat lingering war neuroses, even if he was still unprepared to read and embrace Freudian theory. Following Borys Conrad's initial treatment in Rouen and subsequent therapy at the Neurological Hospital in South London, he continued to suffer from neurasthenic episodes. While hunting near Oswalds in the early fall of 1919, Borys experienced symptoms of shell shock consistent with the classic agoraphobic symptoms of neurasthenia: "I was suddenly overcome by a sensation of exposure to great danger; I felt naked, defenseless and terrified, but eventually succeeded in pulling myself together sufficiently to stagger on to the boundary of the field where I sat down under the shelter of the hedge. I have no idea how long I remained crouching there in a state of semi-consciousness."[5] Borys resolved to say nothing to his parents about this experience and apparently declined to tell the Conrad family physician (whom he disliked) about his neurasthenic episode, consulting instead his brigade medical officer who was then practicing in London.[6] But Conrad must have recognized Borys's precarious health, for Borys reports that "for some weeks I had a dread of being alone and a great reluctance to cross a road or any open space unaccompanied."[7] So too, Conrad must have recognized that the physiologically based, hydro- and electrotherapies to which he was accustomed in the treatment of his own neurasthenic symptoms were inadequate for the treatment of Borys's generation. Such a growing awareness in Conrad is suggested by *The Arrow of Gold,* a novel that was written from the summer of 1917 through the summer of 1918 and published shortly before Borys experienced his neurasthenic attack. *The Arrow of Gold* at once retains many of the characteristic preoccupations of Conrad's earlier fiction, but, as a novel in which war and psychological neuroses serve as the backdrop for a love story, it marks a new, overt portrayal of the connection between hysteria and psychological repression.

Vestiges of pre-Freudian psychology are clearly evident in the atmosphere of *The Arrow of Gold,* set during Marseilles's carnival time, an atmosphere that repeatedly strikes the narrator, early and late in the novel, as reminiscent of "Bedlam" (*AG,* 7, 13, 257, 263). Virtually all of the major characters in the novel are described in varying degrees of nervousness or insanity: Blunt is "slim and elegant . . . a mere bundle of nerves," assumes a "dandified air—nervously" (58), is plagued by "sleeplessness" (123), and is diagnosed by the local physician as a victim of "nervous over-strain" and a "restless brain" (327). Doña Rita is introduced as having "physical perfection in beauty of limb and balance of nerves" (67), but the reader soon witnesses her agoraphobia (103), her claustrophobia (148), and her hysterical actions (204, 306); Monsieur George is, in Rita's company, afflicted with sympathetic claustrophobia (148), "nervous start[s]" (151), "some sort of disease akin to melancholia" (163), exhaustion and fatigue (218); in Ortega's company, M. George has "a sort of nervous fit" (277). Ortega himself is described as an "abominable lunatic" (287). Indeed, during the climactic scenes of the novel—when M. George, Doña Rita, Therese, and Señor Ortega are all in Captain Blunt's house, M. George thinks "there was nobody completely sane in the house" (308). The house itself, owned originally by Allégre (meaning "lively") and then by Captain Blunt ("bluntness" was a medical term sometimes used to describe decreased excitability or paresis [*DPM,* 843]), is peopled with characters that mimic the "contrary stresses" of neurasthenia. Indeed, the phrase "Blunt vibration" occurs repeatedly in the novel to suggest such contrary stresses on the nervous system (*AG,* 175, 178–9). Significantly, Allégre equipped the house with a *salle de bains* for hydrotherapy, which contains "a bath, and a complicated system of shower and jet arrangements" (285–6), which is later described more mysteriously: "Along one of the walls there was the whole complicated apparatus of solid brass pipes, and quite close to it an enormous bath sunk into the floor. The greatest part of the room along its whole length was covered with matting and had nothing else but a long, narrow leather-upholstered bench fixed to the wall. And that was all" (308–9). The room was clearly designed for hydrotherapy but might also serve as a seclusion room in which the nervous inhabitants of the house might be locked and passively restrained. This bath area is adjacent to the setting for the novel's final scene of threatened violence and hysterical paralysis. Many of the preoccupations, characters, and themes of *The Arrow of Gold* thus seem consistent with Conrad's earlier themes of neurasthenia, hysteria, and the fear of madness.

Yet there are significant differences in the way Conrad, in *The Arrow of Gold,* presents his psychological material, differences suggesting that Conrad sensed the inadequacy of enumerating the old themes he once used to narrate his medical history and that he wished to make *The Arrow of Gold* more overtly psychological. Robert Hampson has convincingly shown how Conrad develops the psychology of Rita in Freudian terms, applying Freud's ideas on hysteria to show how the abusive relationship between Ortega and Rita produces the hysterical repression of sexuality in Rita's adult life. His argument is worth summarizing here. Hampson suggests that Rita's response to adult sexuality—her stiffening followed by complete passivity—stems from the early experience in her Basque childhood, when, as a goatherd, she was molested by her older cousin, Ortega: "He got up, he had a switch in his hand, and he walked up to me, saying, 'I will soon show you.' I went stiff with fright; but instead of slashing at me he dropped down by my side and kissed me on the cheek. Then he did it again, and by that time I was gone dead all over" (*AG,* 112). Rita's early traumatic experience of Ortega's repeated attacks are ritually reenacted in a symbolic setting:

> "If I caught sight of him at a distance and tried to dodge out of the way he would start stoning me into a shelter I knew of and then sit outside with a heap of stones at hand so that I daren't show the end of my nose for hours. He would sit there and rave and abuse me until I would burst into a crazy laugh in my hole; and then I could see him through the leaves rolling on the ground and biting his fists with rage. Didn't he hate me! At the same time I was often terrified. I am convinced now that if I had started crying he would have rushed in and perhaps strangled me there. Then as the sun was about to set he would make me swear that I would marry him when I was grown up. ... Oh, I swore ever so many times to be his wife. Thirty times a month for two months. I couldn't help myself. It was no use complaining to my sister Therese. When I showed her my bruises and tried to tell her a little about my trouble she was quite scandalized. She called me a sinful girl, a shameless creature." (112–3)

Hampson argues that Rita's repressed sexuality as an adult stems from possible sexual assault and her early confusion as to whether Ortega intended to do her violence or to make love to her.[8] It surely accounts for her agoraphobic fear for personal safety when she leaves confined space (103) and enters the world in which Ortega, the threat of brutal male sexuality, roams.

The emboldened psychologicality of *The Arrow of God* is apparent in Conrad's rhetorical gestures and parapraxes: his silent inclusions and telling omissions. On the one hand, Conrad quietly includes the hydrotherapy apparatus of Allégre/Blunt in the symbolic landscape of Bedlamite Marseilles; it functions as an objective reminder of the nervousness, even borderland insanity, of the novel's characters. On the other hand, the hydrotherapy apparatus is tellingly omitted from the action of the novel. M. George points out that when Allégre installed it many years ago it was "*then* quite up to date" (*AG,* 286, emphasis mine). The fact that the nervous characters of the novel apparently do not use it for a calming bath is, for an author like Conrad who is so intent on the destructive and curative properties of water, a conspicuous omission in the plot and one that clearly indicates that Conrad considers the therapy it offers to be passé. This telling omission also creates a narrative gap in the text analogous to

Conrad's subjunctive voyeurism in "The Secret Sharer," when the narrator imagines if someone were bold enough to eavesdrop on the captain and Leggatt. Such a narrative strategy depends upon the reader's imaginative construction of an eavesdropper to witness the fictional scene, a fantasy that increases the anxiety and suspense of the story. An analogous narrative strategy is at work in the final sequences of *The Arrow of Gold*. When M. George enters the chamber with Doña Rita stretched on the sofa—like Olympia, but with her back turned, under an animal-skin wrap—it is a missed opportunity for the novelist and ex–spa patron to picture her languishing sensually in a warm-water bath. One might argue that it would be uncharacteristic of Conrad to depict such a scene (even if she were, like Leggatt, in the adjacent bath-room), yet the scene he writes is just as uncharacteristically sensual and voluptuous:

> I only breathed deeply the faint scent of violets, her own particular fragrance enveloping my body, penetrating my very heart with an inconceivable intimacy, bringing me closer to her than the closest embrace, and yet so subtle that I sense her existence in me only as a great glowing, indeterminate tenderness, something like the evening light disclosing after the white passion of the day infinite depths in the colours of the sky and an unsuspected soul of peace in the protean form of life. I had not known such quietness for months; and I detected in myself an immense fatigue, a longing to remain where I was without changing my position to the end of time.

While the bath is literally behind this scene, M. George, in whatever experience he shares with Doña Rita, imaginatively levitates her body above a flood of water:

> It was a strange peace which she shared with me in this unexpected shelter full of disorder in its neglected splendour. What troubled me was the sudden, as it were material, consciousness of time passing as water flows. It seemed to me that it was only the tenacity of my sentiment that held that woman's body, extended and tranquil above the flood. But when I ventured at last to look at her face I saw her flushed, her teeth clenched—it was visible— her nostrils dilated, and in her narrow, level-glancing eyes a look of inward and frightened ecstasy. The edges of her fur coat had fallen open and I was moved to turn away. (294–5)

This telling omission reveals not only the inefficacy of the literal water cure but also points to the inhibition of Doña Rita's sexuality. Although she languishes on the sofa—a gorgeous and sensuous "creature" in animal skins—she is incapable of adult

194

genital sexuality and seems to experience a kind of inwardly directed, orgiastic sexuality that is described, in figurative terms, as the flowing of water. This telling omission no longer requires Conradian restraint; it indicates psychoanalytic repression and symbolic reenactment. The reader who is bold enough to enter the scene almost unavoidably becomes both a voyeur and a practicing analyst, listening to M. George narrate how he knelt next to Rita reclining on her couch.

We witness more obviously the repression and traumatic hysteria of Rita when M. George rejoins her after the ordeal with Ortega and he finds her standing "statuesque in her nightdress, ... indistinctly rigid and inanimate, ... lost on an arctic plain, ... cold, lifeless, but flexible" (*AG,* 328–9). Doña Rita's paralysis is similar to Lord Jim's "hystero-traumatic paralysis" with one critical exception: the exciting cause of Jim's hysteria is physical trauma associated with the simple failure of duty; Rita's original trauma is partly physical but is primarily psychological and her adult hysteria involves the repression of, and the neurotic reenactment of, the fear of sexuality. Conrad knew this, even if he did not know Freud, and he knew also that a temperate, therapeutic bath would not solve Rita's problems. With *The Arrow of Gold,* Conrad consciously rejects the tenets of pre-Freudian medical psychology and embraces instead the modern principles of neurosis and depth psychology. *The Arrow of Gold* is thus a more psychologically graphic novel than Conrad's earlier fiction, and, like another postwar novel, Virginia Woolf's *Mrs. Dalloway,* it focuses on the inadequacy of late Victorian psychology in the modern, shell-shocked world.

From one perspective, *Mrs. Dalloway* may be read less as the story of Clarissa Dalloway than as the contextualized story of Septimus Warren Smith: that is, as the narrative history of a shell-shocked man who survived World War I but falls victim to postwar English culture. Elaine Showalter has shown that Septimus Smith's name probably owes something to Siegfried Sassoon, who visited Woolf while she was writing the novel.[9] But Woolf may also have been thinking of the later works of Conrad, which she admired more than his earlier sea novels. In her essay "Joseph Conrad," written in 1924, Woolf remarks, "For some years . . . it was Marlow who was the dominant partner. *Nostromo, Chance, The Arrow of Gold* represent that stage of the alliance which some will continue to find the richest of all. The human heart is more intricate than the forest, they will say; it has its storms; it has its creatures of the night; and if as novelist you wish to test man in all his relationships, the proper antagonist is man; his ordeal is in society, not solitude. For them there will always be a peculiar fascination in the books where the light of those brilliant eyes falls not upon the waste of waters but upon the heart in its perplexity."[10] *The Arrow of Gold* and *Mrs. Dalloway* are novels that explore "the heart in its perplexity." Septimus, like Doña Rita, finds it difficult to face life without fear and is emotionally paralyzed, unable to love. Both fictional characters are unaided by the therapies of the past that cannot solve more serious contemporary psychological problems such as war neuroses. Septimus's first doctor, the general practitioner Dr. Holmes, brushes aside Septimus's symptoms—"headaches, sleeplessness, fears, dreams—nerve symptoms and nothing more, he said"— and prescribes a sedative that was typically indicated in cases of neurasthenia: "two tabloids of bromide dissolved in a glass of water at bedtime."[11] But Septimus is not merely neurasthenic. He has, like Doña Rita, learned to repress his feelings, first as a defense mechanism commonly developed by men at the front, and then as a consequence of shell shock. But the defense mechanism is also an extension of the English nationalist construction of gender typical of prewar England: "Septimus was one of the first to volunteer. He went to France to save an England which consisted almost entirely of Shakespeare's plays and Miss Isabel Pole. . . . He developed manliness; he was promoted; he drew the attention, indeed the affection of his officer, Evans by name. . . . When Evans was killed . . . Septimus, far from showing any emotion or recognising that here was the end of a friendship, congratulated himself upon feeling very little and very reasonably. The War had taught him" (*MD,* 86). Although the indifference conditioned in war is essential for survival in battle, it is deadly in life, particularly to the life of the affections, and Septimus soon understands that he can no longer taste or feel. In desperation he becomes engaged to Lucrezia "when the panic was on him—that he could not feel"; but like many shell-shocked men, he begins to revile sexuality and, in Septimus's case, validates his loathing by aligning his sexual phobias with those he attributes to the national bard: "Love between man and woman was repulsive to Shakespeare. The business of copulation was filth to him before the end. . . . One cannot bring children into a world like this. One cannot perpetuate suffering, or increase the breed of these lustful animals" (89). If earlier the panic of not feeling was "on him," soon "human nature . . . was on him . . . Holmes was on him" like a ravaging beast "with blood-red nostrils" (92). Though their historical and cultural circumstances are different, Septimus and Doña Rita are both conditioned by violence to abhor sexuality and to become numb to love. And, if the hydrotherapy of medical psychology offers no cure for Doña Rita, the medical solutions proposed by Dr. Bradshaw offer no hope to Septimus.

Dr. Bradshaw, a Harley Street nerve specialist, prides himself on his reputation for "lightning skill, and an almost infallible accuracy of diagnosis," which, in Septimus's case, is a "complete physical and nervous breakdown." Instinctively, Bradshaw recommends a classic Weir Mitchell rest cure:

> rest, rest, rest; a long rest in bed. There is a delightful home down in the country where her husband would be perfectly looked after. Away from her? She asked. Unfortunately, yes; the people we care for most are not good for us when we are ill. But he was not mad, was he? Sir William said he never spoke of "madness"; he called it not having a sense of proportion. (*MD*, 96)

> To his patients he gave three-quarters of an hour; and if in this exacting science which has to do with what, after all, we know nothing about—the nervous system, the human brain—a doctor loses his sense of proportion, as a doctor he fails. Health we must have; and health is proportion; so that when a man comes into your room . . . and threatens . . . to kill himself, you invoke proportion; order rest in bed; rest in solitude; silence and rest; rest without friends, without books, without messages; six months' rest; until a man who went in weighing seven stone six comes out weighing twelve. (99)

The theory behind Bradshaw's therapy echoes, almost verbatim, passages in Sir George Savage's *Insanity and Allied Neuroses,* and the effects of rest, described by the above narrative voice, echo passages from Woolf's letters that reveal her boredom during an eight-month period when Savage, after Woolf's 1904 nervous breakdown, banished her from London.[12] This kind of rest cure is the treatment with which Savage continued to torment Virginia Woolf during her four trips to Burley, a private house (really a small, private asylum) in Twickenham, where Woolf was to be "cured."

The rest cure that proved ineffective and intolerable for Woolf is also anathema for Septimus, who plunges to his death rather than submit to such treatment. Dr. Bradshaw, a kind of guardian of English normalcy, is empowered by the law to either cure the unfit or hide them away: "Worshipping proportion, Sir William not only prospered himself but made England prosper, secluded her lunatics, forbade childbirth, penalised despair, made impossible for the unfit to propagate their views until they, too, shared his sense of proportion" (*MD,* 99). But Septimus will not submit to their views. The accusation that Dr. Holmes hurls after Septimus is perfect—"The Coward!" (149)—for it connects the violence of war, the ideology implicit in the gendered activity of war, and its effect on the psychology of sexuality in the soldiers who survive the events of war but who return unfit for the perpetuation of life. Septimus's "manliness" is lost—in his suggestive intimacy with Evans, as an "English husband" who worries his wife, and in the unmanly act of taking his own life—and as if to emphasize physically her critique of postwar England, Woolf ends Septimus's life with his body being horribly penetrated.

With their novels *The Arrow of Gold* and *Mrs. Dalloway,* Conrad and Woolf mark a stage in the evolution of the medical and literary arts. In these works, the novel is used to narrate personal medical history at a point in time when English culture makes a transition from a pre-Freudian to a Freudian world. Woolf's admiration for that quality in Conrad's art that "tells us something very old and perfectly true" reveals an affinity she has, like Conrad, for the value of stable, traditional forms of beauty. Woolf and Conrad are both, in this sense, romantic Victorians who are on the verge of becoming high moderns. The same may be said for their attitudes toward psychology. Like many of their contemporaries—Ford Madox Ford, Henry and Alice James, T. S. Eliot, and H. G. Wells, among others—Conrad and Woolf suffered from neurasthenia or related nervous instabilities and were treated by pre-Freudian medical psychologists who believed that when the nerves were in disarray, rest for the body was indicated. The second decade of the twentieth century —which, for Conrad, began with a nervous breakdown—was a personal watershed for Conrad just as it was an artistic watershed for Woolf, who famously remarked, "[I]n or about December, 1910, human character changed." Woolf, of course, privately refers to the opening of Roger Fry's Post-Impressionist Exhibition in London.[13] But she also broadens the comment as an observation about English culture: "All human relations have shifted— those between masters and servants, husbands and wives, parents and children. And when human relations change there is at the same time a change in religion, conduct, politics, and literature."[14] While Woolf's statement is clearly ideological, it is also, by implications, psychological, for the "human relations" to which she refers inevitably involve "the heart in its perplexity."

The "shift" and the "perplexity" of which Woolf speaks are metaphors for the reconciled instability that characterizes the modern moment—whether it is Joycean epiphany, Yeatsean unity of being, or Woolf's moment of being. In Woolf's "Mr. Conrad: A Conversation," she notes this characteristic of modernism in Conrad:

> Conrad is not one and simple; no, he is many and complex. That is a common case among modern writers, as we have often agreed. And it is when they bring these selves into relation—when they simplify, when they reconcile their opposites—that they bring off (generally late in life) those complete books which for that reason we call their masterpieces. And Mr. Conrad's selves are particularly opposite. He is composed of two people who have nothing whatever in common. He is your sea captain, simple, faithful, obscure; and he is Marlow, subtle, psychological, loquacious. In the early books the captain dominates; in the later it is Marlow at least who does all the talking. The union of these two very different men makes for all sorts of queer effects. You must have noticed the sudden silences, the awkward collisions, the immense lethargy which threatens at every moment to descend. All this, I think, must be the result of that internal conflict.[15]

The "internal conflict" is surely the "contrary stresses" of which Conrad speaks in his author's note to *An Outcast of the Islands,* written in 1919 about his nervous condition in 1895. After his 1910 breakdown, Conrad sought to resolve such nervousness, such contrary stresses, through allegorical confessions of his medical history, depicted in the emergence of the "composite temperament" of Marlow, in the destruction of plain Mr. Jones, and in the "composite soul" of command that somehow resists contagious disease. In his later novels, Conrad often sought to embed these allegories in tales of human love: in the unions of Flora and Anthony, Lena and Heyst, M. George and Doña Rita. But more often than not, such reconciliations of opposites remain elusive, fragile: denied by the conditions of the modern world or dissolved by the perplexities of the human heart.

Appendix
Joseph Conrad's Medical Entourage

References to sources used to prepare this appendix are self-contained; if they are not used in the body of this book, they do not appear in the Works Cited. Specific information about the academic qualifications, degrees, affiliations, and honors of the physicians listed here is gleaned from various annual volumes of *The Medical Directory* (London: J. & A. Churchill) unless otherwise noted. General information about Conrad and his family is often based on the biographies by Najder and Karl and on Conrad's correspondence. Cross-references are indicated by an asterisk.

Dr. Rayner Derry Batten (1858–1943), born into a prominent medical family (son of John Winterbothan Batten, Q.C., an older brother to F. E. Batten, a neurologist, and to J. D. Batten, artist and illustrator), became a Harley Street general practitioner who attended the Conrad family during their periodic London visits of 1904–5. He advised Conrad on managing his nerves during this difficult period (*CL,* 3:120), treated Borys's scarlet fever (*CL,* 3:301), and probably attended Jessie as well. After his days in general practice, he specialized increasingly in ophthalmology. His obituary reveals that

> [h]e studied medicine at St. Bartholomew's and in Germany, and took his M.D. in Lond. in 1886. He was H.S. at Bart's and R.M.O. at the Brompton and at Addenbrooke's. He was in general practice for a number of years in Kensington, but at the same time did ophthalmic work at Moorfields, where he became assistant surgeon, and in the end gave up general practice for eye work. . . . He became vice-president of the Ophthalmological Society and a member of council of the Oxford Ophthalmological Congress. He was exceedingly happy in his family life. . . . A colleague writes: Rayner Batten was essentially a clinician. Though slow to make up his mind he had the true clinical instinct, compounded of painstaking observation, wide experience, and a retentive memory. The

years spent in general practice gave to his early work (e.g. a paper on the genesis of myopia) a background which may have faded somewhat in later years but was never entirely obliterated. Twenty years ago Batten suggested that the technique of ophthalmic surgery was not for the many but for the few, and should be confined to the few. . . . Batten's own operative skill was considerable. He had a light, sure touch, devoid of tremor, which endured until advancing deafness compelled his retirement. He attached a great importance to "good hands" in all who did ophthalmic work. His life-long hobby was wood-carving, and possibly the "feel" of tools thus acquired inspired the design of some of his instruments. His fixation fork is still of value and a hydrophthalmoscope, originally devised to examine the fundus in high myopia—a forerunner of the contact lens—is often used in the treatment of purulent conjunctivitis by hypertonic solutions. One of his last tasks, under the assistance of his artist-brother, was the training of fundus artists. (Obituary, *British Medical Journal* 13 November 1943, 626. See also Batten obituary notice, *British Journal of Ophthalmology* 27 [1943]: 569–70.)

Dr. Jean-Martin Charcot (1825–93) was director of the clinic of the Salpêtrière; professor of neurology in the Medical Faculty, Paris; and the teacher of Sigmund Freud, Joseph *Grasset (the Conrads' physician at Montpellier), and Paul *Glatz (Conrad's physician at the Champel-les-Bains Hydrotherapeutic Institute). His obituary in the *Journal of Mental Science* observed that "for medico-psychologists his most important works are his *Maladies de Vieillards et Maladies Chroniques,* . . . his *Maladies du Système Nerveux* [and] his 'Lectures on the Localizations of Cerebral and Spinal Diseases.'" The *British Medical Journal* in its notice recognized Charcot's work in hypnotism as a therapy, being reluctant to validate nonpathological nervous phenomena but anxious to give some credit to an Englishman for his advances: "It would have been strange had so far-reaching yet profound a student of the nervous system in health and disease as Professor Charcot failed to include in his range of investigation the phenomena of hypnotism but for the fact that so many neurologists who preceded him had passed them by. It was, we well remember, suggested to him by an English physician some fifteen years ago, when he showed his cases of hystero-epilepsy at the Salpêtrière, that he would obtain great help in his neurological researches from the study of hypnotism." The *British Medical Journal* concluded,

[N]o man was more opposed to quackery, and to him is due the credit of helping to rescue artificial somnambulism from the illegitimate embrace of the charlatan. Fifteen years ago, only a strong man could have given the demonstrations which he gave without endangering his professional status. . . . Never did the illustrious Professor of the Salpêtrière allow himself to be drawn aside from the path of inductive science. His scorn of the frauds and follies which sprang up in a credulous circle outside his own school was only equaled by that which he manifested for the incredulous ignoramuses in his own profession who sneered at phenomena which they could not understand, but in which he recognized, like our own Laycock, a rich source of neurological and psychological knowledge. (*British Medical Journal,* 26 August 1893, quoted in *Journal of Mental Science* 39:615–8)

An important pioneer in hysteria studies, Charcot was crucial to the development of Freud, who wrote in 1885 to his future wife, "'I think I am changing a great deal. I will tell you in detail what is affecting me. Charcot, who is one of the greatest of physicians and a man whose common sense is touched by genius[,] is simply uprooting my aims and opinions. I sometimes come out of his lectures as though I were coming out of Notre Dame, with a new idea of perfection. But he exhausts me; when I come away from him I no longer have any desire to work at my own silly things; it is three whole days since I have done any work, and I have no feelings of guilt." The rest is medical history. (*The Complete Psychological Works of Sigmund Freud* [London: Hogarth Press, 1962], 3:9. See also Freud's "Charcot," *Complete Works,* 3:11–23.)

Dr. Arthur Randall Davis, M.R.L.S. (Middlesex), 1880, was the Hythe partner of Clifford *Hackney. In Jessie Conrad's account in *Joseph Conrad and His Circle,* Davis is surely the unnamed partner of Clifford Hackney who refused to move Conrad the first night of his nervous breakdown or to take medical responsibility for him if Jessie moved him. A member of the British Medical and Royal Archaeological Institute, Davis was also medical referee for Prudential and other Assurance Cos.

Dr. Campbell Tilbury Fox (ca. 1880–1949) attended the Conrad family, was a confidant of Jessie Conrad in the late 1910s, and was one of the two physicians who treated Conrad in the days before his death in 1924. Dr. Fox, who practiced medicine in Ashford, completed his medical training at University College, London, where he received his medical credentials (M.R.C.S. and R.L.C.P) in 1901. A medical officer at Ashford Cottage Hospital, he was also affiliated with the East Ashford Union workhouse and infectious hospital, and was a surgeon and captain in the Royal East Kent Yeomen's Training Corps.

Dr. Paul-Ferdinand Gachet (1828–1909) was an uncle of Marguerite Poradowska; friend and sometime physician to Renoir, Cézanne, Pissarro, Van Gogh, and other artists; amateur painter and engraver; domestic eccentric; and the subject of Conrad's quiet skepticism. Born in Lille, Gachet studied in Paris and—after serving in the military medical corps, in a (medical) campaign against cholera, at the Bicêtre and the Salpêtrière—he took an M.D. at prestigious Montpellier with a doctoral thesis entitled "Étude sur la mélancolie" (1858). He opened his "*cabinet*" in 1859 in Paris at rue Montholon and later moved to 78, faubourg S.-Denis, where he practiced general medicine and eventually focused on electrotherapy and mental disease. In Paris and Auvers-sur-Oise, he often treated members of the arts community and general public without fee, for which he received the Medaille d'Honneur for philanthropy. He was the first president of the Soc. Éclectiques de France and a contributor to the review *Paris-à -l'eau-forte,* which published his articles and original engravings under the name Van Ryssel. Local newspapers recount his heroic activities at the scene of railway accidents when he served as a medical assistant to the Northern Railroad Company. In 1890, Theodore van Gogh placed his brother Vincent under Gachet's care at the recommendation of Pissarro. Van Gogh's letters to Theo suggest that Gachet was a generous and dedicated physician but nervous and rather eccentric. The Gachet residence in Auvers, where it is unlikely Conrad visited, was home not only to Van Gogh, but according Vincent's letters to Theo, "8 cats, 8 dogs, besides chickens, rabbits, ducks, pigeons, etc., in great numbers." (Van Gogh, *Complete Letters,* 3:278, paraphrased from *Dictionnaire de biographie française* [Paris: Librairie Letouzey et Ané, 1979], 1526-7)

Dr. Paul Glatz (1845–1905) was a student of *Charcot and physician to Joseph Conrad during his 1891, 1894, and 1895 visits to Champel-les-Bains, where he was director of the Hydrotherapy Institute. Widely trained in Europe, Glatz studied the classics at Neuchâtel, Switzerland, and later studied medicine at Vienna, Würzburg, Berlin, and the Faculty of Zürich before he received his M.D. at Berne in 1869 with a thesis on Basedow's disease (also called Graves' disease). Later, in Paris, he followed the school of Charcot. In 1874 he was the founding physician of the new hydrotherapeutic establishment of Champel sur Arve (near Geneva, Switzerland), to which he dedicated his summer season activities; during several winter seasons, he also directed a hydrotherapeutic institute in Nice, France.

Glatz would regularly visit other European countries with clinics specializing in nervous disorders to keep abreast of the most recent scientific developments in hydrotherapy, electrotherapy, and massage. A Genevan colleague noted in the *Journal de Genève* that he was especially gifted in treating the special clientele who frequent watering places and who demand special qualities in a physician: amiability, tact, and savoir faire.

Glatz was a member of the Medical Society of Geneva, over which he presided in 1889, and was a correspondent of the Society of Hydrology, Hygiene, and Electrotherapy, Paris. He was regarded as an excellent colleague and recognized for his many publications on the nervous and digestive systems, and most especially for his work on nervous dyspepsia and neurasthenia. In a high compliment, his obituary writer noted that many of his colleagues were also his clients. (Paraphrased from Dr. C. Picot, Obituary of Paul Glatz, *Revue médicale de la Suisse romande*. Reprinted in *Verhandlungen der Schweizerischen Naturforschenden Gesellschaft in Winterthur* [Winterthur, Switzerland: Buchdruckerel von J. Kaufmanns Wwe, 1905], xxxvi–xxxvii)

Dr. Joseph Grasset (1849–1918) attended the Conrad family, most particularly Borys, in the spring of 1907 in Montpellier, France, where he was a professor in the medical faculty. Born into an established Montpellieraine family, he won the general competition for the Emperor's Grand Prize in philosophy with his study "Idea of Causation and the Principle of Causality" (1866). After licensure in physical sciences and chemistry (1868), he took his M.D. degree (1873) with a thesis entitled "Respiratory Ailments of Malarial Origin." He ascended the ranks in the medical faculty at Montpellier as intern (1871), doctor of medicine (1873), professor of therapeutics (1882), clinical medical professor (upon the death of his former professor, Dr. Dupré, 1886), and finally professor of pathology and general therapeutics (1909). During the war he was director of a regional neurological center where he presumably treated cases of shell shock. He was active in his medical career: associate member of the national academy of medicine; *docteur honoris causa* of Geneva and Louvain, member of the scholarly academies or societies of Rome, Moscow, Barcelona, Cambrai, and Bordeaux. He presided over the medical congress of Lille in 1889 and was president of the congress of neurological physicians and alienists (1906). Like Dr. *Glatz of Champel, he had worked with *Charcot in Paris. Dedicated to the treatment of hysteria and neurasthenia and with a medical background in diseases of the lung, he was an ideal specialist to treat Borys's bronchial condition and advise Conrad, given the Korzenioswki medical history. Grasset's publications included *Practical Treatment of Diseases of the Nervous System* (2 vols., 1878–9), *Lessons on Hystero-Traumatism* (1888), *Several Cases of Male Hysteria and Neurasthenia* (1892), and more than a dozen other works. Had Conrad known about the full range of Grasset's eclectic work, he might have been ambivalent about Grasset's interests in occultism, hypnotism, hallucination, and trances. (*Dictionnaire de biographie française,* Dirs., M. Prevost, Roman D'Amat, H. Tribout De Morembert [Paris: Librairie Letouzey et Ané, 1985], 7:1073–4)

Dr. Clifford Hackney (1873–1956), son of John Hackney, was the second medical practitioner to become the Conrad family physician during their years at the Pent Farm. Under the approving eye of Dr. *Tebb, Clifford Hackney became the Conrads' local physician in 1904. Like his father, "young Hackney" (as he was sometimes called by Conrad) was a graduate of University College, London, where, as a matter of course, he would have studied mental disease under William Julius *Mickle, England's leading authority on general paralysis of the insane. Clifford Hackney was the local physician summoned by Jessie Conrad during Conrad's 1910 breakdown, and he consulted with Drs. Tebb and *Mackintosh during Conrad's convalescence. Although Conrad increasingly saw Dr. Mackintosh, Hackney remained Conrad's local physician until he served in the Royal Expeditionary Forces and as medical officer for the Lympne Aerodome. Long-lived, Clifford Hackney retired first to Somerset then to Cambridgeshire, where he died at the age of eighty-two.

Dr. John Hackney, the father of "young Hackney" *(Clifford Hackney), became Conrad's first local physician during the years at the Pent Farm and Aldington. He received his medical training at University College, London, and began practicing medicine in 1865. He took the M.D. degree from St. Andrews in 1887 and became a fellow and vice president of the balneological section of the Royal Society of Medicine. He was, during his career, also house surgeon at the Royal Free Hospital, London, and honorary surgeon at the British Home for Incurables.

Dr. Francis Richard Hinde was probably the "local physician"—the only local practitioner listed for Aldington in the *Medical Directory*—who responded in leisurely fashion to Jessie Conrad's summons for help during the first stages of Conrad's 1910 breakdown and who was indignantly turned away by Jessie after his tardy arrival. He took his M.B. and M.D. from the University of Edinburgh (1890); practiced in Ashford, Aldington, and Hythe; held several appointments in surgery at area hospitals; and in 1910 was "late Deputy-Coroner for East Hertfordshire," which may explain his slow arrival.

Sir Robert Jones (1857–1933) was the most eminent British physician to treat the Conrad family; he performed numerous surgeries on Jessie Conrad's knee and may well have saved the leg from amputation. Jones first operated on Jessie in June of 1918 in London, apparently with success, but he would need to operate again in December of 1919 in Liverpool, in March of 1920 in Canterbury, and again in her own home at Oswalds in May of 1920. Jones operated on Jessie's knee one last time, in mid-June of 1924, less than two months from Conrad's death. But Sir Robert was more than a persistent surgeon; like *Tebb, *Hackney, and *Mackintosh, Sir Robert—whom the *Dictionary of National Biography* noted "made friends equally with duke or docker"— made friends with Conrad and his family, who toured North Wales together in September of 1922 to buoy Conrad's spirits. The *DNB* takes conspicuous note of Jones's achievements in many endeavors:

> Honours came to Jones from many quarters. He was knighted and appointed C.B. [Companion of the Order of the Bath] in 1917, and K.B.E. [Knight Commander of the Order of the British Empire] in 1919 for his services in the war, and created a baronet in 1926. Among other distinctions he received honorary degrees from the universities of Liverpool, Wales, Aberdeen, McGill, Harvard, Smith's College, and Yale, together with that rare honour, the

D.S.M. [Distinguished Service Medal] of the United States of America. He was president of the British Orthopaedic Association (1920–1925); he was the first president of the International Society of Orthopaedic Surgery, and he was elected an honorary fellow of the Royal College of Surgeons in 1919. (499)

His obituary in *The Lancet* emphasized both his professional reputation and his personal kindness:

His fellow orthopaedists . . . soon came to regard him as a pioneer, recognising the practical nature of much of his original technique, and his skill alike in diagnosing the conditions and suggesting the course of treatment to be adopted. In those early days America and the Continent knew Robert Jones better than did his own country. It was not so much by innovations that he attracted attention as by his skilful application of the old knowledge to meet the advance of general therapeutics.

At Jones's seventieth birthday, Lord Moynihan, president of the Royal College of Surgeons,

delivered a short address on Robert Jones, describing him as a prophet, high priest, and practitioner, and setting out his personal qualities in the words: "Robert Jones," said Lord Moynihan, "Speaks ill of no man. He seeks and finds good in all things and in all men. He sets an ideal and a standard of action in friendship which all strive to reach when with him. . . . His personality radiates cheeriness, good temper, and goodwill. All men are attracted to him, and in war-time conflicting temperaments found in him something that appeased their differences, assuaged animosities, and encouraged a desire for friendliness." (Obituary, *The Lancet,* 21 January 1933, 166–7)

Frederick Karl notes that when the collected edition of Conrad's works was published, Conrad reserved only three sets: one for Edward Garnett, one for André Gide, and one for Sir Robert Jones (*Joseph Conrad: The Three Lives,* 839). Jones's biographer, however, noted that after a full day of work Jones found it hard to follow Conrad's fiction. (See Frederick Watson, *The Life of Sir Robert Jones* [Baltimore, Md.: W. Wood, 1935].)

Dr. Izydor Kopernicki (1825–91), a friend of Apollo Korzeniowski, medical anthropologist, folklorist, and translator, supervised Conrad's education from 1871 while Conrad was under the tutorship of *Pulman. Years later, when Kopernicki learned that his former pupil was bound for central Africa, he requested, through Tadeusz Bobrowski, that Conrad collect some human skulls for him: "He [Kopernicki] is engaged on a great work which has already brought him European fame: 'Comparative studies of human races based on types of skulls.' This particular branch of science is called Craniology. He earnestly requests you to collect during your voyages skulls of natives, writing on each one whose skull it is and the place of origin. When you have collected a dozen or so of such skulls write to me and I will obtain from him special information as to the best way of despatching them to Cracow, where there is a special Museum devoted to Craniology" (Najder, *Joseph Conrad: A Chronicle,* 71–2). Kopernicki, the son of Stanisław and Marianna (née Pieńkowska) Kopernicki, was born in Ukraine in Czyżówce, where his father was village administrator. Kopernicki participated in classes of the gymnasium from 1833 to 1844 and studied medicine at the University of Kiev from 1844 to 1849, where he graduated *cum eximia laude*. From 1847 to 1849 he was a member of the Polish student underground and after his studies worked for eight years as a physician in the military, where he was decorated for his service under fire, became a senior physician, and then was counselor to the czar. After his military service (from 1857 to 1863), he worked as a scientist and taught anatomy and surgery to medical students at the University of Kiev, where he was a popular teacher and sympathetic with students in the Polish underground. During this time he was a member of the Secret Union of Scientific Support, which encouraged the organization of Polish schools in Ukraine.

In the early 1860s he was involved in preparation for the insurrection in Ukraine and in this capacity became intimate friends with Apollo Korzeniowski; in April 1863, fearing discovery, he was forced to flee Kiev to Warsaw, where he briefly became chief of the medical staff in the Polish army. In September of 1863 the national government appointed him commissioner in Lwów, but he was arrested in November by the Austrians as a revolutionary. Escaping prison, he fled to Paris, where he attended lectures of Claude Bernarde and P. Broca, the founder of modern anthropology. In the late 1860s, he traveled to Belgrade and Bucharest, where, while serving on the medical faculty, he organized the Museum of Anatomy and wrote papers in anthropology, craniology, and natural history presented at proceedings in Paris, Cracow, Belgium, and Germany. In 1869 he accepted temporary positions at the University of Kiev and Jagiellonian University as a professor of physiology, in a docent (unpaid) position. At this time, he also worked as a physician of balneotherapy at Rabka (1871–80) and Marienbad (1880–8). He eventually received a permanent position at Jagiellonian University and established a distinguished European career as an educator, scientist, and editor.

During his career, he published more than one hundred scientific papers: forty in anthropology, twenty-five in archaeology, twenty in ethnography, and a variety of papers in linguistics, medicine, internal medicine, and balneotherapy. His studies in anthropology led him to a variety of interests in population studies, ethnography, and the folklore and folk music of the Serbian and Roma peoples. Late in his life he looked after the famous and dying ethnographer O. Kolberg, from whom he contracted tuberculosis and died in 1891. (*Polski słownik biograficzny*. Komitet redakcyjny: Władysław Konopczyński et al. [Cracow: Nakł. Polskiej Akademji Umiejetności, 1935–99], 14:1–3. Translation and paraphrase from Polish by Dr. Marian S. Stachowicz.)

Dr. Cesare Lombroso (1835–1909) was referred to implicitly or explicitly in a number of Conrad's works. He was a popularized medical authority on craniology, phrenology, and criminal anthropology. The *British Journal of Psychology,* quoting the *Times* obituary following Lombroso's death on 18 November 1909, reported that

> [h]e was descended from a line of Jews, many of whom had attained to eminence as authors, rabbis, lawyers, and physicians. Among his progenitors on his mother's side was David Levi, the poet, who took part in the struggle for Italian liberty. As a boy Lombroso gave signs of extreme precocity. The monuments of antiquity which he saw around him impelled him to study Roman history with avidity, and he devoured Livy, Sallust, and Tacitus ere he had hardly left the nursery. When he was twelve years old he wrote, and actually obtained publication for, an essay on *The Greatness and Decline of Rome.* A year later his attention was attracted by an obscure work on *The Elucidation of Historic Monuments by Philological Analysis,* written by Paolo Marzolo, of Treviso, a thinker who deserved to be better known, and who in this incomplete work anticipated many later discoveries. . . . Lombroso abandoned the ordinary high-school course and applied himself, under Marzolo's supervision, to the study of Oriental philology. He learnt Hebrew, Chaldee, Egyptian, and Chinese, and endeavoured to discover a common basis for all these tongues. Marzolo recognized however, that owing to the troubled state of the times no living could be earned at philology, and on his advice Lombroso turned his attention to medicine. (*British Journal of Psychology* 56 [1910]: 383)

During Conrad's lifetime, Lombroso was most widely recognized for two texts: *L'Homme criminel* (1888; English edition, *Criminal Man* [1911]) and *The Man of Genius* (1891). Although Conrad loosely employs some of Lombroso's popular theories in his fiction, Conrad seems to dismiss him in *The Secret Agent* and *Chance,* in which Marlow likely refers to *The Man of Genius* as an "idiotic book" (*C,* 184).

Dr. Rudolf Gustav Heinrich Wilhelm Ludwig maintained his medical offices at 119, Finsbury-pavement, E.C., and at the German Hospital in Dalston, North London, where he treated Conrad during his illness in 1891 following the Congo voyage. Dr. Ludwig was trained at the Universities of Heidelberg, Würzburg, Munich, and finally, Leipzig, where he passed the German State Exam and took the M.D. in 1876. He was an assistant in the Munich Clinique and member of the Royal College of

Physicians (M.R.C.P.) of London, 1880. Thereafter, he practiced medicine at the German Hospital.

Dr. Robert Mackintosh (1865–1934) was introduced to Conrad in 1909 by Perceval Gibbon and, in Conrad's words, came "to the rescue of a discouraged man" (*CL,* 4:209). For many years Mackintosh—"a man of scientific attainments" (4:217)—was the primary manager of Conrad's gout and became known as "the good Mac" (4:217) for his efforts, traveling to Kent frequently from his London practice to attend Conrad. He treated Conrad's gout with Solurol (4:261), a proprietary phosphoric acid compound commonly used to dissolve uric acid in Conrad's day. Mackintosh furnished Jessie Conrad with the formula for Conrad's "favourite gout medicine," which she ordered in a Polish pharmacy ingredient by ingredient when she did not have a proper prescription (Jessie Conrad, *Joseph Conrad and His Circle,* 148). Mackintosh remained a family friend for many years, even offering Borys a job after the war in his radio-electric firm that he started after his medical career ended due to deafness (Najder, *Joseph Conrad: A Chronicle,* 457). Mackintosh's great-niece, Janet Jellard, recalls her great uncle as follows:

> Robert Mackintosh was a Scottish doctor of Highland descent. He lived in the borough of Barnes on the south bank of the Thames in London, so he was never Conrad's local physician. He not only had a reputation as a skilful practitioner, but was also a writer of plays and pageants for local production. He appears to have been something of an amateur inventor as well, hence the "metal affair," which Conrad mentions in his first letter, and the foundry in which John Conrad worked during the war. I remember him as a kind and gentle old man. . . . He had lost his hearing as a result of an infection acquired from a patient during the war, which obliged him to give up most of his medical practice. This is no doubt why he later attempted to start a business, with disastrous results. My father told me that he was very sensitive about his deafness and did his best to hide it. In 1924, he published an essay called "Homo Surdus," in which he describes the loneliness of a deaf person's life, and the feeling of separation from the rest of humanity. (*Conradiana* 19 [1987]: 87)

Conrad had a falling out with Mackintosh, when he lost a two-hundred-pound investment in and the hope of secure employment for his sons at Mackintosh's Surrey Scientific Apparatus Company, which failed.

Dr. William Julius Mickle was the lecturer in mental disease of University College Hospital Medical School, where Clifford *Hackney studied medicine. Since Mickle was the leading expert in England on general paralysis of the insane (see *General Paralysis of the Insane,* 1886) and Hackney presumably studied under him in 1896, Mickle may have been the original source of Conrad's concern that he had "incipient softening of the brain" (*CL,* 4:329) after his 1910 breakdown. Mickle took the M.D. from the Toronto (1867), was licensed in London (M.R.C.S., 1868), and became a fellow of the Royal College of Physicians in 1887. In addition to his lecturing on mental physiology and mental disease at University College, Mickle was the medical superintendent of the Grove Hall Asylum; he was a member of the Medico-Psychological Association, the Neurological Society, and the British Medical Association. Before his residence in London, he was assistant physician at the Derby and Warwick County Asylums. In addition to his well-known text on general paralysis, he was widely published on a variety of associated conditions, symptoms, or indications of general paralysis: body temperature, syphilis, necropsy, unilateral sweating, hallucination, and cerebral localization, and knee-jerk in GPI. He also contributed five article entries in *Tuke's *A Dictionary of Psychological Medicine.*

Max Nordau (1849–1923), a Hungarian-born student of medicine and culture critic, was a devotee of Cesare *Lombroso, to whom he dedicated his famous critique of late-nineteenth-century and fin-de-siècle artists and thinkers: his book *Degeneration.* Conrad's use of the term *degeneration* near the beginning of *An Outcast of the Islands* and his leeriness of receiving a compliment from Nordau (*CL,* 2:121) suggest that Conrad was both aware and skeptical of Nordau's theories. (For further discussion of Nordau, see chapter 1.)

Adam Marek Pulman (1846–?) is a shadowy figure in Conrad studies. "Pulman [was] Conrad's private tutor in Cracow from 1870 to 1873. Adam Pulman was a student in medicine at the Jagiellonian University, graduating in 1875. His duties also included escorting the young boy on three summer visits to Krynica, a resort town in the Carpathian Mountains. In May 1873, Conrad, sent to Switzerland for his health, was again accompanied by Pulman on a three-month trip that also took them to Bavaria, Austria, and northern Italy. According to Conrad's later reminiscences, Pulman was given the mission of dissuading him from the 'romantic folly' of leaving Poland to go to sea, but after long arguments, capitulated to his young charge with the words: 'You are an incorrigible, hopeless, Don Quixote. That's what you are' (Joseph Conrad, *A Personal Record,* 43, 44). Pulman and his wife later settled in Sambir, Galicia, where he practiced medicine." (Owen Knowles and Gene Moore, *Oxford Reader's Companion to Conrad* [Oxford: Oxford University Press, 2000], 296)

Dr. Whitehead Reid (1883–1930) was the Canterbury physician and friend to Jessie Conrad who attended the Conrad family after their move to Oswalds, especially in the late 1910s and thereafter. Along with Dr. Campbell Tilbury Fox, Dr. Reid attended to Conrad in the weeks preceding his death. He was a graduate of Cambridge University (M.B.,

1905; B.Ch., 1910) and was licensed in London (M.R.C.P., L.R.C.P., 1909). He became senior surgeon and radiologist for Kent and Canterbury Hospital, consulting surgeon for Hearne Bay Hospital, and lecturer in surgery at St. Augustine's College. His interests in X-ray and electrotherapy and his association with the Royal National Hospital for Consumption may have attracted Conrad. His obituary in the *British Medical Journal* follows:

Dr. Edward Douglas Whitehead Reid of Canterbury, who died on October 20th from injuries received in a flying accident, was one of the first men in this country to own a private aeroplane, and his skill and care as a pilot were recognized in the air service.

He was born in 1883 at Canterbury, where his father, the late Dr. T. Whitehead Reid, F.R.C.P., held a leading position. From Tonbridge School he went to Christ's College, Cambridge, graduating B.A. in the Natural Sciences Tripos, and thence to St. Bartholomew's. Both at Cambridge and at hospital he distinguished himself in athletic sports. After obtaining the English Conjoint diplomas in 1909, he served as house-physician at St. Bartholomew's, and house-surgeon at the London Temperance Hospital, and proceeded to the M.B. and B.Ch. degrees in 1910. He then made several voyages as ship surgeon, and, returning to take up his father's practice, was soon elected to the surgical staff of the Kent and Canterbury Hospital. . . . During the war he served with a temporary commission in the R.A.M.C. at No. 1 British Red Cross (Duchess of Westminster's) Hospital, near Etaples [France], and subsequently in Egypt, where he learnt to fly when acting as surgeon and radiologist to No. 31 General Hospital. After the war he resumed civilian work at Canterbury, and in addition to his hospital duties and a considerable private practice, he undertook the post of surgeon to the local Venereal Disease Clinic. . . .

As may be gathered from this brief record of a life cut short in its prime, Douglas Whitehead Reid was a man of abundant energy; resourceful, enterprising, and businesslike in the arrangement of his day's work. It speaks much for the impression he made upon people that within a few months of his return to the place where he had been known as a boy he was able to hold together a practice built up by his father, and to secure election to the hospital staff. His schoolfellows and contemporaries at Cambridge and Bart's will long remember him as a man always keen, always striving, always living intensely and enjoying life. At the end of the war the ban on his unauthorized enthusiasm for flying was raised, and he was able to join an auxiliary branch of the R.A.F.M.S. This made him extremely happy. (*British Medical Journal,* 15 October 1930, 712)

In another personal tribute in the *British Medical Journal,* Sir Charles Gordon-Watson noted that more than two thousand friends and respectful citizens filled the Canterbury Cathedral at the memorial service following the glider accident that claimed his life. Sir Gordon-Watson noted that Dr. Reid was a surgeon who "was in great demand over a wide area, and his attractive and modest personality made him beloved wherever he went." (*British Medical Journal,* 1 November 1930, 759)

Sir George Savage (1842–1921) was the personal physician of Virginia Woolf during her episodes of neurasthenic collapse and the lecturer in mental diseases at Guy's Medical School, where Conrad's physician, Dr. A. E. *Tebb, trained. During the late nineteenth century, Savage was an expert in moral insanity and a diehard physiologist who advocated with Henry Maudsley the view that mental disease must be based on some organic cause. Woolf's view of Savage as "tyrannical" and the tone of moral condescension evident in his works on mental disease written at the height of his career differ from the portrait sketched by his obituaries, which suggest a more modest and moderate end to his career:

> Though his name is perhaps not directly associated with any remarkable advances in our knowledge of mental disorder, he was, nevertheless, a great psychiatrist, whose name may fittingly be remembered with those of Clauston, Maudsley, and Mercier. . . .
>
> Sir George Savage was born at Brighton in 1842, but his father was a Yorkshireman and his mother of Scottish extraction. He was educated at Brighton, at the Sussex Country Hospital, and Guy's Hospital, where he won the treasurer's gold medal. He took the diploma of the M.R.C.S. Eng. in 1864, and the degree of M.B. in the University of London in 1865; he graduated M.D. in 1867, and took the M.R.C.P. Lond. in 1878, being elected to the Fellowship in 1885. His first appointment outside Guy's Hospital was at Bethlem Royal Hospital; he became assistant medical officer in 1872, and physician-superintendent in 1879, a post he retained for ten years. It was during these seventeen years that his reputation as a psychiatrist became so firmly established in the estimation of the profession. He was well and widely read in the literature of the specialty to which he gave himself; he was a shrewd and careful observer, who made the best use of ample opportunities: he was endowed with much common sense, and had a genial open manner, totally free from pomposity, so that he was socially one of the most popular of men. Though in his early days at Bethlem Hospital he gave much time to the study of the history of the central nervous system, he was primarily a clinical physician. His lecture at Guy's Hospital and his teaching in the wards of Bethlem Hospital were enlivened by stories and anecdotes drawn from an immense store. With all these qualities it is not surprising that he drew large classes, and was visited by many postgraduates from British Dominions and the United States. He retired from Bethlem in 1889 to engage in consulting practice; in this he was very successful, and he was also frequently consulted by the Home Office in difficult cases. He was deeply interested in the medical education of women, and helped not only with sound advice but with money in the early days. For the last thirty years or so he never failed to attend the opening ceremony of the

London School of Medicine for Women, and was present last October. (*British Medical Journal,* 16 July 1921, 98–9)

It is easy to tally the Victorian moralist evident in his medical writing with the portrait of Woolf's Dr. Bradshaw, who is based in part on Savage, but it is hard to reconcile Woolf's portrait with the more egalitarian portrait of Savage from later in life. His obituary in *The Lancet* ends with a personal testimonial that renders him almost endearing in his harmlessness:

> Savage touched life at so many points that [he] was always a delightful companion. He was an alpine climber of no mean achievement, and but for his deafness would have been President of the Alpine Club. He was a fisherman who fished with a dry fly for three years before he caught a trout. . . .
>
>   But . . . it was the man we all loved, the many-sided in his sympathy and understanding, the big-brained vigorous bodied man, with his rich intellect and his strong body who yet had time to think of "the little things that matter." (*The Lancet,* 16 July 1921, 155)

The Lancet obituary likewise affirms that Savage was notable for his support for the medical education of women, "from the start of the movement to the end of his life."

Dr. A. E. Tebb (1863–1943) was the personal friend and physician of the Conrad, Heuffer, and Rothenstein families, Violet Hunt, and some of the Rossettis. He attended Conrad from the early years of the twentieth century through his breakdown of 1910, and Ford Madox Ford lodged with Tebb during periods of his prolonged nervous illnesses of 1904–6. Tebb was educated at Guy's Hospital, where Dr. *Savage taught a course in mental disease and was examined by D. Hack *Tuke, editor of *A Dictionary of Psychological Medicine,* when he sat for the M.D. degree. Tebb, an amateur violinist and collector of avant-garde prints (including Redon and Beardsley), attended many Hampstead artists and members of the Conrad circle, often gratis. He was a physician for the Hampstead Provident Dispensary and became interested in tuberculosis. For a brief period during the war years he served as the medical superintendent of the Benenden National Sanitorium and later conducted research on tuberculosis for the Ministry of Munitions, focusing especially on the rise of the incidence of tuberculosis among women factory workers. Not long after the war, Tebb lost contact with Conrad, though he corresponded with Ford into the mid-1930s. (See chapter 3 above and my own "'What Has Happened to Poor Tebb?': A Biographical Sketch of Conrad's Physician," *The Conradian* 23 [1998]: 1–18.)

Dr. D. Hack Tuke (1827–95) was the editor of *A Dictionary of Psychological Medicine,* an authoritative work often quoted in this study, and an examiner for A. E. *Tebb's M.D. degree from the University of

London (1893). Tuke was the great-grandson of the founder of the York Retreat, a Quaker asylum that pioneered moral treatment for the insane. As a child, Tuke had delicate health, which hindered his study, and he never became proficient in Latin or Greek. He studied for the bar, but ill health prevented his pursuit of a profession in law; instead, he devoted himself to the study of philosophy and poetry. His first published work was an essay that urged the abolition of capital punishment.

At the age of twenty, Tuke began a two-year residence at the York Retreat, where he observed patients and read literature on treatment of the insane. In 1850 he matriculated in London's St. Bartholomew's Hospital Medical School and after two years' study became a member of the Royal College of Surgeons. He took the M.D. from the University of Heidelberg in 1853 and began working and writing on progressive treatments and care for the insane, based in part on his visits to asylums all over Europe. In 1858, he published, with J. C. Bucknell, "A Manual of Psychological Medicine," an essay that remained a classic study for more than two decades. In 1859 his career was interrupted by severe symptoms of pulmonary phthisis, which persisted for many years and caused a fifteen-year hiatus in his medical career.

In 1875 he reentered the profession and began practicing in London, focusing on mental diseases. The balance of his career spanned two decades and resulted in distinguished accomplishments in the field of medical psychology: he was governor of Bethlem Royal Hospital, lecturer in mental diseases at Charing Cross Hospital, coeditor with Sir George *Savage of the *Journal of Mental Science,* presidential chair of the Medico-Psychological Association, author of numerous important publications, and recipient of the L.L.D. from the University of Glasgow. Tuke's 1892 *A Dictionary of Psychological Medicine* was recognized in the 1923 edition of the *Dictionary of National Biography* as being "the authoritative English work on the subject at the present time" (1924), some thirty years after its initial publication. Tuke was well known for his kindness, benevolence, rationality, and mild manner, but he could also be a principled and mordant social critic. William Ireland, writing a tribute to Tuke in the *Journal of Mental Science,* noted that Tuke was a supporter of Irish home rule and reported an anecdote repeated by Dr. Savage: Tuke had once been kept waiting by the eminent surgeon Sir Andrew Clark, who, when he appeared, apologized profusely and explained, "'[M]y life is one of slavery.' 'Yes,' said Tuke. 'On the Guinea Coast.'" (*Journal of Mental Science* 41 [1895]: 386)

Notes

Foreword

1. Jessie Conrad, *Joseph Conrad and His Circle* (London: Jarrolds, 1935), 12.

2. See Tadeusz Bobrowski's letter to Joseph Conrad (20 November/2 December 1891), *Conrad's Polish Background: Letters to and from Polish Friends,* ed. Z. Najder (London: Oxford University Press, 1964), 158.

3. Joseph Conrad, *The Mirror of the Sea* (London: J. M. Dent, 1923), 54.

4. Tadeusz Bobrowski to Joseph Conrad (26 February/10 March 1891), *Conrad's Polish Background,* 136; Joseph Conrad to Marguerite Poradowska (27 February 1891), *Collected Letters,* volume 1, 72.

5. Jessie Conrad to David Meldrum (6 February 1910).

6. Adam Gillon, *The Eternal Solitary: A Study of Joseph Conrad* (New York: Bookman Associates, 1960), 112–7.

7. "The Secret Sharer" in Joseph Conrad, *'Twixt Land And Sea* (London: J.M. Dent, 1923), 130.

8. Elaine Showalter, *The Female Malady: Women, Madness and English Culture, 1830–1980* (London: Virago, 1987), 18.

9. See, for example, Susan Jones, *Conrad and Women* (Oxford: Clarendon Press, 1999) and Andrew Michael Roberts, *Conrad and Masculinity* (New York: St Martin's Press, 2000) for two recent contributions to this debate.

Introduction

1. These illnesses occurred over a five-month period beginning in January 1907 in Montpellier, France, and Geneva, Switzerland. See *CL,* 3:408, 412, 414, 433, 445, 439, 449, 450, 448.

2. Karl, *Joseph Conrad: The Three Lives,* 51, 70; Knowles, *A Conrad Chronology,* 3; and Najder, *Joseph Conrad: A Chronicle,* 24.

3. Karl, *Joseph Conrad: The Three Lives,* 88, 97–100; Najder, *Joseph Conrad: A Chronicle,* 31–5.

4. Najder, *Joseph Conrad: A Chronicle,* 31, 71–2; Najder, ed., *Conrad's Polish Background,* 90.

5. Jessie Conrad, letter to David S. Meldrum, 6 February 1910, in Blackburn, ed., *Letters to William Blackwood and David S. Meldrum,* 192.

6. Meyer, *Joseph Conrad: A Psychoanalytic Biography,* 207–20. See also Najder, *Joseph Conrad: A Chronicle,* 358–65; Karl, *Joseph Conrad: The Three Lives,* 680–5.

7. Jessie Conrad, *Joseph Conrad and His Circle,* 146.

8. For a discussion of calomel treatment as the source of Conrad's various painful limbs, gout-like swelling, and nervousness, see McLendon, "Conrad and Calomel." See also Marsden, "Did Joseph Conrad Have Loiasis?"

9. Joseph Conrad, "The *Torrens:* A Personal Tribute," 24.

10. Hampson, *Joseph Conrad: Betrayal and Identity,* 5. Hampson also cites Jeffrey Berman, who argues that *Chance* is "a kind of encyclopaedia in its detailed case studies of mental illness, including traumas, repressive sexuality, oppressive guilt, Oedipal strife, and hysteria" (Berman, *Joseph Conrad: Writing as Rescue,* 149–50).

Chapter 1. Before Freud

The title of this chapter was used first by Francis G. Gosling in *Before Freud.*

1. Hart, "The Psychology of Freud and His School," 431, 435, 437, 438, 442–3.

2. Ibid., 431.

3. Ibid., 434.

4. Ibid., 451.

5. Frederick Karl, in *Joseph Conrad: The Three Lives,* suggests that Conrad found Freud's ideas "a kind of magic show" (657) and "a jumble" (307).

6. Faulkner quoted in Gwynn and Blotner, *Faulkner in the University,* 268, 147, respectively.

7. See Woolf, *The Letters of Virginia Woolf,* 2:482, 3:134–35; and *The Diaries of Virginia Woolf,* 5:249.

8. See Anderson, introduction to "Joyce and Freud" in *The Seventh of Joyce,* 55; Joyce, *Letters of James Joyce,* 1:166.

9. For recent social histories of modern treatment of the insane, see Scull, MacKenzie, and Hervey, *Masters of Bedlam,* and Scull's earlier "Psychiatry in the Victorian Era," 5–32. See also Foucault, *Madness and Civilization,* and Kathleen Jones, *A History of the Mental Health Services,* 31–149, 176–215. For contemporaneous commentary, see, for instance, Conolly, *Familiar View of Lunacy and Lunatic Life;* Tuke, "Retrospective Glance at the Early History of the Retreat, York"; Tuke, "Historical Sketch of the Insane" in *A Dictionary of Psychological Medicine* (*DPM*), 1:1–26; and, in the United States, Riggs, "An Outline of the Progress in the Care and Handling of the Insane," and Sanborn, "The Progress in the Treatment of Insanity."

10. Scull, "Psychiatry in the Victorian Era," 6.

11. Paton, "The New Munich Clinic," 313.

12. Foucault, *Madness and Civilization,* 65–84.

13. Mary Tuke and Dr. de la Rive quoted in Tuke, "Retrospective Glance," 345, 340, respectively.
14. Tuke, "Retrospective Glance," 347; Bynam, "Rationales for Therapy in British Psychiatry," 43.
15. Tuke, "Retrospective Glance," 344–5, 343.
16. See Conolly, *Familiar View of Lunacy and Lunatic Life,* 137, and Tuke, "Retrospective Glance," 348.
17. Scull, "Moral Treatment Reconsidered," 112.
18. See Tuke, "Retrospective Glance," 349ff, and Bynam, "Rationales for Therapy in British Psychiatry," 42.
19. See Kathleen Jones, *A History of the Mental Health Services,* 83–6, 124–49; Bynam, "Rationales for Therapy in British Psychiatry," 45; and Tuke, *DPM,* 25–6.
20. Corbet, "Ought Private Lunatic Asylums to Be Abolished?" 371.
21. Tuke, *DPM,* 731–45.
22. Arata, *Fictions of Loss in the Victorian "Fin de Siècle,"* 4. Arata argues that decadent erotics and empire were two encumbered ideas in late Victorian culture. Lyn Pykett, in her introduction to *Reading Fin de Siècle Fictions,* suggests that degeneration was one of the "great organizing ideas" at the end of the nineteenth century. William Greenslade, in *Degeneration, Culture, and the Novel,* discusses the relationship between the work of JC and Cesare Lombroso and Max Nordau. See also Spackman, *Decadent Genealogies.*
23. Corbet, "The Progress of Insanity in Our Own Time," *Westminster Review* 165 (March 1906): 269.
24. See, for instance, Drapes, "Is Insanity Increasing?"; Haslett, "Modern Private Asylums"; Bresler, "On the Increase of Insanity, and the Boarding-out System"; Haguch, "Comments on the Report of the Commissioners in Lunacy and the Swing of the Pendulum"; and review of the "Forty-eighth Report of the Commissioners in Lunacy, 19th June, 1894."
25. Corbet, "The Increase of Insanity," *Fortnightly Review* 59 (1893): 14.
26. Corbet, "How Insanity Is Propagated," *Westminster Review* 142 (August 1894): 155.
27. Ibid., 155–6.
28. Respectively, Corbet, "The Increase of Insanity," *Fortnightly Review* 59 (1893): 11; "The Increase of Insanity," *Fortnightly Review* 65 (1899): 431; "The Skeleton at the Feast," *Westminster Review* 159 (January 1903): 1; "Plain Speaking about Lunacy," *Westminster Review* 148 (August 1897): 124; and "How Insanity Is Propagated," *Westminster Review* 142 (August 1894): 162.
29. For a discussion of the emergence of germ theory and its impact on literature, see Otis, *Membranes.* In popular discourse, discussion of germ theory appeared in weekly women's domestic publications. See, for instance, A Lady Doctor, "Something about Germs."
30. Griffith, *Joseph Conrad and the Anthropological Dilemma,* 153–65, 131–52, respectively.

31. From the standpoint of psychological medicine, degeneration theory focuses on the inheritance and transmission of defects that explain "the origin and formation of diseased varieties in the human species" (*DPM,* 331).

32. Cantlie and Freeman-Williams are quoted in Gareth Stedman Jones, *Outcast London,* 172.

33. On Nordau, see Griffith, *Joseph Conrad and the Anthropological Dilemma,* 155ff.

34. Nordau, *Degeneration,* 16.

35. For Nordau on Verlaine's mysticism and Baudelaire's *correspondance,* see *Degeneration,* 119–28 and 286–95, respectively; on pre-Raphaelitism, see 70ff; on Tolstoi's degenerated thought processes, see 148–55; on Nietzsche, see 415ff; and on Ibsen, see 338–415.

36. Ibid., vii–viii.

37. Lombroso, "Nordau's 'Degeneration': Its Value and Its Errors," 936.

38. Ibid., 937.

39. Lombroso, *The Man of Genius,* 57.

40. Prichard, *A Treatise on Insanity,* quoted from Augstein, "J C Prichard's Concept of Moral Insanity," 312.

41. Prichard, *A Treatise on Insanity,* 20, 21.

42. Augstein, "J C Prichard's Concept of Moral Insanity," 313.

43. See Gates, "Kurtz's Moral Insanity."

44. Micale, *Approaching Hysteria,* 162.

45. Oppenheim, *"Shattered Nerves,"* 142.

46. Ibid., 144; Micale, *Approaching Hysteria,* 163–4.

47. See Tuke, *DPM,* 618–41. He notes, "The Editor's intention in asking M. Charcot to contribute an article on HYSTERO-EPILEPSY was to present English readers with a description of an affection which M. Charcot has made his own in an especial manner. The whole range of hysteria has, however, been covered, and the readers of the DICTIONARY will have the advantage of seeing the subject treated by a Paris as well as a London physician—ED" (627).

48. Picot, obituary of Paul Glatz, xxxvi–xxxvii.

49. See, for instance, McComb, "Nervousness in Women: Its Cause and Cure"; Call, "How Women Can Keep from Being Nervous"; and Putnam, "The Nervous Breakdown."

50. Sicherman, "The Uses of a Diagnosis," 42.

51. Rosenberg, "The Place of George M. Beard in Nineteenth-Century Psychiatry," 245–59.

52. Sicherman, "The Uses of a Diagnosis," 34.

53. Rosenberg, "The Place of George M. Beard in Nineteenth-Century Psychiatry," 249–50; Sicherman, "The Uses of a Diagnosis," 34.

54. As early as 1869 Beard predicted that neurasthenia's pathology would eventually be found (Rosenberg, "The Place of George M. Beard in Nineteenth-Century Psychiatry," 249, quoting Beard from "Neurasthenia or Nervous Exhaustion," *Boston M. & S. J.* 80 [1869]: 217; Beard, "The Nature and Diagnosis of Neurasthenia," 229–31).

55. Beard, "The Nature and Diagnosis of Neurasthenia," 225; Beard, "The Sequences of Neurasthenia," 18.

56. Jewell, "The Varieties and Causes of Neurasthenia," 2–3.

57. Rosenberg, "The Place of George M. Beard in Nineteenth-Century Psychiatry," 254.

58. Sicherman, "The Uses of a Diagnosis," 42.

59. Haller, "Neurasthenia: Medical Profession and Urban 'Blahs.'" See also Haller, "Neurasthenia: The Medical Profession and the 'New Woman.'"

60. See "The American Disease," 497.

61. Hughes, "Notes on Neurasthenia," 440.

62. Beard, "The Sequences of Neurasthenia," 19–25.

63. Ibid., 19–20.

64. Poirier, "The Weir Mitchell Rest Cure," 18–20.

65. Savage and Goodall, *Insanity and Allied Neuroses,* 97.

66. Ford, *Return to Yesterday,* 262–4.

67. Najder, *Joseph Conrad: A Chronicle,* 37.

68. See Najder, *Joseph Conrad: A Chronicle,* 16–9.

69. Najder, ed., *Conrad under Familial Eyes,* 92.

70. Ibid., 118, and see 118 n. 44.

71. Osler, *The Principles and Practice of Medicine* (1892), 191–2; Martindale and Westcott, *The Extra Pharmacopoeia,* 1924, 583–4.

72. Martindale and Westcott, *The Extra Pharmacopoeia,* 1924, 585.

73. The major biographers, Karl and Najder, both link illness and depression throughout their interpretations of Conrad's life (see esp. Karl, *Joseph Conrad: The Three Lives,* 63, 305–15, 343–6, 550–1, 673–84, and Najder, *Joseph Conrad: A Chronicle,* 37, 144–6, 262–3, 357–65, 446–7). But their work focuses on Conrad's real and existing depression as opposed to the more abiding and pressing fear of insanity.

74. Quoted in Karl, *Joseph Conrad: The Three Lives,* 70. It should here be noted that "fit" was also a common name for an attack or episode of gout (Osler, *The Principles and Practice of Medicine* [1892], 290).

75. Najder, ed., *Conrad's Polish Background,* 9n.

76. Meyers, *Joseph Conrad: A Biography,* 22–3.

77. Savage and Goodall, *Insanity and Allied Neuroses,* 423.

78. Keith Carabine wonders if Conrad's knowledge of Dostoievski (in French) in the 1880s and 1890s would have exposed him to extreme forms of mental instability and perhaps explains his extremely hostile reaction to Dostoievski, himself a profound psychologist. See Carabine, *The Life and the Art.*

79. Lombroso, *The Man of Genius,* 337–8.

80. Thomas Sydenham, English physician and author of a work on gout, quoted in *DPM,* 548.

81. Although Beard does not start publishing regularly on neurasthenia until 1879, according to Rosenberg, Beard first mentions the disorder in 1869 (see n. 54 above). Berthier and his 1869 work on gout and insanity, published in *Annales médico-psychologiques,* is discussed in Kiernan, "An Historical Case of Gouty Insanity" (27), and in International Medical

Congress, *Transactions* (640–1), which contains an abstracted discussion of Henry Rayner and George H. Savage.

82. Savage and Goodall, *Insanity and Allied Neuroses,* 450–1.

83. Letter to Conrad from Tadeusz Bobrowski in Najder, ed., *Conrad's Polish Background,* 137.

Chapter 2. Conrad's Water Cures

1. Karl, *Joseph Conrad: The Three Lives,* 307.

2. Najder, ed., *Conrad's Polish Background,* 137.

3. Karl, *Joseph Conrad: The Three Lives,* 311; Najder, ed., *Conrad's Polish Background,* 143–5.

4. Weber and Weber, *The Spas and Mineral Waters of Europe,* 9; Weber and Hinsdale, *A System of Physiologic Therapeutics,* 3:168. In the later part of the nineteenth century, the spa was variously referred to as Bains de Champel, Champel, and finally, Champel-les-Bains.

5. Weber and Weber, *The Spas and Mineral Waters of Europe,* 1–9.

6. Ibid., 295, 310.

7. Beard, *A Practical Treatise on Nervous Exhaustion (Neurasthenia),* 134.

8. Hughes, "Notes on Neurasthenia," 440.

9. Weber and Weber, *The Spas and Mineral Waters of Europe,* 301.

10. Hughes, "Notes on Neurasthenia," 440.

11. Weber and Weber, *The Spas and Mineral Waters of Europe,* 318.

12. Beard, *A Practical Treatise on Nervous Exhaustion (Neurasthenia),* 84.

13. In 1879 George M. Beard, in one of his first publications ("The Nature and Diagnosis of Neurasthenia [Nervous Exhaustion]"), concedes that neurasthenia is sometimes thought to be another name for anemia, but he asserts that the two are distinct and that neurasthenia is not necessarily accompanied by anemia. Beard later discusses the relationship between neurasthenia and dyspepsia (*A Practical Treatise on Nervous Exhaustion [Neurasthenia],* 72–3). Hughes cites "impaired nutrition and assimilation" among the "leading symptoms" of neurasthenia ("Notes on Neurasthenia," 440); likewise, Jewell suggests that dyspeptic neurasthenia is characterized by "impaired appetite, . . . imperfect digestion, . . . impoverished blood, and hence a starved, worn, nervous system" ("The Varieties and Causes of Neurasthenia," 5).

14. Weber and Weber, *The Spas and Mineral Waters of Europe,* 307–8 (ultimate emphasis added).

15. See Bruce Johnson's discussion of Schopenhauer and the paralysis of will in *Conrad's Models of Mind,* 11.

16. See Tuke, *DPM,* 519ff. In mid-September? 1900, Conrad writes to Ford Madox Ford with grim humor: "I am at work and beastly seedy with cold, cough, piles and a derangement of the bowels. No doubt paralysis isn't far off" (*CL,* 2:293).

17. Meyer, *Joseph Conrad: A Psychoanalytic Biography,* 220.

18. Tuke, *DPM,* 659–60. At the time of its first publication (1892), the *DPM* distinguished between idiocy and imbecility, which was regarded as a milder form of idiocy. While the classification of the various forms of insanity was an ongoing project, the classification of the forms of idiocy and imbecility was a relatively new undertaking (see *DPM,* 659–65).

19. In May of 1890 Conrad wrote to Karol Zagórski, referring to the weak health of the company's employees in the Congo, "French! Neurotics! (It's very fashionable to be neurotic.)" (Translated by the editors from Conrad's French: "Des Nevrosés! [C'est trés chic d'être nevrosé—]" [*CL,* 1:52]).

20. Kneipp, "My Water Cure," 813. See also Ferro, "The Wörishofen Water-cure and Pfarrer Kneipp."

21. Ralph, "The Famous Cures and Humbugs of Europe," 669–70; see also Rae, "Life at Bohemian Baths."

22. Weber and Weber, *The Spas and Mineral Waters of Europe,* 42–3.

23. Karl, *Joseph Conrad: The Three Lives,* 293.

24. Moore, "Conrad, Dr. Gachet, and the 'School of Charenton,'" 172–3.

25. Doiteau, "La Curieuse Figure du Dr. Gachet," 169–72. The British Library houses a hard copy of Gachet's thesis. See also Rousseau, "Cézanne, Dr. Gachet, and the Hanged Man."

26. Joanna van Gogh-Bonger, "Memoir of Vincent van Gogh by his Sister-in-Law," 1:li.

27. Vincent van Gogh, *The Complete Letters of Vincent van Gogh,* 3:273.

28. Mack, *Paul Cézanne,* 176; Rousseau, "Cézanne, Dr. Gachet, and the Hanged Man," 30.

29. All translations in the text are by the author. In the original, "très fréquenté par les convalescents et les nevropathes." See *Paterson's Guide to Switzerland,* 87; and Baedeker, *La Suisse,* 233.

30. Glatz, *Dyspepsies nerveuses et neurasthénie.* See also his *Sur la melancolie; Des dyspepsies avec suppression de la sécrétion du suc gastrique; Effets physiologiques et thérapeutiques des bains de siège; L'Hydrothérapie aux Bains de Champel près Genève; L'Hydrothérapie: les eaux de l'Arve; L'Hydrothérapie envisagé comme médication tonique et revulsive; Quelques cas d'épilepsie traites avec succès par l'hydrothérapie;* "Quelques réflexions sur l'empirisme en médecine"; "Réflexions sur l'empirisme en médecine à propos d'hydrothérapie"; *Résumé clinique sur le diagnostic & le traitement des différentes espèces de néphrite;* and *Du traitement de la névralgie sciatique par l'hydrothérapie & l'électricité.*

31. See Glatz, *L'Hydrothérapie aux Bains de Champel près Genève .*

32. In the original, "mais l'anémie et l'état nerveux existent le plus souvent simultanément; de là naît une complication et une difficulté dans le traitement, qu'il n'est pas toujours facile de surmonter; ce qui convient à l'un ne convient pas à l'autre, et pourtant nous devons trouver le moyen de vaincre l'un et l'autre, de combiner un traitement s'adaptant à l'un et à l'un autre; c'est dans ces cas que le médecin doit

agir avec la plus grande prudence et beaucoup de discernement"
(Glatz, *L'Hydrothérapie aux Bains de Champel près Genève*, 33–4).
33. Glatz, *Des dyspepsies avec suppression de la sécrétion du suc
gastrique et plus particulièrement de la dyspepsie neurasthénique*.
34. Glatz, *L'Hydrothérapie: les eaux de l'Arve*, 35.
35. In the original, "déprimés et très affaiblis; aux grands fatigués qui
sentent la nécessité d'un repos absolu et complet" (Glatz, *Dyspepsies
nerveuses et neurasthénie*, 4).
36. In the original, "l'usage abusif du lait" (ibid., 6).
37. In the original,
Le matin à 7 h.: friction au drap mouillé (eau froide de 14° à
10° C., friction énergique, drap bien tordu).
A 8h.: deux soucoupes de porridge, deux œufs à la coque,
toast, beurre.
A 9h.: massage de tout le corps de 1/2 heure à 1 heure.
A 10h.: un à deux œufs, bouillie au tapioca, une petite tasse de
lait.
A midi: viandes rôties, légumes verts, purée aux lentilles,
macaronis, riz, pain grillé, un verre de Porto ou de Bordeaux, ou
de Bourgogne, séjour en plein air jusqu'à 3 heures.
A 4 h.: 2me massage, puis: œufs, purée aux lentilles, ou farine
lactée, du thé au lait et pain de Graham (*brown bread* ou pain
complet), beurre. Séjour en plein air, ou promenade de 30 à 60
minutes.
A 5 h.: s'il y a lieu, faradisation de tout le corps avec la brosse
ou le pinceau métallique.
A 6 h.: même repas qu'à midi, puis repos en plein air sur une
chaise longue jusqu'à 8 heures.
A 8 1/2 h.: maillot calmant, ou friction au drap mouillé, suivant
l'indication du moment (ibid., 6–7).
38. In the original, "un drap de grosse toile écrue est trempé dans de
l'eau froide, puis fortement tordu. Le doucheur applique ce drap sur le
corps du baigneur, en ayant sooin de l'enrouler et de le serrer autour
des exrémités inférieures. Avant l'application du drap, comme avant
n'importe quelle opération hydrothérapique (douches, piscines, demi-
bains, etc.), il ne faut pas oublier de mouiller la figure, la poitrine, la
nuque, le dos, les aisselles du malade, de lui poser une compresse
froide sur la tête; et enfin chez les malades, qui se plaignent de
céphalagies et ont facilement le sang à la tête de faire mettre pendant la
douche les pieds dans l'eau chaude, et de finir l'opération par un jet
brisé dirigé pendant quelques secondes et avec force sur les pieds.
Toutes ces précautions sont nécessaires pour prévenir la possibilité
d'une congestion interne, et surtout atténuer dan les limites du possible
la première impression toujours désagréable que chacun ressent, quand
il reçoit le premier jet d'eau froide" (ibid., 24).
39. In the original, "Outre l'hydrothérapie calmante et tonique, nous
avons généralement recours à l'électricité, en particulier à la galvan-
isation de la moelle cervicale et allongée, et à celle du nerf sympathique
au cou, avec des courants très faibles et de courte durée. L'électrisation

produit un effet remarquable sur les mouvements du cœur; et après l'emploi des courants continus, nous avons souvent constaté une diminution notable du nombre des pulsations" (ibid., 31).

40. In the original, "Il est certes incontestable que l'on peut obtenir un effet sédatif de l'usage prolongé de l'eau très froid . . . [C']est dangereuse" (ibid., 33).

41. Ibid., 35.

42. Jean-Aubry, *Joseph Conrad: Life and Letters,* 2:339.

Chapter 3. Conrad's Breakdown

1. For a description of the unhappy honeymoon, see Conrad's letters of the time (*CL,* 1:269–304), especially those to Edward Garnett; Karl, *Joseph Conrad: The Three Lives,* 370–8; Najder, *Joseph Conrad: A Chronicle,* 196–8; and Meyer, *Joseph Conrad: A Psychoanalytic Biography,* 118–9.

2. Bobrowski to JC, 6 June 1891, quoted in Najder, ed., *Conrad's Polish Background,* 141. See also Karl, *Joseph Conrad: The Three Lives,* 215–7, and Najder, *Joseph Conrad: A Chronicle,* 79.

3. Weber and Weber, *The Spas and Mineral Waters of Europe,* 42–3.

4. For the theory on Conrad's difficult adjustment to married life, see Meyer, *Joseph Conrad: A Psychoanalytic Biography,* 118–28.

5. Weber and Weber, *The Spas and Mineral Waters of Europe,* 47, 281.

6. Hueffer [Ford], *The Cinque Ports,* 214–5, viii, respectively.

7. For a discussion of Ford's disparaging comments on his own work, see Saunders, *Ford Madox Ford,* 1:118.

8. Najder, ed., *Conrad's Polish Background,* 226–7; *CL,* 2:131–2.

9. At this time, Wells was treated for a variety of illnesses, including claustrophobia, under the care of Dr. Henry Hick. In a state of ill health, he moved from Romney Marsh to Sandgate in September of 1898, about the same time the Conrads moved into the Pent. See MacKenzie and MacKenzie, *H. G. Wells: A Biography,* 137–40.

10. *The Medical Directory,* 1918, 707.

11. Alfred Clifford John Hill Hackney, student records, Fee Books and Calendars, 1891–6, Records Office, University College, London; *The Medical Directory,* 1896, 418. See also Mickle, "General Paralysis," *DPM,* 519–44, and *General Paralysis of the Insane.*

12. John Conrad, *Joseph Conrad: Times Remembered,* 81. The idea that Tebb was among the first doctors Conrad consulted in England seems dubious, since Tebb probably began his practice in 1890 in Sydenham. Since Tebb was also friends with the Garnett family, it is possible that Conrad was introduced to Tebb by Edward Garnett sometime after their acquaintance in the fall of 1895 (see the appendix to this volume and also Bock, "What Has Happened to Poor Tebb?").

13. A. E. Tebb, letter to Ford Madox Ford, 26 July 1935, Ford Madox Ford Collection (#4605), Division of Rare and Manuscript Collections, Cornell University Library, Ithaca, N.Y.; Tebb Autographs, Letters to A. E.

Tebb, the Brotherton Collection, Leeds University Library, Leeds, England; and Lubbock, *George Calderon,* 139.

14. At the asterisk Conrad glosses Tebb for Ford as "The Doctor, friend of Will R[othenstein], admirer of Your Grandfather" (*CL,* 3:185).

15. Rayner Derry Batten (1858–1943) attended the Conrads during his years as a general practitioner. Later in his career, he became one of the leading ophthalmologic surgeons in England, vice president of the Ophthalmological Society, and inventor of the hydrophthalmoscope. Obituary notices appear in the *British Journal of Medicine,* 13 November 1943, 626, and in the *British Journal of Ophthalmology* 27 (1943): 569–70. See also the appendix.

16. Joseph Conrad, letter to A. E. Tebb, 13 December 1905, in Sutton Manuscripts, Lilly Library, Indiana University, Bloomington, Ind.

17. Martindale and Westcott, *The Extra Pharmacopoeia,* 1910, 50; *The Medical Directory,* 1910, xxxvi; Martindale and Westcott, *The Extra Pharmacopoeia,* 1924, 71.

18. In *Joseph Conrad and His Circle,* Jessie Conrad describes how she procured this compound in Poland (148). John Conrad, in *Joseph Conrad: Times Remembered,* indicates that his father avoided medication, except when absolutely necessary (80). Phenacetin is a mild analgesic that is no longer used due to possible side effects, which include cancer, high blood pressure, heart attack, and kidney disease. Chlorodyne was a tincture of chloroform and morphine, readily available in such proprietary medicines as Freeman's Chlorodyne, which was advertised to treat influenza, diarrhea, dysentery, and even cholera.

19. See McLendon, "Conrad and Calomel."

20. For contemporary medical information on mercury, see Osler, *The Principles and Practice of Medicine* (1902), 1079.

21. Beetham, *A Magazine of Her Own,* 191.

22. "A Fit of the Blues," 280.

23. I have found no evidence that the Conrad household subscribed to or read any of these "penny" weekly magazines. But their proliferation, their low price, their emphasis on domesticity (food, health, hygiene, fashion), and the practice of shared circulation of journals among circles of friends (see Hampson, "Frazer, Conrad, and the 'Truth of Primitive Passion,'" 172) all argue that such publications and the values, ideas, and commodities they promoted were current and available to the sentient.

24. "The Wonders of Phosphorus," 61.

25. *Home Chat,* respectively: 56 (23 January 1909): 281; 56 (13 February 1909): 425; 56 (27 February 1909): 507; 57 (13 March 1909): 603; 57 (27 March 1909): 119; and 57 (8 May 1909): 395.

26. *Guy's Hospital Pupils' Returns,* 1880–1, Records of Guy's Medical School Library, London. Unless otherwise noted, information on Tebb's academic preparation comes from these records.

27. The Tebb Autographs indicate that from his late teens Tebb was becoming a serious amateur violinist. He preserved an 1881 letter from

J. H. B. Dando that suggests that Tebb had written to the violinist inquiring about Dando's lowest fee for lessons, whether receiving lessons with a companion would reduce the fee, and whether it was necessary to furnish his own instrument. A year later, Tebb also corresponded with John Bishop, a translator of several books on the life and work of Stradivarius and other violin makers. Bishop's rather testy letter responding to Tebb suggests that Tebb had put to him some rather difficult or abstruse questions about timbre and the acoustics of the violin, and he may have also sought Bishop's opinion regarding a particular instrument. In 1885 Tebb corresponded with J. B. Paznauskui, a London violin virtuoso, though whether the interview Tebb arranged was to apply as a pupil or appear as an admirer is unclear from the letter. Tebb's autograph letters indicate that in the 1890s his interest in the arts broadens to include a desire to collect fine prints. In 1893 Tebb corresponded with C. J. Middleton Wake about the prints of Dürer and Rembrandt and, more generally, the process of printmaking. Two letters in the collection (dated 1895) are from Frederick Wedmore, who showed Tebb some lithographs by Whistler and with whom Tebb apparently struck up a friendship. The Tebb Autographs also contain a letter from Arthur Symons, answering several questions about Odilon Redon. In subsequent years, Tebb would develop quite an extensive collection of Redon lithographs and prints by Beardsley. Other letters of this time are from men of letters, including the poet Thomas Woolner, London publishers, and booksellers.

28. Certificate of Marriage of Albert Edward Tebb and Bertha Mary Carr, 19 December 1898, Record Keeper's Department, Sumerset House, London; *The Medical Directory,* 1906; Colvin, "Robert Lewis Stevenson in Hampstead," 144; *Kelly's Hampstead and Child's Hill Directory,* 1912–3, 121; Barratt, *The Annals of Hampstead,* 2:66–7.

29. Olive Garnett, "A Bloomsbury Girlhood," unpublished typescript, Harry Ransom Humanities Research Center, University of Texas at Austin, 476, 478, 497, 504, 510; *CL,* 3:337; Speaight, *William Rothenstein,* 222; and Lubbock, *George Calderon.*

30. Olive Garnett expresses concern that Ford was becoming too dependent psychologically on Tebb ("A Bloomsbury Girlhood"). See Moser, *The Life in the Fiction of Ford Madox Ford,* 59.

31. In *The Flurried Years,* Violet Hunt describes Tebb as

> [t]he queer, clever, weedy man who stooped so for despair, not laziness. Himself he could not save. But you called him and he came, hasting, his baggy umbrella in front of him, the flaps of his greatcoat nearly touching the ground, looking like Santa Claus or the Old Clo' Man bringing the babies. He brought several pre-Raphaelite babies into the world and one of Conrad's. He was a magician, a wonder-doctor, as one would have expected from his quack-like appearance, white-complexioned, blue-eyed, bewildered. . . . He took your case home to think out a cure for it—keeping it a terrible time. Say you had something the matter

with your fingers? Weeks hence he would reappear with a bag, put some unknown drug into your shoulder, and, hey presto! you were cured. But how could a man like that make money? He was poor—and likely to remain so. (33–4)

32. Hunt, *The Flurried Years,* 211.

33. For Ford's assertions about his association with Conrad, see his *Return to Yesterday,* 186.

34. Conrad may also have been anxious to have Tebb as his physician because of Tebb's personal and professional interest in tuberculosis. Tebb's son, Robert Palmer Tebb—referred to familiarly as Robin in correspondence between Jessie Conrad and Alice Rothenstein—died in 1913 of basilar meningitis, then thought to be the meningeal form of tuberculosis. Tebb, later in his career, would conduct research and publish on tuberculosis, the disease that killed both of Conrad's parents. See Death Certificate of Robert Francis Palmer Tebb, 7 January 1913, Record Keeper's Department, Sumerset House, London; Jessie Conrad to Alice Rothenstein, 4 August 1904, Papers of Sir William Rothenstein, Houghton Library, Harvard University, Cambridge, Mass.; see Tebb and Greenwood, "An Inquiry into the Prevalence and Aetiology of Tuberculosis among Industrial Workers"; Greenwood, Hudson, and Tebb, "Report on the Metabolism of Female Munition Workers."

35. Office of Student Records, University of London Library, Senate House, London; "The Dean's Report of 1893–4," *Guy's Hospital Medical School, 1894–95,* 71.

36. "Dean's Report," 35.

37. Ibid.

38. Review of *Insanity and Allied Neuroses,* by Savage and Goodall, *British Journal of Psychiatry* 54 (1908): 134–5.

39. Woolf, *The Letters of Virginia Woolf,* 1:147. See also Trombley, *All That Summer She Was Mad,* and Woolf, *Mrs. Dalloway,* 99–100.

40. Savage and Goodall, *Insanity and Allied Neuroses,* 4.

41. Savage, "Moral Insanity."

42. Savage and Goodall, *Insanity and Allied Neuroses,* 96.

43. Professional disagreements about the gender specificity of neurasthenia will be examined in chapter 4.

44. Goldring, *South Lodge,* 83.

45. Ford, *Return to Yesterday,* 261.

46. Ibid., 261.

47. Ibid., 266–8.

48. Savage and Goodall, *Insanity and Allied Neuroses,* 96.

49. For the "prophet of death," see Saunders, *Ford Madox Ford,* 1:191; for the famous teacher's advice, Savage and Goodall, *Insanity and Allied Neuroses,* 96–7.

50. Goldring, *South Lodge,* 83.

51. Jessie Conrad, *Joseph Conrad and His Circle,* 140–1.

52. See Carabine, *The Life and the Art,* 59–60.

53. Moser, *Joseph Conrad: Achievement and Decline.*

54. Jessie Conrad, *Joseph Conrad and His Circle,* 142.

Chapter 4. The Vivid, Nervous Descriptions of Conrad's Fictions

1. Joseph Conrad, "The *Torrens:* A Personal Tribute," 24. Later in the essay, Conrad links his neurasthenia to malaria: "I was then recovering slowly from a bad breakdown, after a most unpleasant and persistent tropical disease which I caught in Africa" (27).

2. Ibid., 24.

3. See, for instance, *CL,* 1:238–40, in which Conrad responds to Sanderson's revelation about a bout with dysentery.

4. Sanderson quoted in Stape and Knowles, eds., *A Portrait in Letters,* 19.

5. *Oxford English Dictionary* (1933 ed.), s.v. "nervous."

6. Recent discussions of Conrad's use of immobility include Billy, "'Nothing to be done': Conrad, Beckett, and the Poetics of Immobility," which suggests that Conrad's depiction of "psychological immobility" in his characters illustrates the "epistemological uncertainty" of modernist fiction; and Boulicaut, "'Action, the barbed hook' (J. Conrad, *Victory*) or the Syndrome of the Motionless Hero," which argues that the isolation of Conradian heroes such as Willems and Lord Jim leads to a disease of "immobilism" that effects the voice of Conrad's characters. Conversely, see also Hubbard, *Theories of Action in Conrad,* on agency in Conrad, and Land, *Paradox and Polarity in the Fiction of Joseph Conrad,* for his theory of purposive action in Conrad's fiction.

7. On the traditional segregation of sexes, see Glatz, "L'Hydrothérapie: les eaux de l'Arve," 8.

8. For the term "constitutional syphilis," see Weber and Weber, *The Spas and Mineral Waters of Europe,* 206–8.

9. Maupassant quoted in Ignotus, *The Paradox of Maupassant,* 239.

10. Glatz quoted in Sherard, *The Life, Work, and Evil Fate of Guy de Maupassant,* 206.

11. See Beard, *Sexual Neurasthenia [Nervous Exhaustion].* Correspondence of 27 June 1891 with his mother indicates that Maupassant planned to take the cure at Champel, for Glatz was "une des meilleurs spécialistes de la Suisse" [one of the leading specialists of Switzerland] and that she should address future correspondence to him at the Hôtel Beau-Séjour, the more expensive hotel associated with the hydropathic institute. Conrad always stayed at the Pension La Roseraie. See Dumesnil, *Chroniques, études, correspondance de Guy de Maupassant,* 406–7; Ignotus, *The Paradox of Maupassant;* and Tassart, *Recollections of Guy de Maupassant,* 290–95.

12. The brochure with the demure woman bears no date, but it does list the title of Dr. Glatz's *Dyspepsies nerveuses et neurasthénie,* which was published in 1898.

13. On male hysteria, Janet Oppenheim quotes Thomas Laycock, who "commented in 1840 that the handful of male hysterics he had observed

were scarcely robust specimens of manhood. 'Of these, two were fat, pale-faced, effeminate-looking men; in the one the affection was attributed to malaria, and he had flabby wasted testicles'" (*"Shattered Nerves,"* 143).

14. For a discussion of complementarity and empire, see Roberts, *Conrad and Masculinity,* 17.

15. Edward Garnett, introduction to *Letters from Joseph Conrad: 1895–1924,* 3, quoted in Najder, *Joseph Conrad: A Chronicle,* 170. For similar references to Conrad's masculinity and femininity, see also Garnett, introduction, 6, 10.

16. Constance Garnett letter quoted in Stape and Knowles, eds., *A Portrait in Letters,* 29.

17. Susan Jones, *Conrad and Women,* 69–98.

18. For scholarship on the gendered views of insanity, see, for instance, two classic works: Showalter, *The Female Malady,* and Gilbert and Gubar, *The Madwoman in the Attic.* More recently, Helen Small in *Love's Madness* examines the love-mad women in the nineteenth-century English novel and in the medical representations of female insanity.

19. See Putnam, "The Nervous Breakdown" (part of a *Good House-keeping* series on "Happiness and Health as promoted by the league of right living"); McComb, "Nervousness in Women"; and Call, "How Women Can Keep from Being Nervous"; and an advertisement in *Home Chat* (28 March 1896: 125), reprinted in Beetham, *A Magazine of Her Own?* 197.

20. Ireland, review of *The Treatment of Neurasthenia,* by Adrien Proust and Gilbert Ballet, 548.

21. Savage and Goodall, *Insanity and Allied Neuroses,* 96; Osler, *The Principles and Practice of Medicine* (1902), 1122.

22. Freud, "On the Grounds for Detaching a Particular Syndrome from Neurasthenia," 3:90–115.

23. Beard, "The Nature and Diagnosis of Neurasthenia (Nervous Exhaustion)," 240–1.

24. Hughes, "Neurasthenia," 363.

25. Oppenheim, *"Shattered Nerves,"* 144.

26. Rankin, "Nervous Break-down," 227, 225, respectively.

27. Ibid., 230–1.

28. Conrad's sense of his feminine self is evident, suggests Susan Jones (*Conrad and Women,* 8), in his comment in a letter to Helen Sanderson that he had wished for a daughter because "she would have resembled me more and would have been perhaps easier to understand" (*CL,* 2:173).

29. Sedgwick, *Epistemology of the Closet,* 48.

30. Sedgwick, *Between Men,* 1.

31. Edward Garnett, introduction to *Letters from Joseph Conrad,* 7.

32. Rothenstein letter quoted in Stape and Knowles, eds., *A Portrait in Letters,* 48.

33. Goldring, *South Lodge,* 83.

34. Fleishman, *Conrad's Politics,* 93, 97.
35. Finn, *Proust, the Body, and Literary Form,* 70.
36. Evelyne Ender, in *Sexing the Mind,* has argued that vocal excess and silence are respectively male and female expressions of hysteria: "[H]ysteria works differently in men and in women: 'powerlessness and excesses of all kinds' for him, 'an ascending and asphyxiating lump'" for her" (137). Tony Tanner, in "'Gnawed Bones' and 'Artless Tales,'" edges toward a similar distinction in Conrad's short story "Falk": "Hermann is verbose, voluble, hysterical, an over-user of words; Falk is invariably silent, and even when he has to talk he is made to seem almost non-lingual" (29).
37. Edward Garnett, introduction to *Letters from Joseph Conrad,* 3.
38. Finn, *Proust, the Body, and Literary Form,* 75.
39. See Meyer, *Joseph Conrad: A Psychoanalytic Biography,* 116–20; Karl, *Joseph Conrad: The Three Lives,* 369–70; Najder, *Joseph Conrad: A Chronicle,* 192–201.
40. Meyer, *Joseph Conrad: A Psychoanalytic Biography,* 118.
41. Jessie Conrad, *Joseph Conrad As I Knew Him,* 105.
42. Meyer, *Joseph Conrad: A Psychoanalytic Biography,* 117.
43. Jessie Conrad recalls that Conrad, before their marriage, asked her to read aloud from his work as he listened critically (*Joseph Conrad As I Knew Him,* 102–3).
44. Edward Garnett, *Letters from Joseph Conrad,* 17–8.

Chapter 5. Restraint
1. Conolly, *Familiar Views of Lunacy and Lunatic Life,* 57.
2. Murchison, "Mechanical Restraint in the Management or Treatment of the Insane," 112–4.
3. Savage, "Notes and News," 154.
4. Campbell, "The Breaking Strain of the Ribs of the Insane."
5. Editorial, *Journal of the British Medical Association,* 23 November 1873, quoting from *Annales médico-psychologiques* (1871): 375–6, in "Reminiscences of Lunacy Practices," *Journal of Psychological Medicine and Mental Pathology* (1875): 215.
6. See Foucault, *Discipline and Punish,* 195–256, and *Madness and Civilization,* 250–61.
7. Putnam, "The Nervous Breakdown," 594–5.
8. Rankin, "Nervous Break-down," 226–7, 228.
9. Maudsley, *Body and Will,* 84, 4, 16, respectively.
10. Ibid., 41–2.
11. Ibid., 95.
12. Ibid., 243–70.
13. Adrien Proust, father of Marcel Proust and a specialist in neurasthenia, observed the high incidence of aboulia in neurasthenic and hysterical French men. In *The Treatment of Neurasthenia,* he notes that, especially in women, "the dominant feature of this neurasthenic state is profound discouragement, powerlessness to exert the will, in one

word, *aboulia,* joined to a degree of *muscular asthenia* that is hardly ever seen except in this form. The patients tire on the slightest effort, and finally they no longer dare to walk. . . . Thenceforward they cease to go out and confine themselves to their room" (73). Finn connects the notion of aboulia with fin-de-siècle ennui (*Proust, the Body, and Literary Form,* 3–4).

14. See Meyer, *Joseph Conrad: A Psychoanalytic Biography,* 112–20, and Moser, *Joseph Conrad: Achievement and Decline,* 71–8.

15. Wiley, *Conrad's Measure of Man,* 25. Celia M. Kingsbury, in "The Novelty of Real Feelings" has seen both "subtlety" and "beauty" in the tale's combination of banality and biting satire. For Conrad's misgivings about the story, see his author's note to *Tales of Unrest* (x) and his correspondence with David Garnett (*CL,* 1:386, 391–4), which both defends and critiques the story, for example.

16. See O'Mealy, "The Herveys and the Verlocs."

17. Mercier, "Vice, Crime, and Insanity," in *A System of Medicine by Many Writers,* 8:853.

18. For comparison, see "The Return" (*TU,* 160). Kingsbury notes that while Hervey "is no Kurtz," he represents "another kind of horror" ("The Novelty of Real Feelings" 38–9). See also Kramer, "Conrad's Experiments with Language and Narrative in 'The Return.'"

19. "[D]enial of feeling in upper middle-class life," from David, "Selfhood and Language in 'The Return' and 'Falk,'" 137.

20. Achebe, "An Image of Africa."Achebe's accusation has prompted a wide-ranging discussion of Conrad's view of civilization and the European civilization that produced Conrad (though all are not specifically in reaction to Achebe). Jacques Berthoud in *Joseph Conrad: The Major Phase,* for instance, examines the concept of restraint as a function of "man's fidelity to the general tradition of civilization" (44); Ian Watt's *Conrad in the Nineteenth Century* studies Conrad in the cultural context of major ideas and cultural influences that helped shape Conrad as a late Victorian and early modern writer; Cedric Watts, in his *A Preface to Conrad,* anatomizes the "cultural background" implied by Conrad's work (42–108); Najder's *Conrad in Perspective* meditates upon the ideas, values, and concepts that characterize Conrad as a European writer in his historical context. For more specific or specialized treatments of Conrad and "civilization," see John Griffith's *Joseph Conrad and the Anthropological Dilemma,* 1–152; Brian W. Shaffer's "'Rebarbarizing Civilization'"; Andrea White's *Joseph Conrad and the Adventure Tradition;* and Robert Hampson's postcolonial reading, *Cross-Cultural Encounters in Joseph Conrad's Malay Fiction* (hereafter cited as *Conrad's Malay Fiction).*

21. For a dialogic discussion of "civilization" and "savagery" in *Heart of Darkness* see Anthony Fothergill's *Heart of Darkness,* 59–85.

22. Andrea White, in *Joseph Conrad and the Adventure Tradition,* argues that Conrad introduces to the discourse on empire a reversal of civilized and savage (140), and in "Conrad and Imperialism" in *The Cambridge Companion to Joseph Conrad,* she observes that "Conrad's

depictions of the white man in the tropics as subversively unheroic [and] his representations of the native also work to destabilize the hegemonic versions of the imperial endeavour" (189).

23. Robert Hampson, in *Conrad's Malay Fiction,* has argued that in *Almayer's Folly* "the novel's initial emphasis on the savage/civilized binary might perhaps be seen as a strategy directed against the European reader. Certainly, with the gradual revelation of the covert plot, and the movement of Malay characters from background to foreground, the savage/civilized binary is problematised" (114). Similarly, Andrew Michael Roberts argues that "Conrad's first two novels . . . raise questions as to how we should read texts which are in many ways in the grip of a stereotyped imperial and misogynistic discourse, and yet deploy irony and ambiguous narrative technique so as to fracture the coherence of that discourse, offering moral and political insight of far greater interest than mere restatement of cliché" (*Conrad and Masculinity,* 38).

24. See Griffith, who sees "the reversion of only partially assimilated people, or people of mixed culture, to savagery . . . [as] another common idea in the period, with clear racial undertones" (*Joseph Conrad and the Anthropological Dilemma,* 137). Hampson, on the other hand, using Homi Bhabha's terms, argues that Nina "finds her identity not through finally choosing (or being forced to choose) her mother's world rather than her father's (that is, by accepting the binaries through which identity is constructed), but rather as a constant performance of identity in the interstices between the different codes and traditions in which she is situated" (*Conrad's Malay Fiction,* 106–7).

25. "Facial expression is much altered, . . . immobile pupils . . . and ataxic conditions . . . replaced by spastic or paralytic ones" (*DPM,* 528) are all later symptoms of general paralysis of the insane (GPI) that transform Almayer into a sexually ambiguous "man-doll."

26. Bannister and Moyer, "On Restraint and Seclusion in American Institutions for the Insane," 463.

27. Gilman, "Black Bodies, White Bodies." For a contemporary discussion of representations of primitive female sexuality, see Ellis, *Studies in the Psychology of Sex,* 4:156–61.

28. Griffith, *Joseph Conrad and the Anthropological Dilemma,* 126.

29. There are numerous treatments of the theme of cannibalism in Conrad. For an overview, see Humphries, "Restraint, Cannibalism and the 'Unspeakable Rites' in *Heart of Darkness.*" See also Tanner, "'Gnawed Bones' and 'Artless Tales,'" 17–36, and Zucherman, "The Motif of Cannibalism in *The Secret Agent.*"

30. Thomson, "The Last of the Cannibal Chiefs," 648; Ward, "Congo Cannibalism," 29; Petrie, "Eaten with Honour," 819. For a discussion of the difference between "cultural cannibalism" and "survival cannibalism" and evidence from contemporary sources on cannibalism in the Congo, see Gill, "The Fascination of the Abomination."

31. Shamming illness was regarded as a typical symptom of hysteria. See Oppenheim, *Shattered Nerves,* 151.

32. Osler identified the dyspeptic and anemic symptoms (*The Principles and Practice of Medicine* [1892], 187–8, 218).

33. In Conrad's works, the police often represent the enforcement of social restraint. One is reminded of Marlow's contempt for Europeans who no longer need "innate strength," surrounded as they are by neighbors, butchers, and police officers who enforce cultural restraints (*HD,* 114, 116).

34. Watts, *Joseph Conrad: A Literary Life,* 49.

35. "Law of Lunacy, 1890 and 1891" (*DPM,* 731).

36. See also other references to nerves and nervousness in *SA,* 156, 176, 182, 187, 193, 211.

37. Steve Ressler, in *Joseph Conrad: Consciousness and Integrity,* observes Conrad's use of the word "horror" and the consequent comparison between Conrad's fear and the revelation of Kurtz in *Heart of Darkness* (15).

38. Frederick R. Karl, in his *Reader's Guide to Joseph Conrad,* suggests the connection between failure of duty and anarchy (112).

39. Tony Tanner, in "'Gnawed Bones' and 'Artless Tales,'" has observed that "the breakdown of a ship and the breakdown of the human body" are analogous (28).

40. Barbara De Mille, in "An Inquiry into Some Points of Seamanship," discusses the analogous activities of the seaman and the narrator of tales in the context of restraint: "Seamanship in the novel is more than the actual art of navigating with which Marlow manages the perilous journey up the Congo River. It is also the art of narrative fabrication with which Marlow is able to call an experience from the profound depths by surrounding it with the necessary symbolic restraint" (97).

41. J. S. Farmer and W. E. Henley, in *Slang and Its Analogues,* cite the nautical meaning of "trick" as "a turn; a spell: *e.g.,* a trick at the helm." But "trick" also carries sexual innuendoes that may prompt the auditor's charge of incivility. "To do the trick" meant "to play the whore" (3:201), and the word "tumble" in venery meant "to possess a woman" or "to be brought to bed" (3:224). Farmer and Henley cite Fletcher's *Woman's Prize* (1615): "Do all the ramping, roaring tricks, a whore Being drunk and tumbling-ripe." That Marlow's sexual punning is intentional is borne out by his contrasting use of the same tight-rope metaphor in a 31 August 1898 letter to Helen Sanderson (*CL,* 2:90), written several months before Conrad began work on *Heart of Darkness* and by a similar metaphor in *The Secret Agent* (92), neither of which carry any secondary, sexual meaning. The sexual subtext in *Heart of Darkness* is introduced by Marlow's inclusion of a price: "'half a crown a tumble'" (*HD,* 94), which was the price of an "East End" (i.e., low class) prostitute who might charge "'three shillings, half a crown, five shillings often occasionally, according to the sort of man'" (quoted in Walkowitz, *Prostitution and Victorian Society,* 23–4).

42. Traditional humanist approaches to *Heart of Darkness* are quite literally too numerous to mention here, but may be represented by such critics as Jerome Thale, "Marlow's Quest," and Garrett Stewart, "Lying as

Dying in *Heart of Darkness*." Peter J. Rabinowitz calls such works "Nature of Man" interpretations; see his "Reader Response, Reader Responsibility: *Heart of Darkness* and the Politics of Displacement," 137–8. Keith Carabine, editor of *Joseph Conrad: Critical Assessments,* collects the following essays under the heading of "'Heart of Darkness': Race, Imperialism and the Third World": Naipaul, "Conrad's Darkness"; Achebe, "An Image of Africa"; Watts, "'A Bloody Racist': About Achebe's View of Conrad"; Hamner, "Colony, Nationhood and Beyond"; Brantlinger, "*Heart of Darkness:* Anti-Imperialism, Racism, or Impressionism?"; Huggan, "Anxieties of Influence: Conrad and the Caribbean"; Nazareth, "Conrad's Descendants"; and Kinkead-Weeks, "*Heart of Darkness* and the Third World Writer." To this selected list, I would add Hampson, introduction to *Heart of Darkness,* ix–xliv; Hawkins, "Conrad's Critique of Imperialism in *Heart of Darkness*"; and Firchow, *Envisioning Africa.*

43. Robert Hampson discusses the Frazerian metaphor of civilization as having a "solid layer of savagery beneath the surface of society" being applicable to both Conrad and *Heart of Darkness* ("Frazer, Conrad, and the 'Truth of Primitive Passion,'" 177). Hampson notes that an analogous metaphor is used by Bertrand Russell in his *Portraits from Memory* to describe Conrad: "I felt, though I do not know whether he would have accepted such an image, that he thought of civilised and morally tolerable human life as a dangerous walk on a thin crust of barely cooled lava which at any moment might break and let the unwary sink into fiery depths" (Russell quoted, 177). The scene in *Heart of Darkness* is analogous in the sense that Marlow feels a precarious attraction to the "incomprehensible frenzy" on the shore, as if walking on a thin veneer of civility.

44. McClure, "The Rhetoric of Restraint in *Heart of Darkness,*" 311. See also De Mille, "An Inquiry into Some Points of Seamanship," 96.

45. See chapter 4.

46. Barbara De Mille argues that "it is through this artist's task of rescue work that Marlow is able to save what he can of Kurtz's memory . . . 'snatching . . . the struggling forms' of the experience of the journey that has involved dangers, temptations, and horrors, into a light, which is the artifice of his narrative. By contrast, Kurtz is noticeably lacking in any form of this work of linguistic conversion, which necessitates restraint" ("An Inquiry into Some Points of Seamanship," 96).

47. McClure, "The Rhetoric of Restraint in *Heart of Darkness,*" 314–5.

48. Savage and Goodall, *Insanity and Allied Neuroses,* 287.

49. One wonders if Conrad was thinking of Darwin's "entangled bank" metaphor in *The Origin of Species,* with its appealing aura of primitive fecundity and interconnection of all life: "It is interesting to contemplate an entangled bank, clothed with many plants of many kinds, with birds singing on the bushes, with various insects flitting about, and with worms crawling through the damp earth, and to reflect that these elaborately constructed forms, so different from each other, and dependent on each other in so complex a manner, have all been produced by laws acting around us. These laws, taken in the largest sense, being growth

and reproduction; inheritance which is almost implied by reproduction" (*The Works of Charles Darwin,* 15:347).

Chapter 6. Solitude/Seclusion

1. Tuke, "Retrospective Glance at the Early History of the Retreat, York," 340.

2. Ibid., 346–7.

3. Quotes from ibid., 348, 345, respectively.

4. Robertson, "Treatment of Mental Excitement in Asylums," 705.

5. Conolly, *Familiar Views of Lunacy and Lunatic Life,* 153–4.

6. Ibid., 154.

7. Robertson, "Treatment of Mental Excitement in Asylums," 705.

8. For a book-length study of the opposition in Conrad between solidarity and solitude, and the ideological and philosophical discussion of that opposition, see Lord, *Solitude versus Solidarity in the Novels of Joseph Conrad.* For more readable treatments of the theme of solidarity and solitude see Manicum, "True Lies/False Truths," which focuses on narration and the dichotomy between "sympathy/detachment and egotism/detachment" (110) in *The Nigger of the "Narcissus,"* and Bruce Johnson's treatment of the ego/sympathy dichotomy in *Conrad's Models of Mind.* For classic treatments of isolation see Paul Wiley's *Conrad's Measure of Man,* which focuses on the opposing figure of the hermit and the incendiary, and Adam Gillon's *The Eternal Solitary: A Study of Joseph Conrad,* which focuses on Conrad's "isolatoes."

9. Paul Kirschner, in "Conrad and Maupassant," suggests that for Maupassant, "the fundamental fact of human existence was moral solitude" (62). Maupassant's story "Solitude" states that confronting this fact can make one "deranged" or "mad" (see Maupassant, *The Complete Short Stories of Guy de Maupassant,* 806–7). Of probable interest to Conrad, and therefore also relevant to this study, are "At the Spa—Diary of the Marquis de Roseveyre," "Mad," "A Madman," "Am I Insane?," "Feminine Men," and "The Spasm."

10. For a systematic treatment of Conrad and existentialism, its major concepts and practitioners, see Bohlmann, *Conrad's Existentialism,* and Bruce Johnson, *Conrad's Models of Mind,* 70–105.

11. The romantic poet John Clare was noted for expressing this thought, especially in "Approaching Night" and "The Exile," respectively:

> Oh, take this world away from me!
> Its strife I cannot bear to see,
> Its very praises hurt me more
> Than e'en its coldness did before,
> Its hollow ways torment me now
> And start a cold sweat on my brow,
> Its noise I cannot bear to hear,
> Its joy is trouble to my ear,
> Its ways I cannot bear to see,
> Its crowds are solitudes to me.

'Tis solitude in city's crowds; all move
Like living death, though all to life still cling.

12. "The Two Solitudes," 593.

13. Ibid., 594.

14. Conrad suggests in a letter to Cunningham Graham that he made the character of Singleton incapable of thought (*CL,* 1:423).

15. Conrad mentions his "hours of solitude" in his author's note to *Youth and Two Other Stories* (x).

16. JC, "Lord Jim: A Sketch." William Blackwood received completed chapters 28–30 and the "beginning of 31" from Conrad by 15 May 1900 (Blackburn, ed., *Letters to William Blackwood and David S. Meldrum,* 93). By 29 June 1900 Conrad was predicting the "last words of Jim" (*CL,* 2:277) might be written before midnight (in fact, it would be late July before he corrected the final typescript [*CL,* 2:286]). Thus, chapter 35 was written sometime between mid-May and late June of 1900.

17. Although Conrad scholars have disagreed about the date of composition of "The Secret Sharer," evidence in the letters (*CL,* 4:296) points to a composition date of early December 1909, after a period of intense depression and about six weeks before his major breakdown of late January 1910. See Najder, *Joseph Conrad: A Chronicle,* 353–4, and Carabine, "'The Secret Sharer': A Note on the Dates of Its Composition."

18. See, for instance, Phelan, "Reading Secrets," 128–44, and Scott, "Intimacies Engendered in Conrad's 'The Secret Sharer,'" 197–210. For articles on Conrad and queer theory, see Ruppel, "Joseph Conrad and the Ghost of Oscar Wilde," and Wilson, "The Best in the Congo: How Victorian Homophobia Infects Marlow's *Heart of Darkness.*"

19. Gillon, *The Eternal Solitary,* 112–7.

20. In his introduction to *Westphal's "Die Agoraphobie"* Terry J. Knapp offers a brief history of the term phobia, from Homer's *Iliad*—whose Ares, the Greek god of war, has a son named Phobos (meaning panic or flight)—through the recognition of phobias by nineteenth-century medical writers, to the discussion of agoraphobia on nationally televised talk shows (1–5).

21. Beard, *A Practical Treatise on Nervous Exhaustion (Neurasthenia),* 50–1; Mercier, "Agoraphobia—A Remedy," 990–1.

22. Beard, *A Practical Treatise on Nervous Exhaustion (Neurasthenia),* 50–1.

23. Ibid., 58.

24. Nordau, in *Degeneration* (242), cites Magnan's "Considérations sur la folie des héréditaires ou dégénerés," with a list of phobias that are symptoms of degeneration, which include agoraphobia and claustrophobia. Even Nordau recognizes that this list is ridiculously long.

25. Haltresht, "The Dread of Space in Conrad's *The Secret Agent,*" 95.

26. Ibid., 89; Ford, *Return to Yesterday,* 261.

27. Conrad discusses the wise simplicity of Singleton in a letter to Cunningham Graham:

Singleton with an education is impossible. But first of all—what education? If it is the knowledge how to live my man essentially possessed it. He was in perfect accord with his life [compare Stein's "how to be"]. . . . Or do you mean the kind of knowledge which would enable him to scheme, and lie, and intrigue his way to the forefront of a crowd no better than himself? Would you seriously, of malice prepense cultivate in that unconscious man the power to think. Then he would become conscious—and much smaller—and very unhappy. Now he is simple and great like an elemental force. Nothing can touch him but the curse of decay—the eternal decree that will extinguish the sun, the stars one by one, and in another instant shall spread a frozen darkness over the whole universe. Nothing else can touch him—he does not think." (*CL,* 1:423)

The elemental simplicity of Singleton is similar, I think, to Yeats's "wise and simple man" imagined in "The Fisherman," that is, one who can embrace the elemental and exist aloof from the "ignorance of the thoroughfares." See Yeats's "The Fisherman" in *The Poems,* 148.

28. Knapp, *Westphal's "Die Agoraphobie,"* 34–5.

29. Mercier, "The Fear of Open and Closed Spaces," 26107.

30. Ibid.

31. Michel Foucault, in *Madness and Civilization,* suggests metaphorically that "madness borrowed its face from the mask of the beast" (72) and that "confinement merely manifested what madness, in its essence, was: a manifestation of non-being" (115).

32. See France, "Abstract of a Paper on the Necessity for Isolating the Phthisical Insane."

33. A classic example of the view of Leggatt's seclusion as the moral protection of an "ideal conception of self" is R. W. Stallman's 1949 essay "Conrad and 'The Secret Sharer,'" later reprinted in his book *The Art of Joseph Conrad* and in Keith Carabine's *Joseph Conrad: Critical Assessments.* Stallman argues, "In terms of the ethical allegory, Leggatt is the embodiment of the captain's moral consciousness. His appearance answers the captain's question—'I wondered how far I should turn out faithful to that ideal conception of one's own personality every man sets up for himself secretly'" (Carabine, ed., *Joseph Conrad: Critical Assessments,* 279–80).

34. For this reading of "The Secret Sharer" see Bruce Harkness's spoof, "The Secret of 'The Secret Sharer' Bared"; see also Barbara Johnson and M. Garber, "Secret Sharing: Reading Conrad Psychoanalytically," and Phelan, "Reading Secrets," 136–40.

35. It should be remembered (at the risk of being simplistic) that Leggatt likes being looked at because of his solitary confinement on the *Sephora:* "I didn't mind being looked at. I—I liked it. And then you speaking to me so quietly—as if you had expected me—made me hold on a bit longer." Leggatt is simply starved for sympathetic companionship, but his phrase "holding on a bit longer" also suggests the restraint and endurance he has needed during his confinement to maintain his

mental balance. "It had been a confounded lonely time," he confessed—"I don't mean while swimming. I was glad to talk a little to somebody that didn't belong to the *Sephora*" (*TLS,* 110–1). Thus the rigorous seclusion of the *Sephora,* slavishly enforced by the unimaginative Archbold, becomes, on the ship of the young captain, a more protective and humanized seclusion offered by the inexperienced officer.

36. Critics who study Conrad's narrative technique include Jakob Lothe (*Conrad's Narrative Method*), who focuses on various methods of narrative distance; Ian Watt, who discusses the "delayed decoding" and Conrad's narrative progress (*Conrad in the Nineteenth Century,* 269–310); and Jeremy Hawthorn (*Joseph Conrad: Narrative Technique and Ideological Commitment*), who focuses on Conrad's narrators, distance, and commitment to/complicity in various ideological positions inscribed in the events of Conrad's fiction. For the linguistic and ideological significance of silence in Conrad's work, see, for instance, Ray, "Language and Silence in the Novels of Joseph Conrad"; Pecora, "*Heart of Darkness* and the Phenomenology of Narrative Voice"; Straus, "The Exclusion of the Intended from Secret Sharing in Conrad's *Heart of Darkness,*" which focuses on the feminist reader who is excluded from the truths spoken by Conrad's masculinist characters and text; and an essay by Myrtle Hooper, who, building on Achebe, asks "Is the silence [of Africans] really there, or is it inscribed into the encounter by the party whose interpretation can predominate?" ("The Heart of Light: Silence in Conrad's *Heart of Darkness,*" 112).

37. Lothe, *Conrad's Narrative Method,* 12–3.

38. Ibid., 133.

39. Regarding Singleton, "who does not think," see chap. 6, n. 27, above.

Chapter 7. Water

1. Regarding the "elemental force" in Conrad's sea novels, Jacques Berthoud, in *Joseph Conrad: The Major Phase,* reminded us in a period of multiplying interpretations that the sea is fundamentally "the element on which the ship sails" (25–6). Although Ian Watt does not specifically discuss the fog in relation to Marlow's delay in perception, his concept of human perception and "delayed decoding" is analogous to fog (Watt, *Conrad in the Nineteenth Century,* 175–80). The fog that enshrouds Marlow as he approaches the inner station delays perception by many hours. See also Bock, *Crossing the Shadow-Line,* 105–7. For a discussion of the reversal of the archetype of water and rebirth (water as contaminated fog and slime in street gutters), see Rosenfield, *Paradise of Snakes,* 94–5.

2. For the "allegorical/mythical threshold," see Thale, "Marlow's Quest." For water as archetypal medium, see Rosenfield, *Paradise of Snakes,* 65–6.

3. Berthoud, "Conrad and the Sea," xx–xxii.

4. See chapter 3.

5. Glatz, *Des dyspepsies avec suppression de la sécrétion du suc gastrique,* 30–1.

6. Glatz, "Champel-les-Bains: établissement hydrothérapique," 4.

7. Glatz, *Dyspepsies nerveuses et neurasthénie,* 7.

8. For treatments of Marlow's homosociality/sexuality, see, for instance, Hodges, "Deep Fellowship: Homosexuality and Male Bonding in the Life and Fiction of Joseph Conrad"; Ruppel, "Joseph Conrad and the Ghost of Oscar Wilde"; and Ruppel, "The Economy of Desire in *Heart of Darkness.*" Marlow's misogyny, gynophobia, and homosexual attractions are discussed by Nina Pelikan Straus ("The Exclusion of the Intended from Secret Sharing," 127, 132–3) and Johanna M. Smith ("'Too Beautiful Altogether': Ideologies of Gender and Empire in *Heart of Darkness,"* 169–84, esp. 177–82).

9. Marlow corrects himself, reflecting on her picture, "She struck me as beautiful—I mean she had a beautiful expression" (*HD,* 154), and then he asserts that he visited her out of curiosity "and also some other feelings, perhaps." Robert Hampson notes that in Conrad's comment to David Meldrum (*CL,* 2:145–6) there is "a mere shadow of love interest just in the last pages" (Hampson, ed., *Heart of Darkness: With "The Congo Diary,"* 117n). See also Watts, *The Deceptive Text,* 138–40.

10. James Phelan, for instance, suggests that this represents a "loss of potency and heat" ("Reading Secrets,"136).

11. Joyce critics identify a "reader-trap" as a textual ploy: the author traps readers by enticing them with received ideas, acceding to their expectations and complacency, and then subverting or reversing the initial expectation.

12. Ted Billy, in *A Wilderness of Words: Closure and Disclosure in Conrad's Short Fiction,* argues that the narrator's belief that "he has achieved a kind of reintegration of the self as a result of Leggatt's plunge . . . cannot be synonymous with authentic maturity" (27).

13. Ambrosini, *Conrad's Fiction as Critical Discourse,* 64ff. See also *CL,* 1:268, 286–7, and Ford, introduction to *The Sisters,* by Joseph Conrad, 6, 3, 16.

14. "The Rescuer" was eventually published as *Rescue* in 1919.

15. Garnett letter in Stape and Knowles, eds., *A Portrait in Letters,* 25.

16. See Ambrosini, *Conrad's Fiction as Critical Discourse,* 65.

17. Ibid., 66.

18. For a discussion of Conrad's use of direct and indirect discourse, see Hawthorn, *Joseph Conrad: Narrative Technique and Ideological Commitment,* 1–66.

19. Berthoud, "Conrad and the Sea," xx.

20. Garnett letter in Stape and Knowles, eds., *A Portrait in Letters,* 25.

21. Willems here seems to anticipate the hysterical rhetoric of Jim in the witness box (*LJ,* 30–1).

22. Because many medical psychologists believed nervous disorders such as neurasthenia were brought on by modern urban life, it was sometimes observed that madness and other diseases of the nervous system were rare in "primitive" civilizations (see *DPM,* 1206). On the

other hand, certain "men of medicine" in what was called "Ethnological Psychiatry" saw a close link between race and mental degeneration. See, for instance the work of James G. Kiernan, who wrote a series of studies, "Race and Insanity," focusing especially on "The Negro Race" for the *Journal of Nervous and Mental Disease* (see 12 [1885]: 174–5, 290–3; 13 [1886]: 74–6, 229–44, 389–92). See also Cesare Lombroso's work on criminal anthropology, for example, *Criminal Man.*

23. In *A Personal Record,* Conrad remembers Jacques in the context of his own Geneva convalescence (14–7).

24. For a balanced discussion of this critical debate, see Lothe, *Conrad's Narrative Method* (87–101), which summarizes important contributions to the discussion of the novel's narrative method.

25. Barthes, *The Pleasure of the Text,*14.

26. This effect is similar to the indeterminate "voice of unrest" described by Charles Eric Reeves in "A Voice of Unrest: Conrad's Rhetoric of the Unspeakable," esp. 304–7.

27. See Najder, *Joseph Conrad: A Chronicle,* 491.

Chapter 8. Medical Allegory in the Later Novels

1. *The Medical Directory,* 1909, 1137. See also Map of Kent, in *Kelly's Directory of Canterbury,* frontispiece.

2. Compare, for instance, Vladimir's comment in *The Secret Agent,* "madness alone is truly terrifying" (*SA,* 31) or Marlow's in *Heart of Darkness,* when he refers to "the holy terror of scandal and gallows and lunatic asylums" (*HD,* 116).

3. Mickle, *General Paralysis of the Insane,* 281–2; Hackney, Fee Books and Calendars, 1891–6. Mickle was the instructor for University College, London's course in mental diseases that Clifford Hackney took in 1895–6. The university calendar describes the course as follows: "The Course of Instruction in Mental Diseases during Summer Session consists of about twelve systematic lectures, of one hour each, at University College; and of 12 (or more) Clinical Demonstrations, of one hour each, on Patients at Grove Hall Asylum." An earlier description from the 1893–4 calendar indicated that course lectures emphasize "mental physiology, esp. in its relation to mental disorder."

4. See, for instance, Watts, "Marketing Modernism: How Conrad Prospered"; Hampson, introduction and "The Wisdom of the Heart: Chance and *Victory,*" both in *Joseph Conrad: Betrayal and Identity;* and Susan Jones, *Conrad and Women.*

5. See Wiley, *Conrad's Measure of Man,* 13 and passim.

6. For divergent readings that Conrad's powers were declining or that there was a shift in Conrad's fictional and career interests, see Moser, *Joseph Conrad: Achievement and Decline,* 1–9, and Susan Jones, *Conrad and Women,* 134–76, respectively.

7. Recently, Susan Jones has argued that "Conrad creates a network of voyeurs, who, tantalised by the object of their view, nevertheless fail to represent her accurately. Marlow, however, believes firmly in his own

authority as interpreter of all he sees and hears" (*Conrad and Women,* 118). Andrew Michael Roberts counters that "Marlow's own role in the events that he narrates. . . [is] largely a passive one of observing and waiting." Such passivity often gives women, in Marlow's view, a "clear vision of reality." But, Roberts, like Jones, concludes that such passive observation and the language Marlow uses "suggests a strong voyeuristic element" and that the exchanges between Marlow and the frame-narrator amount to "a secret sharing of male ignorance, a covert fellowship of fear and desire in relation to the feminine" (*Conrad and Masculinity,* 155, 159).

8. Watts, *The Deceptive Text,* 138–40.

9. For discussions of this paradox, see the chapter entitled *"Chance:* Conrad's Anti-feminine Feminist Novel," in Hawthorn, *Joseph Conrad: Narrative Technique and Ideological Commitment,* esp. 149–55, and also Susan Jones, *Conrad and Women,* esp. 112–23.

10. In the preface to *The Shadow-Line,* Conrad remarks that "the aim of this piece of writing was the presentation of certain facts which certainly were associated with the change from youth, care-free and fervent, to the more self-conscious and more poignant period of maturer life. Nobody can doubt that before the supreme trial of a whole generation" (*SL,* viii). The dedication to the novel reads, "To Borys and all others who like himself have crossed in early youth the shadow-line of their generation; with love" (v). Moreover, the opening page reiterates, "one closes behind one the little gate of mere boyishness" (3), which constructs war as a rite of passage into adulthood.

11. It is interesting to note that Conrad here assigns two character traits of the Marlow of *Chance* to these two insignificant figures, the second engineer and the chief engineer. Indeed, the references to misogynism and indigestion seem almost gratuitous but signatory allusions.

12. For a discussion of how *The Shadow-Line* may be read as a moral allegory on good and evil, on the "disease of idleness," or as a Christian allegory, see Hawthorn, introduction to *The Shadow-Line,* xv–xix.

13. One "whose name is writ in water" is the epitaph, legend has it, that Keats commanded be inscribed on his tombstone.

14. On the theme of guilt, see Hawthorn, introduction to *The Shadow-Line,* xvii.

15. Following is a table from Marr, *Psychoses of the War* (50–1):

Analysis of the Exciting Causes of Neurasthenia in 3000 Soldiers of the Expeditionary Forces

Mental strain	1080
Mental disease	26
Epilepsy	24
Bodily illness, general	45
Shell explosion	274
Shell explosion with burial	83
Shell explosion with g.s.w. and burial	28

Shell explosion with g.s.w. 203
Shell explosion with frost-bite 20
Gunshot wound 102
Injury 168
Immersion in water—shock—torpedoed vessel 7
Malaria 81
Dysentery 103
Malta fever 9
Enteric fever 40
Paratyphoid A & B 184
Trench fever 105
Sand-fly fever 3
Gas poisoning 134
Alcohol 23
Frost-bite 49
Nephritis 22
Ptomaine poisoning 7
Trench foot 15
Pyrexia of unknown origin 149
Sunstroke 11

16. Jean-Aubry, *Joseph Conrad: Life and Letters,* 2:339.

17. This paragraph summarizes materials from Elaine Showalter's chapter "Male Hysteria: W. H. R. Rivers and the Lessons of Shell Shock" in *The Female Malady,* 167–94, esp. 167–76.

18. Borys Conrad, *My Father: Joseph Conrad,* 133, 137.

19. Marr, *Psychoses of the War,* 48. In his "Analysis of the Exciting Causes of Neurasthenia" (see table in note 15 above), 1080 cases (or approximately one-third) were due simply to mental strain; 134 cases were gassed (Borys Conrad was gassed slightly [Jean-Aubry, *Joseph Conrad: Life and Letters,* 2:217]), and 83 cases experienced shell explosion with burial, like Borys. Other frequent exciting causes, among many, included malaria (81 cases) and dysentery (103 cases) (Marr, *Psychoses of the War,* 50–1).

20. For a discussion of this historicist concern, see Levenson, "Secret History in 'The Secret Sharer,'" 168–70.

Conclusion. The Heart in Its Perplexity

Note: The main chapter title is taken from Virginia Woolf's essay "Joseph Conrad" in her *Collected Essays,* 1:306.

1. For "*une ironie méprisante*" and Lenormand's full account of his and Conrad's acquaintance in Corsica, see Lenormand, "Note sur un séjour de Conrad en Corse." For an account of their Corsican adventures, see Jessie Conrad's *Joseph Conrad and His Circle,* 227–35. See also Najder, *Joseph Conrad: A Chronicle,* 460, for a discussion of the Lenormand/Conrad meeting, and Stape and Knowles, eds., *A Portrait in Letters,* for Lenormand's letter to Conrad, acknowledging return of the volumes of Freud.

2. Showalter, *The Female Malady,* 174.

3. Ibid., 180–4.

4. See Knowles, *A Conrad Chronology,* 106. In private correspondence, Professor Knowles has indicated that unpublished letters held in the Berg and Beinecke Libraries (to be published by Cambridge University Press in a forthcoming volume of *Letters*) indicate that Conrad was anticipating a visit from Sassoon in November of 1918 and that he wanted to procure a copy of Sassoon's verse before he met the poet, who may a have been preparing to write a magazine article on Conrad.

5. Borys Conrad, *My Father: Joseph Conrad,* 155.

6. Borys Conrad writes of the former military doctor, "I told him of my recent experience and asked him to take me in hand. This he agreed to do and, as he was familiar with the basic cause of my condition, it was not long before I became much better" (*My Father: Joseph Conrad,* 156).

7. Borys Conrad, *My Father: Joseph Conrad,* 156.

8. Hampson, *Joseph Conrad: Betrayal and Identity,* 260–2.

9. Showalter, *The Female Malady,* 192–3.

10. Woolf, "Joseph Conrad," *Collected Essays,* 1:306.

11. Woolf, *Mrs. Dalloway,* 91, 90, respectively (hereafter cited in the text as *MD*).

12. See Savage and Goodall, *Insanity and Allied Neuroses,* 97, quoted above in chapter 1, and also Virginia Woolf's letter to Violet Dickinson, in which she describes the months she spent in Cambridge after the death of Leslie Stephen in February of 1904: "They don't realize that London means my own home, and books, and pictures, and music from which I have been parted since February now,—and I have never spent such a wretched 8 months in my life" (*Letters of Virginia Woolf,* 1:147).

13. Woolf, "Mr. Bennett and Mrs. Brown," in *Collected Essays,* 1:320. See also Stansky, *On or about December 1910,* 2.

14. Woolf, "Mr. Bennett and Mrs. Brown," in *Collected Essays,* 1:320–1.

15. Woolf, "Mr. Conrad: A Conversation," in *Collected Essays,* 1:310–1.

Works Cited

Archival Materials

Conrad, Joseph. Letter to A. E. Tebb, 13 December 1905. Sutton Manuscripts. Lilly Library, Indiana University, Bloomington, Ind.

Ford, Ford Madox. Collection 4605. Division of Rare and Manuscript Collections, Cornell University Library, Ithaca, N.Y.

Garnett, Olive. "A Bloomsbury Girlhood." Unpublished typescript. Harry Ransom Humanities Research Center, University of Texas at Austin, Austin, Tex.

Hackney, Alfred Clifford John Hill. Fee Books and Calendars, 1891–6. Records Office, University College, London.

Rothenstein, Sir William. Papers. Houghton Library, Harvard University, Cambridge, Mass.

Tebb, A. E. Autographs. Brotherton Collection, Leeds University Library, Leeds, England.

———. Certificate of Marriage to Bertha Mary Carr. 19 December 1898. Record Keeper's Department, Sumerset House, London.

———. Records from Guy's Medical School. Office of Student Records, University of London Library, Senate House, London.

Tebb, Robert Francis Palmer. Death Certificate of 7 January 1913. Record Keeper's Department, Sumerset House, London.

Literary Sources

Achebe, Chinua. "An Image of Africa: Racism in Conrad's *Heart of Darkness*." *Massachusetts Review* 18 (1977): 782–94.

Ambrosini, Richard. *Conrad's Fiction as Critical Discourse*. Cambridge: Cambridge University Press, 1991.

Anderson, Chester G. Introduction to "Joyce and Freud." In *The Seventh of Joyce,* edited by Bernard Benstock. Bloomington: Indiana University Press, 1982.

Arata, Stephen. *Fictions of Loss in the Victorian "Fin de Siècle."* Cambridge: Cambridge University Press, 1996.

Barthes, Roland. *The Pleasure of the Text*. Translated by Richard Miller. New York: Hill and Wang, 1975.

Berman, Jeffrey. *Joseph Conrad: Writing as Rescue*. New York: Astra Books, 1977.

Berthoud, Jacques. "Conrad and the Sea." Introduction to *The Nigger of the "Narcissus,"* by Joseph Conrad. Oxford: Oxford University Press, 1984.

————. *Joseph Conrad: The Major Phase*. Cambridge: Cambridge University Press, 1978.

Billy, Ted. "'Nothing to be done': Conrad, Beckett, and the Poetics of Immobility." *Conradiana* 32 (2000): 66–71.

————. *A Wilderness of Words: Closure and Disclosure in Conrad's Short Fiction*. Lubbock: Texas Tech University Press, 1997.

Blackburn, William, ed. *Letters to William Blackwood and David S. Meldrum,* by Joseph Conrad. Durham, N.C.: Duke University Press, 1958.

Bock, Martin. *Crossing the Shadow-Line: The Literature of Estrangement*. Columbus: Ohio State University Press, 1989.

Bohlmann, Otto. *Conrad's Existentialism*. New York: St. Martin's Press, 1991.

Boulicaut, Yannick Le. "'Action, the barbed hook' (J. Conrad, *Victory*) or the Syndrome of the Motionless Hero." *L'Epoque Conradienne* 25 (1999): 41–57.

Brantlinger, Patrick. "*Heart of Darkness:* Anti-Imperialism, Racism, or Impressionism?" *Criticism* 27 (1985): 363–85. Reprinted in *Joseph Conrad: Critical Assessments,* edited by Keith Carabine. Mountfield, England: Helm Information, 1992.

Carabine, Keith, ed. *Joseph Conrad: Critical Assessments*. 4 vols. Mountfield, England: Helm Information, 1992.

————. *The Life and the Art: A Study of Conrad's* Under Western Eyes. Amsterdam and Atlanta: Rodopi, 1996.

————. "'The Secret Sharer': A Note on the Dates of Its Composition." *Conradiana* 19 (1987): 209–13.

Colvin, Sidney. "Robert Lewis Stevenson in Hampstead." In *The Hampstead Annual,* 1902, edited by Greville E. Matheson and Sydney C. Mayle. London: Priory Press, 1902.

Conrad, Borys. *My Father: Joseph Conrad*. New York: Coward-McCann, 1970.

Conrad, Jessie. *Joseph Conrad and His Circle*. New York: E. P. Dutton, 1935.

————. *Joseph Conrad As I Knew Him*. New York: Doubleday, 1926.

Conrad, John. *Joseph Conrad: Times Remembered*. Cambridge: Cambridge University Press, 1981.

Conrad, Joseph. *Almayer's Folly: A Story of an Eastern River*. Edited by Floyd Eugene Eddelman and David Leon Higdon. Cambridge: Cambridge University Press, 1994.

————. *The Collected Letters of Joseph Conrad*. Edited by Frederick R. Karl and Laurence Davies. 5 vols. Cambridge: Cambridge University Press, 1983–96.

————. *The Complete Works of Joseph Conrad*. New York: Doubleday, Page, 1924.

————. "Lord Jim: A Sketch." *Blackwood's Magazine,* September 1900, 379–83.

————. *The Secret Agent: A Simple Tale*. Edited by Bruce Harkness and S. W. Reid. Cambridge: Cambridge University Press, 1990.

————. "The *Torrens:* A Personal Tribute." In *Last Essays,* by Joseph Conrad. New York: Doubleday, Page, 1926.

David, Deirdre. "Selfhood and Language in 'The Return' and 'Falk.'" *Conradiana* 8 (1976): 137–47.

De Mille, Barbara. "An Inquiry into Some Points of Seamanship: Narration as Preservation in *Heart of Darkness.*" *Conradiana* 18 (1986): 94–104.

Dumesnil, René. *Chroniques, études, correspondance de Guy de Maupassant.* Paris: Librairie Gründ, n.d.

Ender, Evelyne. *Sexing the Mind: Nineteenth-Century Fictions of Hysteria.* Ithaca, N.Y.: Cornell University Press, 1995.

Farmer, J. S., and W. E. Henley. *Slang and Its Analogues.* 3 vols. 1890–4. Reprint, New York: Arno Press, 1970.

Finn, Michael R. *Proust, the Body, and Literary Form.* Cambridge: Cambridge University Press, 1999.

Firchow, Peter Edgerly. *Envisioning Africa: Racism and Imperialism in Conrad's* Heart of Darkness. Lexington: University Press of Kentucky, 2000.

Fleishman, Avrom. *Conrad's Politics: Community and Anarchy in the Fiction of Joseph Conrad.* Baltimore, Md.: Johns Hopkins University Press, 1967.

Ford, Ford Madox. *Return to Yesterday.* New York: Horace Liveright, 1932.

————. Introduction to *The Sisters,* by Joseph Conrad. New York: Crosby Gaige, 1928.

Fothergill, Anthony. *Heart of Darkness.* Milton Keynes, England, and Philadelphia: Open University Press, 1989.

Garnett, Edward. *Letters from Joseph Conrad: 1895–1924.* Indianapolis: Bobbs-Merrill, 1928.

Gates, Barbara. "Kurtz's Moral Insanity." *Victorians Institute Journal* 11 (1982–83): 53–9.

Gilbert, Susan M., and Susan Gubar. *The Madwoman in the Attic: The Woman Writer and the Nineteenth-Century Literary Imagination.* New Haven, Conn.: Yale University Press, 1979.

Gill, David. "The Fascination of the Abomination: Conrad and Cannibalism." *The Conradian* 24 (1999): 1–30.

Gillon, Adam. *The Eternal Solitary: A Study of Joseph Conrad.* New York: Bookman Associates, 1960.

Gilman, Sander. "Black Bodies, White Bodies: Toward an Iconography of Female Sexuality in Late Nineteenth-Century Art, Medicine, and Literature." *Critical Inquiry* 12 (1985): 204–42.

Goldring, Douglas. *South Lodge: Reminiscences of Violet Hunt, Ford Madox Ford, and the English Review Circle.* London: Constable, 1943.

Greenslade, William. *Degeneration, Culture, and the Novel: 1880–1940.* Cambridge: Cambridge University Press, 1994.

Griffith, John W. *Joseph Conrad and the Anthropological Dilemma: "Bewildered Traveller."* Oxford: Clarendon Press, 1995.

Gwynn, Frederick L., and Joseph L. Blotner. *Faulkner in the University: Class Conferences at the University of Virginia, 1957–58*. Charlottesville: University of Virginia Press, 1959.

Haltresht, Michael. "The Dread of Space in Conrad's *The Secret Agent*." *Literature and Psychology* 22 (1972): 89–97.

Hamner, Robert. "Colony, Nationhood, and Beyond: Third World Writers and Critics Contend with Joseph Conrad." *World Literature Written in English* 23 (1984): 108–16. Reprinted in *Joseph Conrad: Critical Assessments,* edited by Keith Carabine. Mountfield, England: Helm Information, 1992.

Hampson, Robert. *Cross-Cultural Encounters in Joseph Conrad's Malay Fiction*. Houndsmills, Basingstoke, Hampshire: Palgrave, 2000.

———. "Frazer, Conrad, and the 'Truth of Primitive Passion.'" In *Sir James Frazer and the Literary Imagination: Essays in Affinity and Influence,* edited by Robert Fraser. New York: St. Martin's Press, 1990.

———. Introduction to *Heart of Darkness: With "The Congo Diary,"* by Joseph Conrad. New York: Penguin, 1995.

———. *Joseph Conrad: Betrayal and Identity*. New York: St. Martin's Press, 1992.

Harkness, Bruce. "The Secret of 'The Secret Sharer' Bared." *College English* 27 (1965): 55–61.

Hawkins, Hunt. "Conrad's Critique of Imperialism in *Heart of Darkness*." *PMLA* 94 (1979): 286–99.

Hawthorn, Jeremy. Introduction to *The Shadow-Line,* by Joseph Conrad. Oxford: Oxford University Press, 1985.

———. *Joseph Conrad: Narrative Technique and Ideological Commitment*. London: Edward Arnold, 1990.

Hodges, Robert R. "Deep Fellowship: Homosexuality and Male Bonding in the Life and Fiction of Joseph Conrad." *Journal of Homosexuality* 4 (1979): 379–93.

Hooper, Myrtle. "The Heart of Light: Silence in Conrad's *Heart of Darkness*." *L'Epoque Conradienne* 40 (1990): 105–13.

Hubbard, Francis A. *Theories of Action in Conrad*. Ann Arbor, Mich.: UMI Research, 1984.

Huggan, Graham. "Anxieties of Influence: Conrad and the Caribbean." *Commonwealth* 11 (1988): 1–12. Reprinted in *Joseph Conrad: Critical Assessments,* edited by Keith Carabine. Mountfield, England: Helm Information, 1992.

Humphries, Reynold. "Restraint, Cannibalism, and the 'Unspeakable Rites' in *Heart of Darkness*." *L'Epoque Conradienne* (1990): 51–78.

Hunt, Violet. *The Flurried Years*. London: Hurst and Blackwell, 1926.

Ignotus, Paul. *The Paradox of Maupassant*. New York: Funk and Wagnalls, 1958.

Jean-Aubry, G. *Joseph Conrad: Life and Letters*. 2 vols. New York: Doubleday, Page, 1927.

Johnson, Barbara, and Marjorie Garber. "Secret Sharing: Reading Conrad Psychoanalytically." *College English* 49 (1987): 628–40.

246

Johnson, Bruce. *Conrad's Models of Mind*. Minneapolis: University of Minnesota Press, 1971.

Jones, Susan. *Conrad and Women*. Oxford: Oxford University Press, 1999.

Joyce, James. *Letters of James Joyce*. Edited by Stuart Gilbert. 3 vols. New York: Viking, 1957.

Karl, Frederick R. *Joseph Conrad: The Three Lives*. New York: Farrar, Straus, and Giroux, 1979.

———. *Reader's Guide to Joseph Conrad*. New York: Noonday Press, 1960.

Kingsbury, Celia M. "'The Novelty of Real Feelings': Restraint and Duty in Conrad's 'The Return.'" *Conradiana* 32 (2000): 31–40.

Kinkead-Weeks, Mark. "*Heart of Darkness* and the Third World Writer." *Sewanee Review* 98 (1990): 31–43. Reprinted in *Joseph Conrad: Critical Assessments,* edited by Keith Carabine. Mountfield, England: Helm Information, 1992.

Kirschner; Paul. "Conrad and Maupassant: Moral Solitude and 'A Smile of Fortune.'" *Review of English Literature* 7 (1966): 62–77.

Knowles, Owen. *A Conrad Chronology*. Boston: G. K. Hall, 1990.

Kramer, Dale. "Conrad's Experiments with Language and Narrative in 'The Return.'" *Studies in Short Fiction* 25 (1988): 2, 6–7.

Land, Stephen K. *Paradox and Polarity in the Fiction of Joseph Conrad*. New York: St. Martin's Press, 1984.

Lenormand, H. R. "Note sur un séjour de Conrad en Corse." *La Nouvelle Revue Française* 23 (December 1924): 666–71.

Levenson, Michael. "Secret History in 'The Secret Sharer.'" In Joseph Conrad, *The Secret Sharer: Complete, Authoritative Text with Biographical and Historical Contexts, Critical History, and Essays from Five Contemporary Critical Perspectives,* edited by Daniel R. Schwarz. Boston: Bedford Books, 1997.

Lord, Ursula. *Solitude versus Solidarity in the Novels of Joseph Conrad: Political and Epistemological Implications of Narrative Innovation*. Montreal and Kingston: McGill-Queen's University Press, 1998.

Lothe, Jakob. *Conrad's Narrative Method*. Oxford: Clarendon Press, 1989.

Lubbock, Percy. *George Calderon*. London: Grant Richards, 1921.

MacKenzie, Norman, and Jeanne MacKenzie. *H. G. Wells: A Biography*. New York: Simon and Schuster, 1973.

Manicum, David. "True Lies/False Truths: Narrative Perspective and the Control of Ambiguity in *The Nigger of the 'Narcissus.'*" *Conradiana* 18 (1986): 105–18.

Maupassant, Guy de. *The Complete Short Stories of Guy de Maupassant*. Translated by Artine Artinian and Francis Steegmuller. New York: Hanover House, 1955.

McClure, John A. "The Rhetoric of Restraint in *Heart of Darkness*." *Nineteenth-Century Fiction* 32 (1977): 311.

McLendon, M. J. "Conrad and Calomel: An Explanation of Conrad's Mercurial Nature." *Conradiana* 23 (1991): 151–6.

Meyer, Bernard C. *Joseph Conrad: A Psychoanalytic Biography.* Princeton, N.J.: Princeton University Press, 1967.

Meyers, Jeffrey. *Joseph Conrad: A Biography.* New York: Charles Scribner's Sons, 1991.

Moore, Gene. "Conrad, Dr. Gachet, and the 'School of Charenton.'" *Conradiana* 25 (1993): 172–3.

Moser, Thomas C. *Joseph Conrad: Achievement and Decline.* Cambridge, Mass.: Harvard University Press, 1957.

———. *The Life in the Fiction of Ford Madox Ford.* Princeton, N.J.: Princeton University Press, 1980.

Naipaul, V. S. "Conrad's Darkness." *New York Review of Books* 19 (19 October 1974): 16–21. Reprinted in *Joseph Conrad: Critical Assessments,* edited by Keith Carabine. Mountfield, England: Helm Information, 1992.

Najder, Zdzisław. *Conrad in Perspective: Essays on Art and Fidelity.* Cambridge: Cambridge University Press, 1997.

———. *Joseph Conrad: A Chronicle.* New Brunswick, N.J.: Rutgers University Press, 1984.

———, ed. *Conrad's Polish Background: Letters to and from Polish Friends.* Translated by Halina Carroll. London: Oxford University Press, 1964.

———, ed. *Conrad under Familial Eyes: Texts.* Translated by Halina Carroll Najder. Cambridge: Cambridge University Press, 1983.

Nazareth, Peter. "Conrad's Descendants." *Conradiana* 22 (1990): 101–9. Reprinted in *Joseph Conrad: Critical Assessments,* edited by Keith Carabine. Mountfield, England: Helm Information, 1992.

O'Mealy, Joseph. H. "The Herveys and the Verlocs: *The Secret Agent's* Debt to 'The Return.'" *Studies in Short Fiction* 20 (1983): 115–20.

Oxford English Dictionary. 20 vols. Oxford: Oxford University Press, 1933.

Pecora, Vincent. "*Heart of Darkness* and the Phenomenology of Narrative Voice." *English Literary History* 52 (1985): 993–1015.

Phelan, James. "Reading Secrets." In Joseph Conrad, *The Secret Sharer: Complete, Authoritative Text with Biographical and Historical Contexts, Critical History, and Essays from Five Contemporary Critical Perspectives,* edited by Daniel R. Schwarz. Boston: Bedford Books, 1997.

Pykett, Lyn. *Reading Fin de Siècle Fictions.* London and New York: Longman, 1996.

Rabinowitz, Peter J. "Reader Response, Reader Responsibility: *Heart of Darkness* and the Politics of Displacement." In Joseph Conrad, *Heart of Darkness: Complete, Authoritative Text with Biographical and Historical Contexts, Critical History, and Essays from Five Contemporary Critical Perspectives,* edited by Ross C. Murfin. 2d ed. Boston: Bedford Books, 1996.

Ray, Martin. "Language and Silence in the Novels of Joseph Conrad." *Conradiana* 16 (1984): 19–40.

Reeves, Charles Eric. "A Voice of Unrest: Conrad's Rhetoric of the Unspeakable." *Texas Studies in Literature and Language* 27 (1985): 284–310.

Ressler, Steve. *Joseph Conrad: Consciousness and Integrity.* New York and London: New York University Press, 1988.

Roberts, Andrew Michael. *Conrad and Masculinity.* London: Macmillan, 2000.

Rosenfield, Claire. *Paradise of Snakes: An Archetypal Analysis of Conrad's Political Novels.* Chicago: University of Chicago Press, 1967.

Ruppel, Richard. "The Economy of Desire in *Heart of Darkness.*" Paper presented at the International Conference of Joseph Conrad Scholars, Texas Tech University, Lubbock, Tex., August 2000.

———. "Joseph Conrad and the Ghost of Oscar Wilde." *The Conradian* 23 (1998): 19–36.

Saunders, Max. *Ford Madox Ford: A Dual Life.* 2 vols. Oxford: Oxford University Press, 1996.

Scott, Bonny Kime. "Intimacies Engendered in Conrad's *The Secret Sharer.*" In Joseph Conrad, *The Secret Sharer: Complete, Authoritative Text with Biographical and Historical Contexts, Critical History, and Essays from Five Contemporary Critical Perspectives,* edited by Daniel R. Schwarz. Boston: Bedford Books, 1997.

Sedgwick, Eve Kosofsky. *Between Men: English Literature and Male Homosocial Desire.* New York: Columbia University Press, 1985.

———. *Epistemology of the Closet.* Berkeley: University of California Press, 1990.

Shaffer, Brian W. "'Rebarbarizing Civilization': Conrad's African Fiction and Spencerian Sociology." *PMLA* 108 (1993): 45–58.

Sherard, Robert Harborough. *The Life, Work, and Evil Fate of Guy de Maupassant (gentilhomme de lettres).* New York: Brentano's Publishers, 1926.

Small, Helen. *Love's Madness: Medicine, the Novel, and Female Insanity, 1800–1865.* Oxford: Clarendon Press, 1996.

Smith, Johanna M. "'Too Beautiful Altogether': Ideologies of Gender and Empire in *Heart of Darkness.*" In Joseph Conrad, *Heart of Darkness: Complete, Authoritative Text with Biographical and Historical Contexts, Critical History, and Essays from Five Contemporary Critical Perspectives,* edited by Ross C. Murfin. 2d ed. Boston: Bedfy. London: Macmillan, 1976.

Spackman, Barbara. *Decadent Genealogies: The Rhetoric of Sickness from Baudelaire to D'Annunzio.* Ithaca, N.Y.: Cornell University Press, 1989.

Stallman, R. W. "Conrad and 'The Secret Sharer.'" *Accent* 9 (1949): 131–43. Reprinted in *The Art of Joseph Conrad: A Critical Symposium,* edited by R. W. Stallman. Ann Arbor: University of Michigan Press, 1960. Also reprinted in *Joseph Conrad: Critical Assessments,* edited by Keith Carabine. Mountfield, England: Helm Information, 1992.

Stansky, Peter. *On or about December 1910: Early Bloomsbury and Its Intimate World.* Cambridge, Mass.: Harvard University Press, 1996.

Stape, J. H., and Owen Knowles, eds. *A Portrait in Letters: Correspondence to and about Conrad.* Amsterdam and Atlanta, Ga.: Rodopi, 1996.

Stewart, Garrett. "Lying as Dying in *Heart of Darkness.*" *PMLA* 95 (1980): 358–74.

Straus, Nina Pelikan. "The Exclusion of the Intended from Secret Sharing in Conrad's *Heart of Darkness.*" *Novel* 20 (1987): 123–37.

Tanner, Tony. "'Gnawed Bones' and 'Artless Tales': Eating and Narrating in Conrad." In *Joseph Conrad: A Commemoration,* edited by Norman Sherry. New York: Barnes and Noble Books, 1976.

Tassart, François. *Recollections of Guy de Maupassant by His Valet François.* Translated by Mina Round. London: John Lane, The Bodley Head, 1912.

Thale, Jerome. "Marlow's Quest." *University of Toronto Quarterly* 24 (1955): 351–8. Reprinted in *The Art of Joseph Conrad: A Critical Symposium,* edited by R. W. Stallman. Ann Arbor: University of Michigan Press, 1960.

Trombley, Stephen. *All That Summer She Was Mad: Virginia Woolf, Female Victim of Male Medicine.* New York: Continuum, 1982.

Watt, Ian. *Conrad in the Nineteenth Century.* Los Angeles: University of California Press, 1799.

Watts, Cedric. "'A Bloody Racist': About Achebe's View of Conrad." *Yearbook of English Studies* (1983): 196–209. Reprinted in *Joseph Conrad: Critical Assessments,* edited by Keith Carabine. Mountfield, England: Helm Information, 1992.

———. *The Deceptive Text: An Introduction to Covert Plots.* Sussex, England: Harvester Press, 1984.

———. *Joseph Conrad: A Literary Life.* New York: St. Martin's Press, 1989.

———. "Marketing Modernism: How Conrad Prospered." In *Modernist Writers and the Marketplace,* edited by Ian Willison, Warwick Gould, and Warren Chernaik. New York: St. Martin's Press, 1996.

———. *A Preface to Conrad.* London and New York: Longman, 1993.

White, Andrea. "Conrad and Imperialism." In *The Cambridge Companion to Joseph Conrad,* edited by J. H. Stape. Cambridge: Cambridge University Press, 1996.

———. *Joseph Conrad and the Adventure Tradition: Constructing and Deconstructing the Imperial Subject.* Cambridge: Cambridge University Press, 1993.

Wiley, Paul. *Conrad's Measure of Man.* Madison: University of Wisconsin Press, 1954.

Wilson, Donald S. "The Best in the Congo: How Victorian Homophobia Infects Marlow's *Heart of Darkness.*" *Conradiana* 32 (2000): 96–118.

Woolf, Virginia. *Collected Essays.* 4 vols. New York: Harcourt, 1967.

———. *The Diaries of Virginia Woolf.* Edited by Ann Oliver Bell. 5 vols. New York: Harcourt, 1977–84.

———. *The Letters of Virginia Woolf.* Edited by Nigel Nicholson and Joanne Trautmann. 6 vols. New York: Harcourt, 1975–80.

———. *Mrs. Dalloway.* New York: Harbrace, 1925.

Yeats, William Butler. "The Fisherman." In *The Poems,* edited by Richard J. Finneran. New ed. New York: Macmillan, 1983.

Zucherman, Jerome. "The Motif of Cannibalism in *The Secret Agent.*" *Texas Studies in Literature and Language* 10 (1968): 295–9.

Medical History and Cultural Studies Sources

"The American Disease." *American Monthly Review of Reviews* 32 (1905): 497–8.

Augstein, Hannah Franziska. "J C Prichard's Concept of Moral Insanity: A Medical Theory of the Corruption of Human Nature." *Medical History* 40 (1996): 312–3.

Baedeker, Karl. *La Suisse.* Paris: Ollendorff, 1891.

Bannister, H. M., and H. N. Moyer. "On Restraint and Seclusion in American Institutions for the Insane." *Journal of Nervous and Mental Disease* 9 (1882): 457–78.

Barratt, Thomas J. *The Annals of Hampstead.* 3 vols. London: Adam and Charles Black, 1912.

Batten, Dr. Rayner Derry, obituary notice. 13 November 1943. *British Journal of Ophthalmology* 27 (1943): 569–70.

Beard, George M. "The Nature and Diagnosis of Neurasthenia (Nervous Exhaustion)." *New York Medical Journal* 29 (1879): 225–51.

———. *A Practical Treatise on Nervous Exhaustion (Neurasthenia): Its Symptoms, Nature, Sequences, Treatments.* New York: E. B. Treat, 1905.

———. "The Sequences of Neurasthenia." *Alienist and Neurologist* 1 (1880): 18–29.

———. *Sexual Neurasthenia [Nervous Exhaustion]: Its Hygiene, Causes, Symptoms, and Treatment.* New York: E. B. Treat, 1898.

Beetham, Margaret. *A Magazine of Her Own? Domesticity and Desire in the Woman's Magazine, 1800–1914.* London: Routledge, 1996.

Bresler, J. "On the Increase of Insanity, and the Boarding-out System." *Journal of Mental Science* (April 1896): 315–20.

Bynam, William. "Rationales for Therapy in British Psychiatry, 1780–1835." In *Madhouses, Mad-Doctors, and Madmen: The Social History of Psychiatry in the Victorian Era,* edited by Andrew Scull. Philadelphia: University of Pennsylvania Press, 1981.

Call, Annie Payson. "How Women Can Keep from Being Nervous." *Ladies' Home Journal* 25 (March 1908): 8.

251

Campbell, Alfred W. "The Breaking Strain of the Ribs of the Insane." *Journal of Mental Science* 41 (1895): 254–74.

Conolly, John. *Familiar Views of Lunacy and Lunatic Life: With Hints on the Personal Care and Management of Those Who Are Afflicted with Temporary or Permanent Derangement.* London: John W. Parker, 1850.

Corbet, W. J. "Holocaust at Colney Hatch." *Westminster Review* 159 (1903): 383–93.

———. "How Insanity Is Propagated." *Westminster Review* 142 (August 1894): 153–63.

———. "The Increase of Insanity." *Fortnightly Review* 59 (1893): 7–19.

———. "The Increase of Insanity." *Fortnightly Review* 65 (1899): 431–2.

———. "Is Insanity Increasing?" *Fortnightly Review* (1897): 321–4.

———. "Is the Increase of Insanity Real or only 'Apparent'?" *Westminster Review* 147 (1897): 539–50.

———. "Lunacy Reform." *Westminster Review* 147 (1897): 200–10.

———. "Ought Private Lunatic Asylums to Be Abolished?" *Westminster Review* 142 (1894): 369–80.

———. "Plain Speaking about Lunacy." *Westminster Review* 148 (August 1897): 117–25.

———. "Progress of Insanity in Our Own Time." *Westminster Review* 163 (1905): 198–211.

———. "Progress of Insanity in Our Own Time." *Westminster Review* 166 (1906): 408–17.

———. "The Progress of Insanity in Our Own Time." *Westminster Review* 165 (March 1906): 269–83.

———. "The Skeleton at the Feast." *Westminster Review* 159 (January 1903): 1–14.

Darwin, Charles. *The Works of Charles Darwin.* Edited by Paul H. Barrett and R. B. Freeman. New York: New York University Press, 1988.

"The Dean's Report of 1893–4." In *Guy's Hospital Medical School, 1894–95.* London: Office of Student Records, University of London Library, 1894–5.

Doiteau, Victor. "La Curieuse Figure du Dr. Gachet." *Aesculape* (1923): 169–72.

Drapes, Thomas. "Is Insanity Increasing?" *Fortnightly Review* (1896): 483–93.

Ellis, Havelock. *Studies in the Psychology of Sex.* 7 vols. Philadelphia: F. A. Davis, 1920.

Ferro, A. de. "The Wörishofen Water-cure and Pfarrer Kneipp." *Blackwood's Magazine* 66 (1890): 816–28.

"A Fit of the Blues." *Home Chat,* 12 April 1902, 280.

Foucault, Michel. *Discipline and Punish: The Birth of the Prison.* Translated by Alan Sheridan. New York: Random House, 1979.

———. *Madness and Civilization: A History of Insanity in the Age of Reason.* Translated by Richard Howard. New York: Vintage, 1965.

France, Eric. "Abstract of a Paper on the Necessity for Isolating the Phthisical Insane." *Journal of Mental Science* 46 (1900): 1.

Freud, Sigmund. "On the Grounds for Detaching a Particular Syndrome from Neurasthenia under the Description of 'Anxiety Neurosis.'" In vol. 3 of *The Complete Psychological Works of Sigmund Freud.* Translated by James Strachey. 24 vols. London: Hogarth Press, 1962.

Gachet, Paul-Ferdinand. "Etude sur la mélancolie." Thesis, Académie de Montpellier, 1858.

Glatz, Paul. "Champel-les-Bains: établissement hydrothérapique de premier ordre fondé sous le patronage du Corps médical de Genève." Promotional brochure, n.d.

———. *Des dyspepsies avec suppression de la sécrétion du suc gastrique et plus particulièrement de la dyspepsie neurasthénique.* Geneva: Imprimerie Charles Schuchardt, 1889.

———. *Dyspepsies nerveuses et neurasthénie.* Bale and Geneva: Georg & Cie. Libraires-Éditeurs, 1898.

———. *Effets physiologiques et thérapeutiques des bains de siège et de traitement de la spermatorrhée par l'hydrothérapie et l'électricité.* Geneva: Schuchardt, 1881.

———. *L'Hydrothérapie: les eaux de l'Arve, leur action hygiénique et curative, l'établissement hydrothérapique de Champel-sur-Arve.* Paris: Genève Librairie Desrogis, 1875.

———. *L'Hydrothérapie aux Bains de Champel près Genève.* Geneva: Georg, 1879–82.

———. *L'Hydrothérapie envisagé comme médication tonique et revulsive: conclusion du rapport de M. le Dr. Glatz.* Geneva: Imprimerie Ramboz et Schuchardt, 1878.

———. *Quelques cas d'épilepsie traites avec succès par l'hydrothérapie et les bromures à hautes doses.* Geneva: n.p., [1886].

———. "Quelques réflexions sur l'empirisme en médecine: à propos de l'abbé Kneipp." *Tribune de Genève,* 1893.

———. "Réflexions sur l'empirisme en médecine à propos d'hydro-thérapie." Geneva: n.p., 1894.

———. *Résumé clinique sur le diagnostic & le traitement des différentes espèces de néphrite et de la dégénérescence amyloïde des reins: mémoire lu à la Société de Médecine de Genève.* Geneva and Paris: [n.p.], 1872.

———. *Sur la melancholie: dissertation inaugurale (sur la maladie de Basedow).* Paris: Pichon, 1869.

———. *Du traitement de la névralgie sciatique par l'hydrothérapie & l'électricité.* Paris: Alcan, 1894.

Gosling, Francis G. *Before Freud: Neurasthenia in the American Medical Community.* Urbana: University of Illinois Press, 1987.

Greenwood, M., C. Hudson, and A. E. Tebb. "Report on the Metabolism of Female Munition Workers." *Proceedings of the Royal Society of London* 91 (November 1920): 62–82.

Guy's Hospital Pupils' Returns, 1880–81. London: Guy's Medical School Library.

Haguch. "Comments on the Report of the Commissioners in Lunacy and the Swing of the Pendulum." *Westminster Review* 148 (1897): 672–81.

Haller, John S. "Neurasthenia: The Medical Profession and the 'New Woman' of Late Nineteenth Century." *New York State Journal of Medicine* 71 (1971): 473–81.

———. "Neurasthenia: Medical Profession and Urban 'Blahs.'" *New York State Journal of Medicine* 70 (1970): 2489.

Hart, Bernard. "A Philosophy of Psychiatry." *British Journal of Psychology* 54 (1908): 473–90.

———. "The Psychology of Freud and His School." *British Journal of Psychology* (July 1910): 421, 434–43, 451.

Haslett, W. J. Handfield. "Modern Private Asylums: A Defence." *Westminster Review* 143 (1894): 307–15.

Home Chat. London: Harmsworth, 1895–1958.

Hueffer, Ford Madox. *The Cinque Ports: A Historical and Descriptive Record.* Edinburgh and London: William Blackwood and Sons, 1900.

Hughes, C. H. "Neurasthenia." *Alienist and Neurologist* 15 (1894): 354–66.

———. "Notes on Neurasthenia." *Alienist and Neurologist* 1 (1880): 436–49.

International Medical Congress. *Transactions.* London: Klockmann, 1881.

Ireland, William W. Review of *The Treatment of Neurasthenia,* by Adrien Proust and Gilbert Ballet. *Journal of Nervous and Mental Disease* (1902): 548.

Jewell, J. S. "The Varieties and Causes of Neurasthenia." *Journal of Nervous and Mental Disease* 7 (1880): 1–16.

Jones, Gareth Stedman. *Outcast London: A Study in the Relationship between Classes in Victorian Society.* Oxford: Clarendon Press, 1971.

Jones, Kathleen. *A History of the Mental Health Services.* London: Routledge and Kegan Paul, 1972.

Kelly's Hampstead and Child's Hill Directory, 1912–13. London: Kelly's High Holburn, 1912.

Kiernan, James G. "An Historical Case of Gouty Insanity." *Journal of Nervous and Mental Disease* 10 (1883).

———. "Psychological Aspects of the Sexual Appetite." *Alienist and Neurologist* 12 (1891): 188–217.

———. "Race and Insanity." *Journal of Nervous and Mental Disease* 12 (1885): 174–5.

———. "Race and Insanity." *Journal of Nervous and Mental Disease* 12 (1885): 290–3.

———. "Race and Insanity." *Journal of Nervous and Mental Disease* 13 (1886): 74–6.

———. "Race and Insanity." *Journal of Nervous and Mental Disease* 13 (1886): 229–44.

———. "Race and Insanity." *Journal of Nervous and Mental Disease* 13 (1886): 389–92.

———. Review of *The Insane in the United States and Canada,* by D. H. Tuke. *Journal of Nervous and Mental Disease* 13 (1886): 187–90.

Knapp, Terry J. Introduction to *Westphal's "Die Agoraphobie."* Lanham, Md.: University Press of America, 1988.

Kneipp, Sabastian. "My Water Cure." Translated by A. de F[erro]. *The Spectator* 67 (1891): 813.

A Lady Doctor. "Something about Germs." *Home Chat* 1 (1895): 431, 471.

Lombroso, Cesare. *Criminal Man.* New York: G. P. Putnam's Sons, 1911.

———. *The Man of Genius.* London: Walter Scott, 1891.

———. "Nordau's 'Degeneration': Its Value and Its Errors." *Century Illustrated Monthly Magazine* (October 1895): 936–7.

Mack, Gerstle. *Paul Cézanne.* New York: Knopf, 1936.

Magnan. "Considérations sur la folie des héréditaires ou dégénerés." *Progrès Médical,* 1886.

Map of Kent. *Kelly's Directory of Canterbury.* London: Kelly's Directories, 1909.

Marr, H. C. *Psychoses of the War: Including Neurasthenia and Shell Shock.* London: Henry Frowde, Oxford University Press, 1919.

Marsden, Philip Davis. "Did Joseph Conrad Have Loiasis?" *Transactions of the Royal Society of Tropical Medicine and Hygiene* 89, no. 2 (1995): 464.

Martindale, W. Harrison, and W. Wynn Westcott. *The Extra Pharmacopoeia.* London: H. K. Lewis, 1883–.

Maudsley, Henry. *Body and Will: Being an Essay Concerning Will in Its Metaphysical, Physiological, and Pathological Aspects.* New York: D. Appleton, 1884.

McComb, Samuel. "Nervousness in Women: Its Cause and Cure." *Harper's Bazaar* 41 (October 1907): 962–4.

The Medical Directory. London: J. & A. Churchill, 1857–.

Mercier, Charles. "Agoraphobia—A Remedy." *The Lancet,* 13 October 1906, 990–1.

———. "The Fear of Open and Closed Spaces." *Scientific American Supplement,* no. 1629 (23 March 1907): 26107.

———. "Vice, Crime, and Insanity." In vol. 8 of *A System of Medicine by Many Writers,* edited by Sir Clifford Allbutt and Humphrey Davy Rolleston. Rev. ed. 9 vols. London: Macmillan, 1910.

Micale, Mark S. *Approaching Hysteria: Disease and Its Interpretations.* Princeton, N.J.: Princeton University Press, 1995.

Mickle, William Julius. *General Paralysis of the Insane.* London: H. K. Lewis, 1886.

Murchison, F. "Mechanical Restraint in the Management or Treatment of the Insane." *Journal of Psychological Medicine and Mental Pathology* 2 (1876): 112–4.

Nordau, Max. *Degeneration*. New York: D. Appleton, 1895.

Oppenheim, Janet. *"Shattered Nerves": Doctors, Patients, and Depression in Victorian England*. New York and Oxford: Oxford University Press, 1991.

Osler, William. *The Principles and Practice of Medicine: Designed for the Use of Practitioners and Students of Medicine*. 1892. Reprint, Birmingham, England: The Classics of Medicine Library, 1978.

———. *The Principles and Practice of Medicine: Designed for the Use of Practitioners and Students of Medicine*. 4th ed. New York and London: D. Appleton, 1902.

Otis, Laura. *Membranes: Metaphors of Invasion in Nineteenth-Century Literature, Science, and Politics*. Baltimore, Md.: Johns Hopkins University Press, 1999.

Paterson's Guide to Switzerland. London: Edward Stanford, 1885.

Paton, Stewart. "The New Munich Clinic." *Science* 22 (1905): 313.

Petrie, W. M. F. "Eaten with Honour." *Contemporary Review* 71 (1897): 819.

Picot, C. Obituary of Paul Glatz. *Verhandlungen der Schweizerischen Naturforschenden Gesellschaft in Winterthur*. Winterthur, Switzerland: Buchdruckerel von J. Kaufmanns Wwe, 1905.

Poirier, Suzanne. "The Weir Mitchell Rest Cure: Doctor and Patients." *Women's Studies* 10 (1983): 18–20.

Prichard, James. *A Treatise on Insanity and Other Disorders Affecting the Mind*. London: Sherwood, Gilbert, and Piper, 1835.

Proust, Adrien, and Gilbert Ballet. *The Treatment of Neurasthenia*. Translated by Peter Campbell Smith. London: Henry Kimpton, 1902.

Putnam, J. J. "The Nervous Breakdown." *Good Housekeeping* 49 (November 1909): 594–8.

Rae, W. Fraser. "Life at Bohemian Baths." *Blackwood's Magazine* 148 (1890): 515–29.

Ralph, Julian. "The Famous Cures and Humbugs of Europe." *Cosmopolitan* 34 (1903): 669–70.

Rankin, Guthrie. "Nervous Break-down." *Contemporary Review* 89 (1906): 223–32.

Review of "The Forty-eighth Report of the Commissioners in Lunacy, 19th June, 1894." *Journal of Mental Science* (January 1895): 100.

Review of *Insanity and Allied Neuroses: A Practical and Clinical Manual,* by George Savage with Edwin Goodall. *British Journal of Psychiatry* 54 (1908): 134–5.

Riggs, C. Eugene. "An Outline of the Progress in the Care and Handling of the Insane in the Last Twenty Years." *Journal of Nervous and Mental Disease* 20 (1893): 620–8.

Robertson, George. "Treatment of Mental Excitement in Asylums." *British Journal of Psychology* 56 (1910): 700–14.

Rosenberg, Charles E. "The Place of George M. Beard in Nineteenth-Century Psychiatry." *Bulletin of the History of Medicine* 36 (1962): 240–59.

Rothenstein, William. *Men and Memories.* 3 vols. New York: Coward-McCann, 1931–40.

Rousseau, Claudia. "Cézanne, Dr. Gachet, and the Hanged Man." *Notes in the History of Art* 6 (1986): 30.

Sanborn, F. B. "The Progress in the Treatment of Insanity during the Past Half-Century." In *The Social Welfare Forum: Official Proceedings of the Annual Meeting.* New York: National Conference on Social Welfare, 1909.

Savage, George. "Moral Insanity." *Journal of Mental Science* 27 (1881): 147–55.

———. "Notes and News." *Journal of Mental Science* 33 (1887): 154.

Savage, George H., and Edwin Goodall. *Insanity and Allied Neuroses: A Practical and Clinical Manual.* New enlarged ed. New York: Funk and Wagnalls, 1910.

Scull, Andrew. "Moral Treatment Reconsidered: Some Sociological Comments on an Episode in the History of British Psychiatry." In *Madhouses, Mad-Doctors, and Madmen: The Social History of Psychiatry in the Victorian Era,* edited by Andrew Scull. Philadelphia: University of Pennsylvania Press, 1981.

———. "Psychiatry in the Victorian Era." In *Madhouses, Mad-Doctors, and Madmen: The Social History of Psychiatry in the Victorian Era,* edited by Andrew Scull. Philadelphia: University of Pennsylvania Press, 1981.

Scull, Andrew, Charlotte MacKenzie, and Nicholas Hervey. *Masters of Bedlam: The Transformation of the Mad-Doctoring Trade.* Princeton, N.J.: Princeton University Press, 1996.

Showalter, Elaine. *The Female Malady: Women, Madness, and English Culture, 1830–1980.* New York: Pantheon Books, 1985.

Sicherman, Barbara. "The Uses of a Diagnosis: Doctors, Patients, and Neurasthenia." *Journal of the History of Medicine* 32 (1977): 33–54.

Speaight, Robert. *William Rothenstein: The Portrait of an Artist in His Time.* London: Eyre & Spottiswoode, 1962.

Tebb, A. E., and Greenwood, M. "An Inquiry into the Prevalence and Aetiology of Tuberculosis among Industrial Workers, with Special Reference to Female Munitions Workers." London: Great Britain National Health Insurance Joint Committee, Medical Research Committee, 1918.

Thomson, Basil. "The Last of the Cannibal Chiefs." *Blackwood's Magazine,* May 1890, 648–54.

Tuke, D. Hack. *A Dictionary of Psychological Medicine: Giving the Definition, Etymology, and Synonyms of the Terms Used in Medical Psychology with the Symptoms, Treatment, and Pathology of Insanity and the Law of Lunacy in Great Britain and Ireland.* 2 vols. London: J. & A. Churchill, 1892.

257

————. "Retrospective Glance at the Early History of the Retreat, York: Its Objects and Influence." *Journal of Mental Science* 38 (1892): 333–59.

"The Two Solitudes." *The Spectator,* 25 April 1896, 593.

Van Gogh-Bonger, Joanna. "Memoir of Vincent van Gogh by His Sister-in-Law." In *The Complete Letters of Vincent van Gogh.* 2d ed. 3 vols. Greenwich, Conn.: New York Graphic Society, 1959.

Van Gogh, Vincent. *The Complete Letters of Vincent van Gogh.* 2d ed. 3 vols. Greenwich, Conn.: New York Graphic Society, 1959.

Walkowitz, Judith R. *Prostitution and Victorian Society: Women, Class, and the State.* Cambridge: Cambridge University Press, 1980.

Ward, Herbert. "Congo Cannibalism." *Current Literature* 27 (1900): 29.

Weber, F. P., and Guy Hinsdale. *A System of Physiologic Therapeutics.* Edited by Solomon Solsis Cohen. 4 vols. London: Rebman, 1901.

Weber, Hermann, and F. Parkes Weber. *The Spas and Mineral Waters of Europe: With Notes on Balneo-Therapeutic Management in Various Diseases and Morbid Conditions.* London: Smith, Elder, 1896.

"The Wonders of Phosphorus." *Home Chat,* 31 December 1904, 61.

Index